RESEARCH HIGHLIGHTS IN SOCIAL WORK 44

Women Who Offend

Research Highlights in Social Work series

This topical series examines areas of particular interest to those in social and community work and related fields. Each book draws together different aspects of the subject, highlighting relevant research and drawing out implications for policy and practice. The project is under the general direction of Professor Joyce Lishman, Head of the School of Applied Social Studies at the Robert Gordon University.

Working with Offenders
Edited by Gill McIvor
ISBN 1 85302 249 7
Research Highlights in Social Work 26

Addictions and Problem Drug Use
Issues in Behaviour, Policy and Practice
Edited by Mike Bloor and Fiona Wood
ISBN 1 83502 438 4
Research Highlights in Social Work 33

Risk Assessment in Social Care and Social Work
Edited by Phyllida Parsloe
ISBN 1 85302 689 1
Research Highlights in Social Work 36

Managing Front Line Practice in Social Care
Edited by Daphne Statham
ISBN 1 85302 886 X
Research Highlights in Social Work 40

RESEARCH HIGHLIGHTS IN SOCIAL WORK 44

Women Who Offend

Edited by Gill McIvor

Jessica Kingsley Publishers
London and New York

Research Highlights in Social Work 44

Editor: Gill McIvor
Secretary: Anne Forbes
Editorial Advisory Committee:

Prof. J. Lishman	Robert Gordon University, Aberdeen
Prof. I. Broom	Research and Development Office, Grampian University Hospitals NHS Trust
Mr P. Cassidy	Formerly Social Work Department Aberdeen City Council, representing the Association of Directors of Social Work
Ms A. Connor	Scottish Human Services Trust
Ms M. Coutts	The Scottish Executive
Mr D. Cox	Robert Gordon University, Aberdeen
Prof. G. McIvor	University of Stirling
Dr A. Kendrick	University of Strathclyde
Mr C. Mackenzie	Social Work Department, Aberdeenshire Council
Mr S. McLean	Management Consultant
Dr A. Robertson	University of Edinburgh

Robert Gordon University
School of Applied Social Studies
Faculty of Health and Social Care
Garthdee Road, Aberdeen AB10 7QG

First published in the United Kingdom in 2004 by
Jessica Kingsley Publishers Ltd
116 Pentonville Road
London N1 9JB, England
and
29 West 35th Street, 10th fl.
New York, NY 10001-2299, USA
www.jkp.com

Library of Congress Cataloging in Publication Data
A CIP catalog record for this book is available from the Library of Congress

British Library Cataloguing in Publication Data
A CIP catalogue record for this book is available from the British Library

ISBN 1 84310 154 8

Printed and Bound in Great Britain by
Athenaeum Press, Gateshead, Tyne and Wear

Contents

Part Three: Contemporary Issues

Preface

This volume in the Research Highlights series brings together contributions that together aim to elucidate the nature of women's offending and responses to it. Such a volume was considered timely for a number of reasons. First, there continues to be a relative dearth of literature on women who offend and, in particular, on the effectiveness of responses that have been developed to meet offending women's needs. At the same time as the 'what works?' literature claims to provide increasing insight into what constitutes effective intervention aimed at reducing reoffending, it is becoming increasingly apparent that women's offending is in many ways distinctive and therefore demands a distinctive response.

Second, the contributions in this volume are set against a backdrop of increasingly punitive responses to women's offending by the courts, with the female prison populations throughout the UK having risen to unprecedented levels over the last few years. Third, a number of policy and legislative developments in different parts of the UK will impact in differing ways and to differing degrees upon women who offend. To better understand the likely implications of these developments it is necessary to consider the nature and circumstances of women's offending and to chart how the criminal justice system has dealt with women who break the law both historically and in more recent years.

The contributions to the volume have been organised thematically in three parts. Part I examines the nature of women's offending and the sentencing of women who offend. In Chapter 1, Loraine Gelsthorpe provides an overview of theoretical perspectives on women who offend. Michele Burman examines, in Chapter 2, how women's offending compares with offending by men and whether, as media representations would suggest, women are becoming more criminal and more violent. In Chapter 3, Jackie Tombs describes the transformations that have taken place in penal policy in relation to women who offend, especially in Scotland, while Carol

Hedderman focuses, in Chapter 4, on the rising female prison population in England and Wales.

Part II of the book focuses more specifically upon women's experiences of the criminal justice system. The contribution by Judith Rumgay (Chapter 5) focuses upon the supervision of women in the community, which itself has been redefined through an increasing emphasis upon change programmes, with those designed for women not sitting easily alongside the criteria for accreditation against which they must now be assessed. Gill McIvor highlights in Chapter 6 the difficulties that have accompanied attempts to maximise the use of community service with women in order to impact on the numbers of women entering prison under sentence. The characteristics of women in prison are discussed by Nancy Loucks in Chapter 7. In Chapter 8 Chris Wilkinson outlines the challenges faced by women on leaving prison and speculates as to the likely implications of proposed changes in early release arrangements in England and Wales. Black women's experiences at different stages of the criminal justice system are described by Ruth Chigwada-Bailey in Chapter 9.

The final part of the volume addresses broader contemporary issues that impact upon women's offending and how it is responded to by criminal justice professionals. In Chapter 10, Hazel Kemshall discusses the limitations of existing risk assessment tools for predicting the risk of serious offending for women and suggests that energies might better be directed towards gaining a fuller understanding of the nature and context of serious offending by women. In a similar vein, Carol Hedderman argues in Chapter 11 that different factors have a bearing upon women's offending than upon offending by men. This therefore means that programmes that focus upon addressing male 'criminogenic needs' are unlikely to be effective in reducing reoffending among women. In Chapter 12, Margaret Malloch focuses upon drug misuse, one of the factors most often associated with women's offending and increasingly so. Finally, in Chapter 13, Susan Batchelor and Michele Burman discuss the challenges in developing effective work with girls.

This volume is wide ranging in its scope, but its aim overall is to equip practitioners with up-to-date knowledge and debates about women who offend and how their offending is responded to by policy-makers and by the courts. It is hoped that it will make a useful contribution to the small but growing literature on 'what works' with women who offend, but that it will equally importantly highlight the plight of women who commit offences and the continuing challenges involved in providing appropriate resources for them in the community.

PART I

Female Offending and Responses to It

CHAPTER 1

Female Offending

A Theoretical Overview

Loraine Gelsthorpe

Introduction

This chapter is concerned with pathways into crime and the explanations for women's involvement in crime, but the most obvious starting point is what we know about women's involvement in crime. One of the most persistent and universal findings in criminological research has been that women commit less crime than men. Indeed, while criminal convictions in England and Wales are relatively common for males they are still unusual for females (Home Office 2001). In Scotland too, women constitute a relatively small percentage of the criminal cases coming before the courts and the same situation pertains in Northern Ireland. Such findings are not uncommon across the world (Steffensmeier and Allan 1996).

There are, however, some interesting historical fluctuations in the amount of crime committed by females; for instance, there was a surge in the prosecution of females in the late seventeenth and early eighteenth centuries, resulting in a unique moment of female domination among recorded offenders (Beattie 1995), but for the most part women's involvement in crime has been lower than men's. In the twenty-first century this claim perhaps requires further analysis and qualification because of the social transformations brought about by late modernity (Giddens 1990). Perceptions of increased crime among women have perhaps never been greater, at least within the media, and the burgeoning prison population (Gelsthorpe and Morris 2002) seemingly supports such perceptions. But the situation is more complex than this and it is important to separate out public, media and criminal justice system responses to women who commit crimes from the actualities of involvement.

Following an extensive self-report survey of over 2500 young people, Graham and Bowling (1995) indicate that an increasing number of young women are lured by crime and drug use. Every other male and every third female in their sample admitted to committing offences and the same numbers admitted using drugs at some time. More recent studies rehearse similar arguments. Flood-Page *et al.* (2000) carried out a youth lifestyle survey in 1998 to 1999 as a development of the 1998 British Crime Survey. From nearly 5000 young people aged 12 to 30 (with a response rate of 69%) they learned that almost a fifth (19%) admitted to one or more offences in the previous 12 months, though males (26%) were more likely to admit offending than females (11%). In Jamieson, McIvor and Murray's (1999) Scottish study, using a slightly broader definition of offences than in the studies by Graham and Bowling and Flood-Page *et al.*, the majority of boys and girls between 14 and 15 years of age admitted to having committed an offence in the previous 12 months, though the incidence of offending was higher among the boys (85% compared with 67% of girls). Thus a reassessment of females' involvement in crime is important, but there is nothing here to suggest that the overall picture is changing. Indeed, from self-report studies such as these we learn that although there may be more females involved in crime than hitherto (or at least more reporting involvement) the basic male/female discrepancy in rates of involvement in crime pertains.

Another key question is whether women and men commit the same kinds of crimes. While offenders such as Myra Hindley and Rose West have attracted enormous media and public attention because of the commission of sexual crimes and violent murders, and while female offenders over 21 years are found in all other offence types (ranging from burglary, robbery, criminal damage, and drug offences to motoring offences, for instance), they form a numerical majority in only two: offences relating to prostitution and failing to pay for a television licence. When women are convicted it is more likely to be for offences involving theft and handling stolen goods, drug offences, and fraud and forgery than anything else (see also Chapter 2 this volume).

Women seem to have lower rates of involvement in murder, serious violence and professional crime. In none of the categories does the female share reach even half the total (Home Office 1999). Developmental studies on crime and delinquency seem to support the general claim that women's crime broadly reflects the same pattern of men's crime, however, noting that the gender gap is more a question of differences in the degree of participation, frequency and variety, than in types of behaviour (Loeber *et al.* 1993).

Theories of women's offending

At once we can learn that the differential involvement in crime between males and females goes beyond official processing and agency responses and is still there even when looking at self-report studies. We learn that female 'criminal careers' are perhaps shorter than those of their male counterparts, and with some guidance as to the kinds of crimes that women typically commit we can begin to see that there might be distinctive reasons why males and females become involved in crime in the first place, not to mention distinctive pathways out of crime (McIvor, Jamieson and Murray forthcoming).

Interestingly, however, there has been relatively little theorising about women and crime and this point is as relevant today as it was in the nineteenth century. Rather, it is often the case that theories put forward to explain men's crime have been presented as general theories of crime and have included women without real questioning as to whether or not this is appropriate (Heidensohn 1996). Barbara Wootton's early plea for more research into sex differences in crime has oft been repeated (1959, p.318).

While criminological theorising about crime and pathways into crime has been abundant then, criminology has seemingly had almost nothing to say of interest or importance about women. Whether this reflects the apparent rarity of the female offender, simple neglect, sexism on the part of theorists, or some other reason it is difficult to say, but it has meant that the trajectory of theories relating to women has been unusually conservative (Leonard 1982; Morris 1987; Smart 1976). In addition to outlining some of these conservative theories and highlighting some critical theoretical developments, with brief examples along the way I conclude with some contemporary understandings of women's pathways into crime.

Biological theories

Early theorists argued that the true nature of women was antithetical to crime. Reflecting dominant ideas about biological determinism, epitomised in Freud's widely quoted phrase 'anatomy is destiny' (1924, p.178)[1] it was thought that criminality was linked to 'maleness' and 'masculine' traits such as aggression and physicality. Cesare Lombroso, one of the most influential of the biological theorists, analysed the physical characteristics of prisoners and concluded that offenders were atavistic – throwbacks to a more primitive evolutionary stage of development. With William Ferrero, Lombroso asserted that women were even less evolved than men and that female criminality resulted from biological inferiority (Lombroso and Ferrero 1895). As a result of this she was seen as 'doubly deviant', both biologically and socially, for she was anomalous compared with other typically male offenders, and as a woman she was 'odd' because she was acting against her biological nature. If crime were to be explained by primitive traits, of course, we might expect women to commit more crime than men. Lombroso explains this apparent anomaly by arguing that prostitution was the female substitution for crime and by attributing the lower crime rate of women to their proximity to lower life forms (being less intelligent, they could not commit as much crime as men). (See Smart 1976 and Williams 1991, for a fuller explanation of early biological theories.)

Some modern theorists have continued this line of thinking, imagining that there are essential biological differences which account for differential involvement in crime. In their review of differences between men and women Maccoby and Jacklin (1975) highlight that the main differences which stood up to testing were aggression, verbal ability and spatial or mathematical ability. They argue that men are more aggressive than women in all human societies for which evidence is available; that such differences are found in early infancy; that levels of aggression are straightforwardly related to levels of sex hormones and that similar differences in aggression exist in all subhuman primates. Each of these points can be questioned, however.

Criticisms include the fact that notions of natural 'masculine' or 'feminine' behaviour are culturally bound, that socialisation begins at birth (if not before), that not only do men and women have 'male' and 'female' hormones, but hormone levels vary for any one person in moments of stress and at different times in life, and hormone levels can be stimulated according to social situations. Thus aggressive behaviour can affect the production of testosterone (the so-called 'male' hormone). (See Caplan 1975 for a critique of 'sex difference' research.)

Thus each of Maccoby and Jacklin's arguments can be put aside, but belief in the biological basis of differences in aggression remains strong. Wilson and Herrnstein, for example, conclude their discussion by arguing that while aggression is often situationally controlled and the forms which it takes are shaped by social learning, 'the durability, universality and generality of the relative aggressiveness of males cannot plausibly be blamed entirely on arbitrary sex roles' (1985, p.121). They believe that constitutional (that is, biological) sex differences in aggression are of a magnitude sufficient not only to explain differences in the commission of violent crime, but possibly also in the commission of crime generally.

A further notable strand to the biology and crime debate has revolved around menstruation and crime. The main advocate of a link between menstruation and crime is Katherina Dalton (1961, 1977). Dalton interviewed incarcerated women, obtaining information about their menstrual cycles. From their self-reported information, Dalton calculated that the women's menstrual cycle phases occurred at the times their crimes were committed. A number of studies followed, with sometimes contradictory results (Epps 1962; Horney 1978) and it should be noted that methodological problems have led other researchers to question the results which point to a link between menstrual cycles and crime – largely because of inaccuracies in self-reported menstrual cycles and because social context can influence the onset and cessation of menstruation. Nevertheless, it is clear that the law has taken such generative phases as menstruation and the menopause into account in some cases (Edwards 1988). In similar vein it has been suggested that there are links between post-natal depression and crime (especially infanticide). Put simply, it is thought that as the female body fluctuates in terms of hormonal activity, women may engage in a wide variety of antisocial and criminal activity (see Smart 1976).

Some theorists (for example, Otto Pollak 1961) have addressed female criminality in terms of physiological differences between the sexes. Pollak thought that because women are capable of concealing sexual arousal (unlike men) they are inherently deceitful and manipulative. In this way, they are likely to conceal the true nature of their offending behaviour. Other research on women and crime includes biological and neurological studies which explore hereditary factors (through family, twin and adoption studies for example; see Widom and Ames 1988).

In many theoretical overviews, biological approaches to antisocial behaviour are either ignored or vilified, rightly so in many cases (cf. Brown 1990). It is certainly the case that arguments that there is a single biological factor or genetic predisposition which produces criminal behaviour would be shortsighted. Nevertheless, from recent research findings it is possible that biological factors are involved in the aetiology of at least some antisocial behaviour. It is widely thought that early central nervous system trauma may contribute to the development of antisocial or criminal behaviour for instance (Widom and Ames 1988). We might add that there has been surprisingly little research on psychophysiological factors, but one promising avenue of research appears to be the relation between the personality trait of sensation seeking and the physiological/biological phenomena associated with it (Zuckerman 1994).

Psychological theories

Psychological theories of crime emerged during the latter half of the nineteenth century in conjunction with the development of medical models of crime and deviance. Proponents of early psychological theories attributed criminality to mental disease or defect that could be treated and potentially cured through the assistance of psychologists and/or psychiatrists. Interestingly, psychological dysfunction among women was often thought to have a biological basis. For example, nineteenth-century explanations for kleptomania attributed women's shoplifting to a mental disease associated with reproductive functions. Sigmund Freud (1933) attributed women's deviance to their inability psychologically to adjust to their biological inferiority to men. As a consequence, he suggested that they develop a masculinity complex, exhibiting exaggerated masculine characteristics and engaging in masculine behaviours, including crime, as a way of compensating for their inferiority. Deutsch (1944), developing some of this work, emphasised the normal passivity of women and their determination to be wives and mothers and argued thus that women offenders were personality disordered (see also Gibbens 1957; Glover 1969). However, such theories reflect cultural and gender assumptions as much as anything.

Several studies of girls and young women in institutions in the 1960s and 1970s addressed the relationship between psychology and delinquency. For example, Konopka (1966), Cowie, Cowie and Slater (1968), Richardson (1969), Gibbens (1971) and Hoghughi (1978) all pointed to the high levels of emotional instability, poor self-image, and psychological disturbance of girls. Critics have questioned the methodology of theorists in this area, however, since institutionalised samples are notoriously suspect. Certain kinds of offenders may be selected for official processing in the first place and the institutionalisation itself may have led to the psychological behaviour viewed as pathological. Moreover, it has been suggested that definitions of 'mental health' and 'ill-health' reflect gendered stereotypes (see, for instance, Broverman *et al.* 1970; Chesler 1972).

Some theories see women's crime as a kind of 'acting out' (Blos 1969; Pollak and Friedman 1969). It has been thought that women have been traditionally socialised to be passive and to need affection. However, if they have been poorly or under-socialised, then they may be susceptible to manipulation by men (for example, through promiscuity or prostitution; Davis 1971; Gibbens 1957; Glueck and Glueck 1934; Morris 1964; Rosenblum 1975; Thomas 1923) and may 'act out' the faulty socialisation.

Recent research includes social psychological research on motivational constructs. Such research has involved researchers examining gender differences in relation to sexuality, emotion, competition and aggression, for example (Bernstein 1999). Personality research too is much in evidence. As indicated above, one such example involves a focus on sensation seeking, creativity and differences in social attitudes (Zuckerman 1994). There is a good deal of North American research which looks at psychosocial profiles of males and females too, especially work which compares the degree and quality of social and personal adaptations between adolescent males and females (Lanctot and LeBlanc 2002). Linked to this, more recent research still has focused on gender differences in social cognition (those factors which affect an individual's capacity for encoding information, interpreting and considering the risks and benefits of a particular action, and determining appropriate responses in any one situation). It is thought that one of the reasons that women have lower rates of offending is because they acquire social cognitive skills earlier in life than males and because they have better pro-social skills (Bennett, Farrington and Huesmann 2002).

Sociological theories

Explanations of female criminality in terms of social differentiation of gender roles which emerged in the 1960s and 1970s were heralded as a major advance on the early conservative physiological and psychological theories. Reference to differential opportunities for illegitimate activity, differential patterns of socialisation and differential expectations of behaviour all point to how the social environment of a person limits or facilitates access to illegitimate means to achieve social goals or status (see Williams 1991 for a review). Ruth Morris (1964) in particular pursued a line of thinking that linked obstacles to economic power status to delinquency in boys, and obstacles to positive affective relationships to delinquency in girls. Sutherland and Cressey (1970) make a similar point in revealing that the rates of arrest for women are lowest in those societies in which they are most closely supervised and highest in those societies where women have achieved some equality with men in terms of the opportunities to operate in 'public space' and commit crime. Hoffman-Bustamante (1973) reiterated the link between sex roles and criminal activity, suggesting that girls are induced to be much more passive and domesticated than boys, who are encouraged instead to be ambitious, aggressive and outward-going. Moreover, sex-role theorists suggest that sex roles not only structure opportunity and the degree of participation in crime, but that crime is also seen as either an extension or expression of the female role; her domestic role is seen as shaping both the object and the means of the crime (see Morris

1987 for a review of such ideas). Thus the fact that women shop is used to account for their prevalence among detected shoplifters, not only in terms of opportunity but also with reference to the motive for the offence. It is often said that women steal food or 'extras' to improve their image as 'mothers' or 'homemakers', for instance. Prostitution is similarly explained with reference to sex role and is seen as an attempt to gain status or emotional security through dependency (see also Smart 1976).

There is a common theme in all of this which is to do with public/private space and social control and it is perhaps in the direction of control theories that we find particularly helpful insights regarding women. Hirschi's ground-breaking theoretical framework which revolved around attachment, commitment, involvement and belief (1969) has sparked off a number of ideas which reflect the differential socialisation of males and females (Smith and Paternoster 1987; Tortensson 1990). Harriet Wilson (1980), looking at 'socially deprived' families in Birmingham, England, noted that what differentiated delinquent and non-delinquent children was what she called the exercise of 'chaperonage' and it is here that we can discern key differences affecting males and females and interest in the 'conforming' female. Hagan (1987) and Hagan, Simpson and Gillis (1979, 1985), looking at variants of social control theory, came to the conclusion that crime and delinquency as a form of excitement was more often open to males than females, because females were more frequently subject to intense and diffuse family control in the private, domestic sphere. That control led to the removal of girls from public purview of agents of both informal and formal social control. It followed that the more women were confined to the domestic sphere, the greater the disparity between rates of male and female offending. The implications of this 'power-control' theory are interesting insofar as we might imagine 'house arrest' as an effective control over women: a cruel and usual punishment many would say.

A new line of sociological thinking is developing in the direction of gender, structural disadvantage and crime (the search for links between aggregate characteristics and rates of crime has a long tradition in the social sciences – with some of the work of Durkheim, Marx and the early Chicago ecologists – of course). The question is whether embedded structural factors such as poverty and family disruption influence female offending levels in the same way that they appear to influence those of males. Steffensmeier and Haynie (2000), for example, in their study of US cities, provide strong evidence that structural disadvantage is a source of high levels of female offending (see also Broidy and Agnew 1997). This is work which supports earlier US-based feminist work in this vein (Chesney-Lind 1997; Daly 1994). I return to the idea of social disadvantage later.

Women's emancipation and crime

In 1975 two controversial books, Freda Adler's *Sisters in Crime* and Rita Simon's *Women and Crime*, proposed ideas about women's criminality based on analyses of female arrest trends at that time. Adler suggested that the lifting of restrictions on women's opportunities in the economic marketplace gave them the chance to be as greedy, violent and crime prone as men. Similarly, Simon concluded that women's increased share of arrests for property crime (she found no increase for violent crime) might be explained by their increased opportunities in the workplace to commit crime. Both books attracted critical attention, and several scholars called into question many of the issues raised by the two authors. Steffensmeier (1978), for example, found that the research contradicted the view at that time that women were committing more violent ('masculine type') crimes. Box and Hale (1983) also raised questions as to how the 'women's movement' can be measured and its impact assessed.

A major assumption underlying the suggestion that increased opportunities lead to increases in women's crime is that women's roles have changed, that women now play an equal part in social, economic and political life. But women continue to feel excluded from areas of public life. Moreover, women's earnings continue to be lower than those of men, and women remain a minority in high-ranking positions in society. Women also continue to bear the brunt of domestic and childcare responsibilities even when they are in full-time employment (Office for National Statistics 2000). Thus women may be more involved in crime than hitherto, but this may be due to reasons of poverty, economic marginalisation and so on, and not due to women's emancipation. Such factors would explain race and class differences in women's crime rates (where these are discernible). It is obviously hard to separate out public and criminal justice responses which may be based on stereotypes rather than on the actualities of crime.

Feminist contributions to understandings of women's involvement in crime

In 1961 Walter Reckless, an American criminologist, questioned whether any theory of crime and delinquency would be accepted if a criminologist paused to consider if it applied to women. It was nearly a decade later, however, before Heidensohn (1968) drew attention to the 'omission of women from general theories of crime' and the awakening of criminology from its male-centred (androcentric) slumber was begun. Numerous feminist reviews of theories of women's crime followed (for example, Heidensohn 1996; Leonard 1982; Morris 1987; Naffine 1987; Smart 1976) which point out that theories of women's offending have often been based on studies of men, and that images of female offenders have been distorted because of ideological reasoning. As Scraton suggests: 'An excursion through the twentieth-century's developments in criminology is a journey through communities inhabited only by men' (1990, p.17).

While there is no space to describe these studies in detail here, it is relevant to mention that a key feminist contribution has been to highlight that our knowledge of female offenders has been beset with myths, muddles and misconceptions which often reflect ideological concerns rather than objective evidence and that even self-consciously 'objective' scientific approaches reflect men's knowledge. Klein (1973), Rasch (1974), Smart (1976), Pollock (1978), Gelsthorpe and Morris (1990), Naffine (1997) and Gelsthorpe (2002) have all contributed to discussion in this way. Smart, for example, states:

> ideologically informed studies have become 'leading' works by default...
> The main thrust of theories of female criminality, even more than those
> concerned with male criminality, support and justify the prevailing
> methods of treatment and the ideology of social control adhered to by the
> administrators of legal and penal policy. (Smart 1976, p.4)

The collective endeavours of feminist criminologists and supporters in other disciplines have offered trenchant critiques of the accumulated wisdom about female offenders and demonstrated that theories of criminality 'developed by, and validated on men had limited relevance for explaining women's crime' (Gelsthorpe and Morris 1988, p.98).

The emancipation thesis had value in focusing attention on female crime, and the feminist critique of existing theories made an immense contribution in terms of leading to proper evaluation of theories and their relevance in explaining women's crime, but these insights only went so far. Other feminist contributions have shifted attention towards an understanding of the role of patriarchy and its role in relation to crime. A key theme in current feminist theories of crime is the pervasiveness of male dominance in patriarchal society and its impact on crimes committed both by and against women (Naffine 1997). Here then we can see that power differentials lead women into types of crime that are perhaps 'powerless' such as small-scale fraud and prostitution (Messerschmidt 1986). These crimes involve little reward because women are marginalised economically.

Some of the questions left unanswered by feminist analysts of crime revolve around the precise ways in which patriarchy might contribute to women's crime. The problem here is that as a concept 'patriarchy' is difficult to measure so that its explanatory value cannot be determined in different settings; nor is it realised how patriarchy is made manifest by powerless men (Gelsthorpe 1986). Nevertheless, if there is weakness in defining how precisely patriarchy contributes to routes into crime, the concentration on power in feminist analyses has contributed enormously to an understanding of the gender biases built into and demonstrated by knowledge construction, legal and criminal justice processes (see Naffine 1997; Walklate 2001 and Heidensohn 2002). Feminist contributions have reminded us that even the questions as to what is an 'offence' and who is a 'victim' are often intertwined with gender stereotypes and biases which reflect a general inequality between the sexes (that is, male dominance) in society. Recent feminist work has focused on social–structural influences which mark women's pathways towards crime (Chesney-Lind 1997; Daly 1994) and some relevant points are made below under the heading of contemporary understandings of women's crime.

Women's own explanations for their involvement in crime

One theme that is evident in both conventional and feminist writings about women and crime concerns gender role conditioning (whether as the result of biology, psychology or patriarchy so to speak). In *Criminal Women*, Carlen (1985) suggested that the autobiographical accounts of women's careers demonstrate how 'under certain material and ideological conditions...law-breaking may indeed comprise rational and coherent responses to women's awareness of the social disabilities imposed on them by discriminatory and exploitative class and gender relations' (1985, p.8). She describes the women as rejecting conventional gender roles (as Freud did within a very different theoretical framework) and finding, through crime, roles which 'lift them above the social disabilities imposed on them as women' (1985, p.11). Each woman, Carlen claims, 'deliberately engaged in lawbreaking as a way of either achieving some satisfaction as a person or of resolving some of the problems facing her as a woman' (1985, p.11). With respect to shoplifting, for example, Christina's own explanation was, in part, the provision of an income for her family: 'I never saw enormous compatibility of the situation of being a full-time mother and a full-time thief...I thought of it as my work time' (1985, p.78). This seems to bear out Carlen's claims and, unwittingly perhaps, fuels belief that crime is a rational (almost political) response to oppression. But later, Christina offers a much less rational explanation: 'I have since realised that I was overestimating my capacity to control my own weakness. It was the same as when an alcoholic takes that second drink. The stealing just snowballed' (1985, p.94). Thus financial circumstances may contribute, but not provide the sole answer. Moreover, insurmountable social and economic difficulties lead some women towards crime, but not others, and there may be a particular individually shaped psychological motivation (not necessarily gendered perhaps) as well. Chris Tchaikovsky's (2000) review of *One Hundred Women* highlights similar contradictions. Many of the 100 female offenders whose voices are heard in this volume indicate child sexual and violent abuse and other deprivations in their early lives, but of course not all who are abused go on to commit crime. Nevertheless, it is arguable that women's accounts about pathways into crime, with all their contradictions, are no less valid than others.

Contemporary understandings of women's crime

Holding in mind what women themselves say about their pathways into crime, we can see that the 1980s saw high unemployment, benefit cuts and reductions in services; for example, in health, social services and housing, (Alcock, Payne and Sullivan 2000; Townsend, Davidson and Whitehead 1992; Walker and Walker 1997). Indeed, Smith and Stewart (1998) suggest that the financial and other circumstances of offenders has got worse over the last 30 years or so leading to the (somewhat cynical) comment that imprisonment has become an effective way of managing the unemployed. This point can be readily extended to cover the management of women who are socially and economically marginalised. The notion of 'the feminisation of poverty' seems pertinent here (Glendinning and Millar 1992).

Thus precisely why some women commit crimes can perhaps be approached by referring to the broad features of women's structural positions and lifestyles in society. (A considerable amount of the work in this area, but not all, has been feminist inspired.) It is possible to see that many women are vulnerable to financial difficulties and to the stresses and strains that go along with childcare responsibilities, domestic violence and high levels of childhood victimisation. Indeed, one might refer to these vulnerabilities as 'indirect pathways towards crime'. Numerous researchers and publications have drawn attention to the particular needs of female offenders in relation to childcare responsibilities (often they are single parents), drug and/or alcohol abuse (which is often directly linked to their offending), limited qualifications, lack of work skills or experience, low income, and histories of abuse (Chesney-Lind 1997; Gilfus 1992; Loucks 1998; Morris *et al.* 1995; Walmsley, Howard and White 1992; Widom 1995; and Chapter 8 this volume). Her Majesty's Chief Inspector of Prisons' thematic review of women in prison (HM Inspectorate of Prisons for England and Wales 1997, pp. 14–16)[2] and Mair and May's (1997) study of offenders on probation also confirm the picture of female offenders as having distinctive needs which relate to their general poverty and deprivation.[3] Judith Rumgay (1996, 2000), drawing on an analysis of women on probation in the mid-1990s and on pre-sentence report descriptions of the women, similarly reports that a high proportion of the women offenders had been abused, had psychological problems, and were in or had been in abusive relationships with partners, or had drug and/or alcohol problems.

A key question from all of this research is the extent to which these social characteristics can be said to be offending related. In particular, there have been relatively few attempts really to get to the heart of the relationship between childhood sexual abuse and routes into crime and yet, as indicated above, this is frequently mentioned as central to our understanding of women and crime. At a general level, Cathy Widom (1995) has argued that early exposure to crime as bystander or victim in families or neighbourhoods can increase the probability of becoming an offender. Jacqui Saradjian (1996) has drawn attention to the connections between childhood sexual abuse and becoming a perpetrator. Others recognising connections have suggested that criminal lifestyles are imbued with the risk of victimisation (Baskin and Sommers 1998).[4] But generally, the nature of the connections remains under-theorised. This is not to suggest that such connections do not hold, but rather to suggest that more research is needed to support the observations of professionals and practitioners on the ground and academics alike. At present we are left with the difficulty that many women are abused and socially disadvantaged in other ways, but not all go on to commit crime. It could well be that the low self-esteem engendered by the abuse and disadvantage fosters movement towards crime simply because crime provides a way of establishing some kind of autonomy in otherwise disempowered lives, but this is an idea which needs solid evidence behind it (Pollack 2000). Also, this point should not lead us to assume (as some feminist analyses imply) that offenders are acting as self-consciously political agents when they commit crime.

Recent research on offender-related (criminogenic) factors points towards the importance of: poor cognitive skills, antisocial attitudes and feelings, strong ties to and identification with antisocial/criminal models, weak social ties, difficulty with self-management, dependency on drugs and alcohol, adverse social or family circumstances, unemployment and literacy problems. However, while some of these factors will be relevant to women, as I have suggested, the specific contributory factors in women's offending have received comparatively little research attention in Britain as elsewhere beyond the broad 'pathways into crime' described above (but see Chapter 11 this volume).

At the same time, it is tempting to assume that the social and individual characteristics of female offenders, whether imprisoned or on probation, are predictive of offending. But, of course, prediction is not straightforward. Without wishing to overdo the point, many of the studies of female offenders show 'associations' between the particular needs and circumstances of female offenders (low self-esteem, accommodation and financial problems and so on) and their routes into crime, but this is not the same thing as showing 'causal mechanisms'. Part of the problem here is that classification and risk prediction instruments have been designed and validated exclusively in relation to male offenders (Gelsthorpe 2001; Kemshall, Chapter 10 this volume; Rex 2001). The HM Prison Service review of the literature on female offenders (Howden-Windell and Clarke 1999) helps a little in this regard by sifting through the evidence to indicate which factors can be said to be more predictive of offending and reoffending than other factors. They concluded that the criminogenic factors associated with male offenders are clearly relevant for female offenders too, but their level of importance and the nature of the association may differ; that additional criminogenic needs exist in the female offender population, although their exact relationship to recidivism is not known; and that different criminogenic factors may be relevant for adult female offenders and for juvenile female offenders (see, for example, Jamieson *et al.* 1999).

Notwithstanding the difficulties of prediction studies, and the fact that there have been too few comparisons with women in the general population to help sort out which factors might be predictive of offending (that is, which factors indicate the precise *causes* of crime) we can, at the very least, argue that all the social and individual factors which characterise women on probation and in prison may be *sources* of crime (that is to say, these circumstances contribute to crime). Crime is but one response, but there may be other responses too. As Cook (1997) indicates, crime may be chosen for a variety of complex reasons, which include:

- *an act of desperation:* for example, the offence may be the only way for those in debt 'to keep their heads above water'

- *taking a chance:* for example, the offence may be the result of an impulsive response to illegitimate opportunities which are presented

- *nothing to lose:* for example, the offence may be the product of disillusionment and social exclusion

- *a rational economic choice:* for example, the offence may be a response to the fact that the woman is not able to perceive a legitimate way of gaining the same benefits

- *a means of asserting economic or emotional independence:* for example, an abused woman may 'see' no other option to gaining her 'freedom' than to kill her abusive partner

- *a narrowing of options* for employment or social/personal stability.

It is for these reasons then that one can argue that criminal justice practice needs to focus not just on the immediate lead-up to the crime of an individual female offender (the psychological processes involved) but on the broad social and individual factors which may contribute to and which, so to speak, put the female offender on the pathway to crime. These *sources* of crime need to be tackled as well as any immediate psychological motivation (arising from *particular* stresses or reasons). Indeed, it may be argued that the need to address underlying issues is fundamental to any attempts to reduce crime. As Rumgay (1996, 2000) has argued, the backgrounds and circumstances of women's lives are inseparable from their involvement in crime. Far from being irrelevant to an understanding of women's offending, personal difficulties and welfare problems are inextricable from it. This point is nicely emphasised in Chesney-Lind's (1997) recent review of the literature where she indicates 'the importance of viewing female offenders as people with life histories'.

Conclusion

As indicated earlier, theories on women and crime have been scant compared with the number and range of theories on men and crime. Those theories that have developed over time have been accused of being distorted or reflecting 'ideological reasonings'. Recent empirical research indicates some change. Indeed studies often now include mixed gender samples though sometimes women are relegated to control groups and are not really the focus of attention (Lanctot and LeBlanc 2002). To sum up, let me offer four observations in relation to theories about women's offending. First, some researchers maintain that mainstream criminological theories can explain women's crime even if those theories derive from work on males (Gottfredson and Hirschi 1990; Smith and Paternoster 1987). Though the issue of whether gender-neutral or gender-specific theories hold the most explanatory promise is unresolved. Second, some researchers focus on gender differences, whether biological, psychological or social, to understand disparities regarding involvement in crime (Steffensmeier and Allan 1996). Here it is thought that a gendered perspective helps clarify the gendered nature of both female and male patterns of crime (that is, crime reflects the way in which we 'operationalise gender' in everyday life). Third, some researchers suggest that the male construction of knowledge about female offenders should be challenged from feminist perspectives (Daly and Chesney-Lind 1988; Heidensohn 2002; Scraton 1990; Smart 1976).

Recent research on women and crime includes a number of statistical studies which focus on variance in delinquency prevalence (for example, Wikström and Svensson 2001) and which conclude that gender is not as important as other factors in explaining crime. At the same time, developmental studies (Moffitt *et al.* 2001) suggest that sex difference is the most robust fact known about antisocial behaviour and that there are sound empirical bases for continuing explorations at a critical individual level – looking at neuro-developmental factors alongside research on influential social contexts. A new genre of developmental theoretical approaches of this sort appear to have much credence (Lanctot and LeBlanc 2002; Moffitt *et al.* 2001). Certainly the integrated approach which is presupposed here would seem to have much to commend it, as long as social context is taken to include broad social–structural and political factors and not simply immediate social groupings or environment. Thus my fourth point is that in the move towards integrated theories of pathways into crime, it is important not to neglect feminist ideas about pathways. Feminist ideas are important because of their emphasis on structural social pathways and inequalities, disempowerment and low self-esteem which conceivably affect women and their emphasis on the social institutions and processes which control them. If there could be some way of developing the connections and integrating all these different strands of theories, this would seem to be a promising way forward.

Acknowledgements

I would like to thank Judith Rumgay for her helpful comments on an earlier draft of this chapter, and Gill McIvor for her general help and patience.

Notes

1   Freud's view has often been misinterpreted however. He claimed that boys and girls initially demonstrated both masculine and feminine behaviours as a result of their bisexuality. Thus he did not view 'masculinity' and 'femininity' as innate, but rather as developing from the way the child interpreted the fact of biological sex differences. It was in this sense that he asserted that 'anatomy is destiny'.

2   This was based on Prison Service information and interviews with 234 randomly selected prisoners. It was clear that many of the women had childcare responsibilities (with the majority having at least one child under 16), accommodation problems, financial problems (with over a third of the women indicating that they were in debt – and survived largely on state benefits augmented by casual work and crime) and poor employment and education histories. (See also Carlen *et al.* 1985; Carlen and Cook 1989.)

3   See also similar research findings relating to imprisoned women in the USA produced by feminist theorists (Chesney-Lind 1997; Hannah-Moffat 1999; Pollock 1978). The literature tends not to distinguish between violent, persistent or serious female offenders much: they too are shown to have been subject to child sexual abuse, poverty, physical abuse, financial problems, and so on in the same way as the 'typical' female offender. Chesney-Lind and Laidler (1997), for example, in an analysis of women engaged in heavy drug use, point to background situations of family turmoil and parental drug and alcohol abuse, and argue that women may 'drift' into drug use as they attempt to escape early victimisation and neglect in the home. Daly (1994, p.47) found a varied pattern of women's entry into serious crime in her content analysis of probation officers' reports on 40 women appearing in New Haven's felony court. Four categories of female offenders emerged: street women (who were sexually abused, ran away as girls, and got involved in prostitution); harmed and harming women (who were abused or neglected as children and were probably drug addicted and likely to become violent when under the influence); battered women (who were in a

relationship with a violent man and acted in response to this violence); drug-connected women (who used and sold drugs in connection with boyfriends or family members).

4   See Maher (1997) and Rumgay (2001) for important brief reviews of studies in this area.

References

Adler, F. (1975) *Sisters in Crime: The Rise of the New Female Criminal.* New York: McGraw-Hill.

Alcock, C., Payne, S. and Sullivan, M. (2000) *Introducing Social Policy.* Harlow: Pearson Education.

Baskin, D. and Sommers, I. (1998) *Casualties of Community Disorder: Women's Careers in Violent Crime.* Boulder, CO: Westview Press.

Beattie, J. (1995) 'Crime and inequality in eighteenth-century London.' In J. Hagan and R. Peterson (eds) *Crime and Inequality.* Stanford: Stanford University Press, pp.116–139.

Bennett, S., Farrington, D.P. and Huesmann, L.R. (2002) 'Explaining gender differences in crime and violence: The importance of social cognitive skills.' *Aggression and Violent Behaviour* (forthcoming, 7).

Bernstein, D. (ed) (1999) *Gender and Motivation.* Nebraska: University of Nebraska Press.

Blos, P. (1969) 'Preoedipal factors in the aetiology of female delinquency.' *Psychoanalytic Studies of the Child 12,* 229–249.

Box, S. and Hale, C. (1983) 'Liberation and female criminality in England and Wales.' *British Journal of Criminology 23,* 1, 35–49.

Broidy, L. and Agnew, R. (1997) 'Gender and crime: A general strain theory perspective.' *Journal of Research in Crime and Delinquency 34,* 3, 275–306.

Broverman, I., Broverman, D., Clarkson, E., Rosencrantz, P. and Vogel, S. (1970) 'Sex role stereotypes and clinical judgements of mental health.' *Journal of Consulting and Clinical Psychology 34,* 11, 1–7.

Brown, B. (1990) 'Reassessing the critique of biologism.' In L. Gelsthorpe and A. Morris (eds) *Feminist Perspectives in Criminology.* Buckingham: Open University Press.

Caplan, P. (1975) 'Sex differences in antisocial behaviour: Does research methodology produce or abolish them?' *Human Development 18,* 444–460.

Carlen, P. (ed) (1985) *Criminal Women: Autobiographical Accounts.* Cambridge: Polity Press.

Carlen, P. and Cook, D. (1989) *Paying for Crime.* Milton Keynes: Open University Press.

Carlen, P., Hicks, J., O'Dwyer, J., Christina, D. and Tchaikovsky, C. (1985) *Criminal Women: Autobiographical Accounts.* Oxford: Blackwell.

Chesler, P. (1972) *Women and Madness.* London: Allen Lane.

Chesney-Lind, M. (1997) *The Female Offender: Girls, Women and Crime.* Thousand Oaks, CA: Sage.

Chesney-Lind, M. and Laidler, K. (1997) 'Drugs, violence and women's crime.' In M. Chesney-Lind (ed) *The Female Offender: Girls, Women and Crime.* Thousand Oaks, CA: Sage.

Cook, D. (1997) *Poverty, Crime and Punishment.* London: Child Poverty Action Group.

Cowie, J., Cowie, V. and Slater, E. (1968) *Delinquency in Girls.* London: Heinemann.

Dalton, K. (1961) 'Menstruation and crime.' *British Medical Journal 2*, 1752–1753.

Dalton, K. (1977) *The Premenstrual Syndrome and Progesterone Therapy.* London: Heinemann.

Daly, K. (1994) *Gender, Crime and Punishment.* New Haven: Yale University Press.

Daly, K. and Chesney-Lind, M. (1988) 'Feminism and criminology.' *Justice Quarterly 5*, 4, 101–143.

Davis, K. (1971) 'Prostitution.' In R. Merton and R. Nisbet (eds) *Contemporary Social Problems.* New York: Harcourt Brace Jovenovich.

Deutsch, H. (1944) *The Psychology of Women: A Psychoanalytic Interpretation.* New York: Grune and Stratton.

Edwards, S. (1988) 'Mad, bad or pre-menstrual?' *New Law Journal 138*, 456–458.

Epps, P. (1962) 'Women shoplifters in Holloway Prison.' In T. Gibbens and J. Prince (eds) *Shoplifting.* London. ISTD.

Flood-Page, C., Campbell, S., Harrington, V. and Miller, J. (2000) *Youth Crime: Findings from the 1998/99 Youth Lifestyles Survey.* Home Office Research Study no. 209. London: Home Office.

Freud, S. (1924) 'The dissolution of the Oedipus complex.' In *Standard Edition of the Complete Psychological Works of Sigmund Freud*, vol. 19. London: Hogarth Press.

Freud, S. (1933) 'The psychology of women.' Lecture 33 in J. Strachey and A. Richards (eds) *New Introductory Lectures on Psychoanalysis.* Harmondsworth: Penguin.

Gelsthorpe, L. (1986) 'Towards a sceptical look at sexism.' *International Journal of the Sociology of Law 14*, 2, 125–152.

Gelsthorpe, L. (2001) 'Accountability: Difference and diversity in the delivery of community penalties.' In A.E. Bottoms, L.R. Gelsthorpe and S. Rex (eds) *Community Penalties: Change and Challenges.* Cullompton: Willan.

Gelsthorpe, L. (2002) 'Feminism and criminology.' In M. Maguire, R. Morgan and R. Reiner (eds) *The Oxford Handbook of Criminology*, 3rd edn. Oxford: Clarendon Press.

Gelsthorpe, L. and Morris, A. (1988) 'Feminism and Criminology in Britain.' *British Journal of Criminology 28*, 2, 93–110.

Gelsthorpe, L. and Morris, A. (eds) (1990) *Feminist Perspectives in Criminology.* Buckingham: Open University Press.

Gelsthorpe, L. and Morris, A. (2002) 'Women and imprisonment: A penal paradox.' *Criminal Justice 2,* 3, 277–301.

Gibbens, T. (1957) 'Juvenile prostitution.' *British Journal of Delinquency 8,* 1, 3–12.

Gibbens, T. (1971) 'Female offenders.' *British Journal of Hospital Medicine 6,* 279–286.

Giddens, A. (1990) *The Consequences of Modernity.* Cambridge: Polity Press.

Gilfus, M. (1992) 'From victims to survivors to offenders: Women's routes of entry and immersion into street crime.' *Women and Criminal Justice 4,* 1, 63–89.

Glendinning, C. and Millar, J. (eds) (1992) *Women and Poverty in Britain: The 1990s.* London: Harvester Wheatsheaf.

Glover, E. (1969) *The Psychopathology of Prostitution.* London: ISTD.

Glueck, S. and Glueck, G. (1934) *Five Hundred Delinquent Women.* New York: Knopf.

Gottfredson, M. and Hirschi, T. (1990) *A General Theory of Crime.* Palo Alto, CA: Stanford University Press.

Graham, J. and Bowling, B. (1995) *Young People and Crime.* Home Office Research Study no. 145. London: HMSO.

Hagan, J. (1987) *Modern Criminology: Crime, Criminal Behaviour and its Control.* New York: McGraw-Hill.

Hagan, J., Simpson, J. and Gillis, A. (1979) 'The sexual stratification of social control: A gender-based perspective on crime and social control.' *British Journal of Sociology 30,* 1, 25–38.

Hagan, J., Simpson, J. and Gillis, A. (1985) 'The class structure of gender and delinquency: Toward a power-control theory of common delinquent behavior.' *American Journal of Sociology 90,* 1151–1178.

Hannah-Moffat, K. (1999) 'Moral agent or actuarial subject: Risk and Canadian women's imprisonment.' *Theoretical Criminology 3,* 1, 71–94.

Heidensohn, F. (1968) 'The deviance of women: A critique and enquiry.' *British Journal of Sociology 19,* 2, 160–175.

Heidensohn, F. (1996) *Women and Crime,* 2nd edn. Basingstoke: Macmillan.

Heidensohn, F. (2002) 'Gender and crime.' In M. Maguire, R. Morgan and R. Reiner (eds) *Oxford Handbook of Criminology,* 3rd edn. Oxford: Clarendon Press.

Hirschi, T. (1969) *Causes of Delinquency.* Berkeley: University of California Press.

HM Inspectorate of Prisons for England and Wales (1997) *Women in Prison: A Thematic Review by HM Chief Inspector of Prisons.* London: Home Office.

Hoffman-Bustamante, D. (1973) 'The nature of female criminality.' *Issues in Criminology 8,* 2, 17–136.

Hoghughi, M. (1978) *Troubled and Troublesome: Coping with Severely Disordered Children.* London: Burnett.

Home Office (1999) *Statistics on Women and the Criminal Justice System: A Section 95 Publication under the Criminal Justice Act 1991.* London: Home Office Research, Development and Statistics Directorate.

Home Office (2001) *Criminal Statistics: England and Wales 2000.* London: The Stationery Office.

Horney, K. (1978) *The Neurotic Personality of our Time.* London: Routledge and Kegan Paul.

Howden-Windell, J. and Clarke, D. (1999) 'The criminogenic needs of women: A literature review.' Unpublished paper. London: HM Prison Service.

Jamieson. J., McIvor, G. and Murray, C. (1999) *Understanding Offending Among Young People.* Edinburgh: The Stationery Office.

Klein, D. (1973) 'The etiology of female crime: A review of the literature.' *Issues in Criminology 8,* 3–30.

Konopka, G. (1966) *The Adolescent Girl in Conflict.* Englewood Cliffs, NJ: Prentice Hall.

Lanctot, N. and LeBlanc, M. (2002) 'Explaining deviance by adolescent females.' In M. Tonry (ed) *Crime and Justice: A Review of Research,* vol. 29. Chicago: University of Chicago Press.

Leonard, E. (1982) *Women, Crime and Society.* New York: Longman.

Loeber, R., Wung, R., Keenan, K., Giroux, B., Stouthamer-Loeber, M., van Kammen, W. and Maughan, B. (1993) 'Developmental pathways in disruptive child behaviour.' *Development and Psychopathology 5,* 101–133.

Lombroso, C. and Ferrero, W. (1895) *The Female Offender.* London: Fisher Unwin.

Loucks, N. (1998) *HMP Cornton Vale: Research into Drugs and Alcohol, Violence and Bullying, Suicides and Self-Injury and Backgrounds of Abuse.* Scottish Prison Service Occasional Papers no. 1/98. Edinburgh: Scottish Prison Service.

Maccoby, E. and Jacklin, C. (1975) *The Psychology of Sex Differences.* Oxford: Oxford University Press.

McIvor, G., Jamieson, J. and Murray, C. (forthcoming) 'Is desistance from crime different for girls?' In R. Immarigeon and S. Maruna (eds) *After Crime and Punishment: Ex-offender Reintegration and Desistance from Crime.* Cullompton: Willlan.

Maher, L. (1997) *Sexed Work.* Oxford: Clarendon Press.

Mair, G. and May, C. (1997) *Offenders on Probation.* Home Office Research Study no. 167. London: The Stationery Office.

Messerschmidt, J. (1986) *Capitalism, Patriarchy and Crime.* Totowa, NJ: Rowman and Littlefield.

Moffitt, T., Caspi, A., Rutter, M. and Silva, P. (2001) *Sex Differences in Antisocial Behaviour.* Cambridge: Cambridge University Press.

Morris, A. (1987) *Women, Crime and Criminal Justice.* Oxford: Blackwell.

Morris, A., Wilkinson, C., Tisi, A., Woodrow, J. and Rockley, A. (1995) *Managing the Needs of Female Prisoners.* London: Home Office.

Morris, R. (1964) 'Female delinquency and relational problems.' *Social Forces 43,* 1, 82–89.

Naffine, N. (1987) *Female Crime: The Construction of Women in Criminology.* London: Allen and Unwin.

Naffine, N. (1997) *Feminism and Criminology.* Cambridge: Polity Press.

Office for National Statistics (2000) *Social Trends 31.* London: The Stationery Office.

Pollack, S. (2000) 'Reconceptualising women's agency and empowerment: Challenges to self-esteem discourse and women's lawbreaking.' *Women and Criminal Justice 12,* 1, 75–89.

Pollak, O. (1961) *The Criminality of Women.* New York: A. S. Barnes.

Pollak, O. and Friedman, A. (eds) (1969) *Family Dynamics and Female Sexual Delinquency.* Palo Alto, CA: Science and Behavior Books.

Pollock, J. (1978) 'Early theories of female criminality.' In L. Bowker (ed) *Women, Crime and the Criminal Justice System.* Ann Arbor: Michigan State University Press.

Rasch, C. (1974) 'The female offender as an object of criminological research.' *Criminal Justice and Behaviour 1,* 4, 301–320.

Reckless, W. (1961) *The Crime Problem,* 3rd edn. New York: Appleton-Century-Crofts.

Rex, S. (2001) 'Beyond cognitive-behaviouralism? Reflections on the effectiveness literature.' In A. E. Bottoms, L. R. Gelsthorpe and S. Rex (eds) *Community Penalties: Change and Challenges.* Cullompton: Willan.

Richardson, H. (1969) *Adolescent Girls in Approved Schools.* London: Routledge and Kegan Paul.

Rosenblum, K. (1975) 'Female deviance and the female sex role: A preliminary investigation.' *British Journal of Sociology 26,* 2, 169–185.

Rumgay, J. (1996) 'Women offenders: Towards a needs based policy.' *Vista,* September, 104–115.

Rumgay, J. (2000) 'Policies of neglect: Female offenders and the Probation Service.' In H. Kemshall and R. Littlechild (eds) *User Involvement and Participation in Social Care.* London: Jessica Kingsley Publishers.

Rumgay, J. (2001) 'Accountability in the delivery of community penalties: To whom, for what and why?' In A. E. Bottoms, L. R. Gelsthorpe and S. Rex (eds) *Community Penalties: Change and Challenges.* Cullompton: Willan.

Saradjian, J. in association with Hanks, H. (1996) *Women Who Sexually Abuse Children: From Research to Clinical Practice.* Chichester: Wiley.

Scraton, P. (1990) 'Scientific knowledge or masculine discourses? Challenging patriarchy in criminology.' In L. Gelsthorpe and A. Morris (eds) *Feminist Perspectives in Criminology.* Buckingham: Open University Press.

Simon, R. (1975) *Women and Crime.* Lexington, MA: Lexington Books.

Smart, C. (1976) *Women, Crime and Criminology.* London: Routledge and Kegan Paul.

Smith, D. and Paternoster, R. (1987) 'The gender gap in theories of deviance: Issues and evidence.' *Journal of Research in Crime and Delinquency 24,* 2, 140–172.

Smith, D. and Stewart, J. (1998) 'Probation and social exclusion.' In C. Jones Finer and M. Nellis (eds) *Crime and Social Exclusion.* Oxford: Blackwell.

Steffensmeier, D. (1978) 'Crime and the contemporary women: An analysis of changing levels of female property crime 1960-75.' *Social Forces 57*, 566–584.

Steffensmeier, D. and Allan, A. (1996) 'Gender and crime: Toward a gendered theory of female offending.' *Annual Review of Sociology 22*, 459–487.

Steffensmeier, D. and Haynie, D. (2000) 'Gender, structural disadvantage, and urban crime: Do macrosocial variables also explain female offending rates?' *Criminology 38*, 2, 403–438.

Sutherland, E. and Cressey, D. (1970) *Criminology*, 8th edn. Philadelphia: Lippincott.

Tchaikovsky, C. (2000) *One Hundred Women*. Cropwood Occasional Papers no. 24. Cambridge: University of Cambridge, Institute of Criminology.

Thomas, W. (1923) *The Unadjusted Girl*. New York: Harper & Row.

Torstensson, M. (1990) 'Female delinquents in a birth cohort: Tests of some aspects of control theory.' *Journal of Quantitative Criminology 6*, 1, 101–115.

Townsend, P., Davidson, N. and Whitehead, M. (1992) *Inequalities in Health: The Black Report and the Health Divide*. London: Penguin.

Walker, A. and Walker, C. (eds) (1997) *Britain Divided. The Growth of Social Exclusion in the 1980s and 1990s*. London: Child Poverty Action Group.

Walklate, S. (2001) *Gender, Crime and Criminal Justice*. Cullompton: Willan.

Walmsley, R., Howard, L. and White, S. (1992) *The National Prison Survey 1990*. Home Office Research Study no. 128. London: HMSO.

Widom, C. Spatz (1995) 'Victims of childhood sexual abuse: Later criminal consequences.' Research in Brief. Washington, DC: National Institute of Justice, US Department of Justice.

Widom, C. Spatz, and Ames, A. (1988) 'Biology and female crime.' In T. Moffitt and S. Mednick (eds) *Biological Contributions to Crime Causation*. Dordrecht: Martinus Nijhoff.

Wikström, P.-O. and Svensson, R. (2001) 'Does gender matter? A study of gender, social situation, morals and prevalence of juvenile delinquency.' Unpublished paper.

Williams, K. (1991) *Textbook on Criminology*. London: Blackstone.

Wilson, H. (1980) 'Parental supervision: A neglected aspect of delinquency.' *British Journal of Criminology 20*, 3, 203–235.

Wilson, J. and Herrnstein, R. (1985) *Crime and Human Nature*. New York: Simon and Schuster.

Wootton, B. (1959) *Social Science and Social Pathology*. London: Allen and Unwin.

Zuckerman, M. (1994) *Behavioural Expressions and Biosocial Bases of Sensation Seeking*. New York: Cambridge University Press.

CHAPTER 2

Breaking the Mould

Patterns of Female Offending

Michele Burman

'Women Behaving Badly'
(*The Herald*, 14 February 1998)

'When Did Girls Get So Brutal?'
(*The Independent on Sunday*, 1 August 1999)

'Surge in Women's Prisons Puts Jails in Crisis'
(*The Guardian*, 27 November 2001)

'Twisted Sisters'
(*The Guardian*, 15 August 2000)

Misrepresenting female offenders

Crime is a news staple, and crimes committed by women, especially violent crimes, make for compelling news. A recurring feature in our newspapers, these kinds of media headlines, with their accompanying text documenting the lives and deeds of the women involved, combine to present a disturbing picture of growing numbers of criminally minded females, increasingly engaging in more violent offences. Media images and representations encourage a particular discourse of female offenders, typically profiling them as unstable or out of control, and their actions as irrational, emotional or driven by stress or duress. Nowhere is this more evident than in depictions of violently criminal women, which tap into (real and imaginary) fears of the growing antisocial behaviour of uncontrollable females which almost rival concerns about volatile young men (Batchelor, Burman and Brown 2001). Yet such images of female offenders and the crimes that they commit are far from accurate. Whilst newspapers have a powerful role to play in the construction of gender in generating understandings of the roles and capabilities of women (Naylor 1995, 2001), news reporting of female offending reflects neither the 'reality' of female offending nor its incidence.

Plotting the contours of female offending, however, is not straightforward. Like crime in general, the 'true' facts of the scale and patterning of female offending are, in all probability, unknowable. But we do know, incontrovertibly, that female offenders, of all ages, are far outnumbered by males. A universally established fact about crime is that it is overwhelmingly committed by men, particularly young men. All available sources of information about crime – official statistical data, self-report studies, research studies and victimisation surveys – point to a marked gender ratio in patterns of crime and victimisation. Women's participation in virtually all forms of criminal activity is far lower than their male counterparts, and this renders them far less visible in systems of criminal justice.

We know too that one of the most robust predictors of non-offending is female gender (Heidensohn 1997). That said, we need to be as wary of asserting gender to be the single most significant factor explaining crime (Muncie 1999) as we are of characterising women as non-offenders. Media accounts often wildly exaggerate female criminality, yet there is some compelling evidence, based on self-report studies, to suggest that the difference between male and female offending rates may be smaller than thought (Flood-Page *et al.* 2000; Graham and Bowling 1995; Jamieson, McIvor and Murray 1999), and that women, especially young women, are increasingly being drawn into the criminal justice system (Batchelor *et al.* 2001; Chesney-Lind 1997, 2001; Chesney-Lind and Shelden 1998; Worrall 2000, 2001).

'Facts' and figures about female offending

The most commonly cited evidence for women's consistently low participation in crime are national official statistics: those figures compiled by the police, the courts, and other criminal justice agencies and routinely published by the government.[1] Police-generated statistics provide data on particular categories of recorded crimes which are taken to be the official indicators of levels and patterns of crime, and from which trends in crime over time are charted.

Official statistics provide the 'authorised version of crime and criminals' (Coleman and Moynihan 1996, p.23) and a good part of their significance lies in the fact that they are used as the main source of information about the extent of crime by the media, politicians and the general public, as well as academics and those who work in the criminal justice system. Strong criticism has been directed at the reliability and validity of these statistical measures, though, and the silences and limitations inherent in them have been thoroughly documented (Coleman and Moynihan 1996; Maguire 1997; Walker 1995). It is not proposed to go over that well-trodden ground here, but it is always worthwhile bearing in mind that official statistics represent only the tip of the iceberg when it comes to documenting criminal behaviour. Their production is a social process reflecting wider institutional, political and organisational contexts (Walker 1995). They are not an objective measure of criminal behaviour, but only measure those crimes reported to, and recorded by the police (and hence rely to a large degree on crimes being reported by the public). Not all crimes and offences are recorded. This is most marked in relation to England and Wales, where only notifiable offences[2] are recorded, with no statistics provided on the incidence of most summary offences. However, in Scotland, unlike England and Wales, national statistics are published on more minor infractions (known as 'offences') as well as more serious ones (known as 'crimes'). It is also important to remember that official statistics provide scant information about the nature of the offence or the circumstances in which it was committed, or about the characteristics of the person who committed the offence, apart from their sex and age group.[3] Furthermore, there is no necessary correspondence between the number of crimes recorded and the number of known offenders (Walklate 1995, p.2). It is important in this regard to distinguish between offence- and offender-based data. Basically the former refers to crimes recorded by the police and the latter to those individuals who have been either found guilty (data produced by the courts) or cautioned (formally warned by the police) and who are termed 'known offenders'.

Offender-based criminal statistics also provide data about the sex and age of known offenders, and the overall male:female gender ratio is calculated from this information. Statistics on offenders also provide some information on those offences which are not notifiable (and hence not recorded by the police). Official crime data on 'known offenders' resoundingly shows the 'typical' offender to be young and male; year after year, in all jurisdictions within Britain, official statistics consistently show that over four-fifths of offenders are male and approximately half are aged under 21 years (Muncie 1999). To take each jurisdiction in turn, in 2000, in England and Wales, there were 1.7 million persons found guilty or cautioned of which just 19 per cent (or 316,000) were women (Home Office 2001a). Similarly, in Scotland, women make up a very small proportion of the criminal cases coming before the courts. Although 52 per cent of the overall Scottish population is female, in 2000 women accounted for 14 per cent of the 137,000 persons proceeded against in Scottish courts (Scottish Executive 2001a, p.5), and just under 14 per cent of those with a charge proved (Scottish Executive 2001a, pp.22–23). In Northern Ireland, in 1999, 12 per cent (n = 3500) of all court prosecutions were female; women, therefore, are approximately eight times less likely to be prosecuted than men (Northern Ireland Office 2002).

It is evident from these figures that *actual* numbers of female offenders are low, compared to men, and this is the case even in those categories of offending where women figure most prominently. There are some important implications arising from the relatively small number of female offenders, particularly in terms of the dangers to which interpretations of female criminality are subject (Heidensohn 1997). On the one hand, when aggregate crime data (totals including both males and females) are used, patterns (and differences in patterns) of female criminality are very difficult to detect, and can go unnoticed. So, for example, a claim based on statistics that shows that the total number of persons proceeded against in court decreased may effectively mask the actual increase in numbers of women proceeded against in the same period. Similarly, data presented on female offenders, which in turn is not broken down in terms of age groups, can also mask trends and patterns specific to particular age groups. Patterns of young female offending show some key differences, in terms of prevalence, than those of older women and these can be obliterated altogether when aggregate female data is employed. In addition, differences in terms of race and ethnicity are particularly prone to erosion because of the relatively small numbers involved. This is particularly pertinent in Scotland where absolute numbers of ethnic minority women are so low.[4] A key message, therefore, is not to view female offenders as a homogeneous group. Yet, obtaining fully disaggregated female data is difficult even though, in recent years, a much wider range of statistical information about female offending from official reports has become available. For example, under the Criminal Justice Act 1991 Section 95, the Home Office is obliged to publish information on gender and race in the criminal justice system. Separate publications are produced on each, however, neither contain information on women that is broken down by age and race (Home Office 2000b; 2001b).

On the other hand, because the raw numbers are so low, they are highly susceptible to shifts in policing, recording and other policies, and this can have a considerable knock-on effect. A recent example involves the increase in convictions for TV licence evasion amongst women aged 21 and over, and which in the course of a year (1999 to 2000) pushed up the proportion of females cautioned or found guilty of summary non-motoring offences from 40 per cent to 48 per cent (Home Office 2001a). Low numbers also mean that even infinitesimal rises in numbers of female offenders can have a radical effect in overall percentage terms. Fluctuations, up or down, can therefore appear very marked. In illustration and, admittedly, to use a rather extreme example, if we take the homicide figures for Scotland, we can see that nine women were accused of homicide in 1997; in 1998 this figure had risen to 21 – a staggering increase of 133 per cent, but a numerical increase of only 12 (Scottish Executive 2001b). It is often this kind of calculation that is employed in media accounts which point to the 'rising tide' of female offenders (Batchelor 2001).

The predominance of males is a characteristic of the official crime statistics of all modern countries, and is not confined to the jurisdictions within Britain (Harvey *et al.* 1992). Heidensohn (1991) found that in most European countries women accounted for less than 20 per cent of those dealt with in criminal proceedings. The pattern is broadly similar in North America. Females constitute approximately 22 per cent of all arrests in the USA (Federal Bureau of Investigation 2001), and account for approximately 16 per cent of all criminal charges (excluding traffic offences) in Canada (Canadian Crime Statistics 1997, cited in Chunn 2000). Australia does not collate national crime statistics because the various states are responsible for police and courts. However, figures from New South Wales (the state with the largest population) show clearly that women make up a small proportion of all offenders convicted; in 1998 women made up approximately 16 per cent of all those found guilty in local courts (which have jurisdiction over both state statutes and summary offence matters), and an even smaller proportion of all convictions in the Higher Criminal Court, which has jurisdiction over indictable offences (NSW Bureau of Crime Statistics and Research 2000).

The pattern has also endured over time. For as long as official statistics relating to crime have been collated,[5] they have consistently shown significant overall differences in terms of numbers of males and females, pointing to the maleness of criminal behaviour and the relative rarity of female criminality. Historical studies of crime show that, statistically, offences by women were always in the minority (Emsley 1997) and that female crime patterns generally paralleled those of today (Rafter 2000). Indeed, the overall gender ratio of convictions in England and Wales was precisely the same in 1892 as in 1992 (Home Office 1993, cited in Emsley 1997). Then, as now, women committed less serious crimes than men, and their involvement in serious violence or serious property crime was rare (Rafter 2000). However, there have been some notable fluctuations. For example, there was an upward surge in female prosecutions in the late seventeenth and early eighteenth centuries, but thereafter the percentage of women prosecuted fell sharply (Emsley 1997; Feeley and Little 1991). Zedner's (1991) detailed study of female crime in Victorian England confirms that women constituted a minority of those who came to the attention of the police and courts. She notes that females constituted a steady 17 per cent of all summary convictions, with drunkenness, larceny and assault the most common types of offences (1991, p.34), but points to the sharp decline (from 27% in 1867 to 19% in 1890) in women prosecuted by means of indictment for more serious offences (1991, p.36). The historical evidence also points to the selectivity by which women came to the attention of the authorities. Most were young, single, working class and living in urban areas (Emsley 1997; Rafter 2000). Unsurprisingly, given the moral climate of the time, the campaigns directed at the 'evils of prostitution' and the ensuing state regulation (Walkowitz 1980), prostitutes constituted a considerable component of female offenders.

Less serious offending

The official figures also yield a picture of the types of crimes and offences for which males and females are charged, and gender differences are marked here as well. Women tend to commit a relatively narrow range of offences in comparison to men. That is not to say, however, that women do not feature in all offence groups. Official statistics reveal that men and women engage in more or less the same range of 'street crimes' but, crucially, they differ markedly in respect of the total number of charges laid each year, and women are more likely to be convicted for less serious offences, such as those involving theft and handling stolen goods, drug offences, prostitution, fraud and forgery and more minor motoring offences. Table 2.1, which shows the actual numbers of male and female offenders with a charge proven in Scotland, makes this point about numerical difference forcefully. Women are in the minority in all categories of offending behaviour.

Table 2.1 Males and females with a charge proven by main crime/offence and age Scotland 2000

Crime or offence	All offenders	Females					Males				
		Total	%	<21	21–30	30+	Total	%	<21	21–30	30+
All crimes and offences	117,574	16,366	13.92	3,059	6,203	6,765	101,208	86.08	24,392	38,523	37,548
All crimes	39,815	6,013	15.10	1,542	2,661	1,809	33,802	84.90	11,360	14,209	8,232
Crimes of violence	4,123	315	7.64	96	111	108	3,808	92.36	1,445	1,431	931
Crimes of indecency	651	202	31.03	28	117	57	449	68.97	85	112	252
Crimes of dishonesty	20,853	3,813	18.29	989	1,707	1,117	17,040	81.71	5,939	7,454	3,647
Fire-raising and vandalism	3,949	352	8.91	122	105	125	3,597	91.09	1,558	1,190	849
Other crimes *	10,239	1,331	13.00	307	621	402	8,908	87.00	2,333	4,022	2,553
All offences	77,759	10,353	13.31	1,517	3,622	4,956	67,406	86.69	13,032	24,314	29,316
Miscellaneous offences	33,297	5,349	16.06	1,102	1,890	2,260	27,948	83.94	7,610	9,798	10,455
Motor vehicle offences	44,462	5,004	11.25	415	1,732	2,696	39,458	88.75	5,422	14,516	18,861

* includes drugs offences

Source: Adapted from Scottish Executive (2001a, Tables 6a, 6b).

Women Who Offend

Figure 2.1 plots the same information as that displayed in Table 2.1, but shows the relative proportions, in percentage terms, of the gender breakdown within each offence category. Again, this reveals a stark picture.

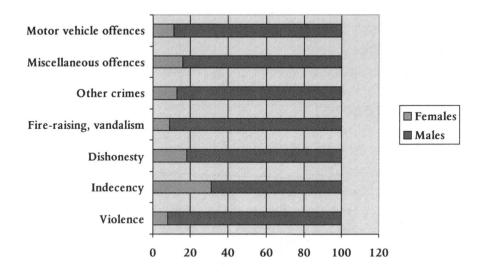

Figure 2.1 Percentage of males and females with a charge proven by main crime/offence Scotland 2000
Source: Adapted from Scottish Executive (2001a).

Table 2.1 shows that in Scotland in 2000 males accounted for just over 86 per cent and women for almost 14 per cent of all convictions (crimes and offences together). We can also see that of the total 16,366 female convictions, 6013 (37%) were for (the more serious) crimes and 10,353 (63%) were for (the less serious) offences. This is much the same for men: 33,802 (33%) and 67,406 (67%) respectively of a total of 101,208 convictions. However, the size of the gender gap varies significantly by type of offence. As Coleman and Moynihan (1996) point out, wide variations between offence categories can distort the overall picture of female offending. If we break down the larger categories, we can see the variation in offending rates. In some offence categories, women form a higher than average proportion of those convicted. In order to see this more clearly, it is necessary to look more closely at the types of crimes and offences that comprise the larger categories. For example, grouped within the category of 'crimes of indecency' are the crimes of sexual assault (rape, indecent assault, etc.), lewd and indecent behaviour and offences related to prostitution. Overall, two-thirds (69%) of offenders in the category of 'crimes of indecency' were male; but more females than males were proceeded against for offences related to prostitution (although this was the only offence where women formed the majority). Other categories where women formed a higher than average proportion of those proceeded against (but did not form a numerical majority) in 2000 include shoplifting (28%), fraud (26%), 'other' theft (19%) – which all fall within the category of 'crimes of dishonesty' – and non-payment of TV licences (24%), which falls under 'miscellaneous offences' (Scottish Executive 2002).

Table 2.2 Arrests of notifiable offences by offence group, England and Wales 2000–2001

Offence group	Total arrests	% Male	% Female
Violence against the person	259,000	86	14
Sexual offences	24,100	95	5
Robbery	31,200	90	10
Burglary	106,500	92	8
Theft and handling stolen goods	442,700	79	21
Fraud and forgery	1,100	73	27
Criminal damage	131,700	89	11
Drug offences	111,300	88	12
Other notifiable offences	116,200	88	12
Total	1,264,200	84	16

Source: Taken from Home Office (2001b, Table 3.1).

Using official data in England and Wales, it is possible to obtain information on arrests for different offence groups disaggregated by gender. Disappointingly, this is not possible in Scotland, as the recorded crime figures are not broken down by gender. The data from England and Wales shows that women are far less likely than men to be arrested for notifiable offences. In 2000 to 2001, 84 per cent of such arrests were male and 16 per cent were female. As Table 2.2 shows, women form a very small proportion of those arrested for sexual offences (5%) and burglary (8%). On the other hand, they form a larger than average proportion of arrests for fraud and forgery (27%) and theft and handling (21%) (Home Office 2001a).

Again, because there are wide variations in offending rates across offence categories, it is useful, in relation to known female offenders in England and Wales, to distinguish first between these broad categories and then look more closely at the types of offending behaviour within the categories. As Figure 2.2 reveals, in 2000, 81 per cent of known offenders were male and 19 per cent were female. Roughly similar proportions of men *and* women were cautioned or found guilty of indictable offences (just under 30%) and summary offences (just over 70%). Looking more closely at the types of summary offences however, is more revealing of gender differences. Summary motoring offences accounted for just under a quarter (24%) of female offending, compared to 29 per cent of male offending. However,

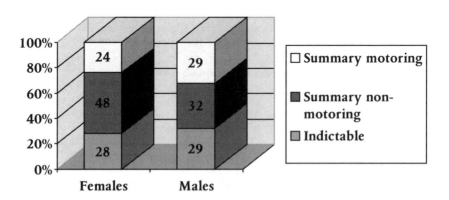

Figure 2.2 Female and male involvement in offending, England and Wales 2000
Source: Adapted from Home Office (2001b, Figure 2.2).

summary non-motoring offences (which include prostitution offences, drunkenness, criminal damage, common assault and TV licence evasion) account for almost half of all female offending (as opposed to just under a third (32%) of male offending).

The official statistics tell us, quite clearly, that female offenders are largely involved in the commission of summary offences. To reiterate a point made earlier, it is perhaps interesting to note that, in 1999, 40 per cent of female known offending related to summary non-motoring offences (Home Office 2000a), and this figure rose dramatically in 2000 to nearly half (48%). This sharp rise can be attributed to increased numbers of convictions for TV licence evasion amongst females aged 21 and over (Home Office 2001a). Like offences relating to prostitution, women form a numerical majority in this offence category. As Carol Hedderman (1995) points out, the person who 'opens the door' is the one who is prosecuted, and the female householder is both more likely to be at home, and the one who answers the door. Not dissimilarly, in the USA and Canada, women are more likely to be charged with welfare fraud (the so-called 'spouse in the house' rule). As Chunn (2000) remarks, the (highly dubious) assumption that if a woman lives with a man he is supporting her and she is not eligible for welfare is *not* made with men who live with women and collect social assistance.

Table 2.3 shows offenders (of all age groups) found guilty of indictable and summary offences in England and Wales over the decade 1990 to 2000. We can see the overall increases in both offence categories, as well as the differences in the proportions of female offenders in both categories, and the large fluctuations in female involvement at both the beginning and the end of the decade. Table 2.3 also reveals that, in terms of indictable offences, theft and handling is consistently the most common offence amongst female offenders (reaching an all-time high in 1992), as it is also amongst males. Female involvement in sexual offences is the only offence group that has seen no variation across the decade. Women's involvement in motoring offences fluctuated in the mid-1990s, but was the same at the end of the decade as it was at the beginning. With some notable peaks and troughs, theft and handling and burglary have seen an overall steady decline and, following a steep incline and a sharp dip in the mid-1990s, so too has violence against the person. Robbery, fraud and forgery, 'other' offences and

Table 2.3 Male and female offenders cautioned or found guilty by type of offence, England and Wales 1990-2000

England and Wales	Number of offenders (thousands)						
Sex and offence type	1990	1992	1994	1996	1998	1999	2000
MALES Indictable offences							
Violence against person	60.6	57.3	51.5	43.9	51.7	48.7	47.1
Sexual offences	9.9	8.3	7.4	6.4	6.2	5.7	5.2
Burglary	52.2	56.1	47.5	40.5	37.2	35.0	31.0
Robbery	5.1	5.4	5.1	6.0	5.6	5.7	5.9
Theft and handling	174.7	186.7	169.0	153.7	152.6	151.5	142.1
Fraud and forgery	20.4	20.5	19.1	17.6	19.1	19.3	17.6
Criminal damage	14.0	12.6	13.0	11.7	12.4	12.5	12.0
Drug offences	39.0	45.4	65.1	72.8	96.0	87.1	76.5
Other (exc. motoring offs)	30.6	35.4	37.6	41.6	48.1	46.1	42.9
Motoring offences*	10.6	10.3	11.4	9.4	8.5	7.6	7.2
Total indictable offences	423.0	439.9	428.2	405.1	437.3	419.1	387.5
Summary offences (exc. motoring offences)	429.6	412.5	392.0	414.2	430.1	415.4	428.8
All offences (exc. motoring offences)	852.6	852.5	820.2	819.3	867.4	834.5	816.3

drugs offences in particular have all seen an increase. However, these figures must be read bearing in mind the need for caution, stated earlier in the chapter, concerning the interpretations of female criminality that can be made from them. Aggregated female data such as this can obscure important

Sex and offence type	1990	1992	1994	1996	1998	1999	2000
FEMALES Indictable offences							
Violence against person	8.6	9.7	9.7	7.9	8.9	8.2	8.1
Sexual offences	0.1	0.1	0.1	0.1	0.1	0.1	0.1
Burglary	2.7	2.5	2.0	1.8	2.0	2.0	1.8
Robbery	0.3	0.4	0.4	0.5	0.6	0.5	0.6
Theft and handling	59.4	71.5	63.4	54.5	56.8	55.2	53.5
Fraud and forgery	6.1	7.0	6.9	6.2	8.0	8.2	7.8
Criminal damage	1.3	1.3	1.3	1.2	1.3	1.4	1.4
Drug offences	4.2	4.9	7.0	8.7	11.5	11.0	9.3
Other (exc. motoring offs)	2.9	3.4	4.4	4.8	6.5	6.4	6.1
Motoring offences*	0.4	0.4	0.6	0.5	0.5	0.5	0.4
Total indictable offences	86.1	101.1	95.7	86.3	96.1	93.4	88.9
Summary offences (exc. motoring offences)	140.1	164.3	161.4	169.6	128.9	113.8	150.0
All offences (exc. motoring offences)	226.6	265.4	257.1	255.9	225.0	207.0	239.0
* offenders found guilty only							
Source: Adapted from Home Office (2000a).							

variations amongst offenders of different age groups; it is also necessary to look at the actual types of offending behaviour within each of the larger offences groups. For example, the figures show a sharp rise in drugs offences committed by women, from 5 per cent of their indictable offending in 1990 to 12 per cent in 1999 (although this came down slightly in 2000 to 10.5%). In fact, the drugs offences for which women are convicted relate to unlawful possession of (mostly class B) drugs, rather than more serious offences, such as the sale of controlled drugs (Home Office 2000a).

Figure 2.3 indicates the relative proportion of male and female offenders found guilty or cautioned for indictable offences in 2000. Depicted this way, one can see the degree to which theft and handling outstrips all other indictable offences. This accounted for 60 per cent of all females found guilty of indictable offences, and 37 per cent of male offenders (Home Office 2001a). But looking at actual numbers, Table 2.3 shows that, numerically, over two and a half times as many men as women were found guilty of or cautioned for this offence. Next to theft and handling, drug offences are the most common for women, with 10 per cent of female offenders found guilty of drugs offences (compared to 20% of male offenders).

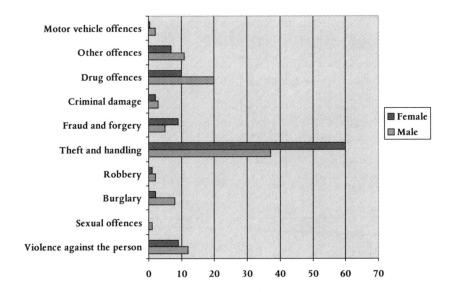

Figure 2.3 Offenders found guilty at all courts or cautioned for indictable offences, England and Wales 2000
Source: Adapted from Home Office (2001b, Table 2.3).

In Northern Ireland, 27 per cent of females and 30 per cent of males were proceeded against for indictable offences in 1999. However, within that category, females were more likely to be proceeded against for acquisitive crime (such as theft, fraud and forgery) than males (61% compared to 41%). On the other hand, males were more likely to be proceeded against for violent offences than were females (29% as compared to 21%) (Northern Ireland Office 2002).

Looking across the Atlantic, the patterning is broadly similar. Females comprised 22 per cent (n = 2,020,780) of all those arrested in the USA in 2000, and accounted for 26 per cent of arrests for 'index' crimes[6] (Federal Bureau of Investigation 2001). Males constituted 83 per cent of those arrested for violent crimes, and 70 per cent of property crimes. In the USA, males are most commonly arrested for drug abuse violations and driving under the influence. Arrests for these two offence groups totalled 23 per cent of all male arrests, compared to 17 per cent of overall female arrests. More than three-quarters of female arrestees were arrested for non-index crimes, and violent crimes constituted a very small proportion of index crime arrests for women. When arrests for index crimes are examined by type, women are arrested approximately five times more for index property crimes than for index violent crimes. Economic crimes such as larceny-theft, fraud and forgery/counterfeiting have higher percentages of female perpetrators than other index property crimes. For example, in 2000, larceny-theft arrests totalled 71 per cent of female arrests for index offences, and 14 per cent of all female arrests. The FBI's Uniform Crime Reports record just two categories of offences with more females arrested than males; prostitutes and juvenile runaways. Females accounted for 59 per cent of runaways arrested in 2000, and 62 per cent of prostitution and commercialised vice arrests (Federal Bureau of Investigation 2001).

The picture is much the same in Canada. In 1999, adult women made up 17 per cent of those charged with a criminal offence. The most common crime amongst women is theft. In the same year, 25 per cent of charges against adult women and 32 per cent of charges against young women were for theft (Canadian Centre for Justice Statistics 2001). In most instances, this was shoplifting and the stolen property was worth $5000 or under. Minor assault accounted for 16 per cent of charges laid against adult women, and 29 per cent of charges against female juveniles.

In all jurisdictions, women have much lower rates of involvement in murder, serious violence and professional and organised crime. This led Walklate (1995) to conclude that 'while men and women commit similar crimes, albeit at different rates, women appear to commit the more serious crimes at a much lesser rate than men' (1995, p.6). Reviewing trends in the USA, Kathleen Daly similarly remarked that 'in general, as offenses increase in seriousness, the gender gap widens for both prevalence and incidence' (Daly 1998). This is even more apparent when the 'hidden crimes' of sexual and physical violence are taken into account. Some crimes are overwhelmingly 'male', most evidently sexual offences, many of which, like the crime of rape in Scotland and the statutory sexual offences, are gender specific. The gender distribution of those involved in business fraud and market manipulation and other forms of 'white-collar' crime is also skewed towards males, although these crimes are not recorded by official statistics.

Changing patterns?

There has been a gradual upward trend since the early 1960s in the proportion of women amongst those charged and found guilty or cautioned. In the late 1950s the gender ratio between men and women for overall convictions was approximately 7:1. By the beginning of the 1990s this had come down to 5:1 (Walklate 1995). These trends caused some commentators in the 1970s and 1980s to argue that female crime was rising at a faster rate than male crime, and that female emancipation was responsible for the greater involvement of women in criminal activity (Adler 1975; Simon 1975), but these arguments are difficult to sustain (Box and Hale 1983).

More recently, statistical evidence has suggested that female patterns in crime are changing. Throughout the 1990s there have been small upward shifts in the pattern of female convictions, especially those involving young women, for robbery, burglary and, more markedly, drug and violent offences. For example, in England and Wales, the proportion of female involvement in violence against the person increased from the late 1980s to the late 1990s, although a closer look at the figures shows that the highest increase has been amongst young women, especially those in the 14- to 18-year-old age group (Home Office 2000a). Trends like this, which show apparent increases in more serious offending by young women, have been the cause of much consternation in recent years, and bear closer inspection.

The relationship between age and offending has been the subject of much attention, although this attention has focused primarily on males. Like males, the official data on criminally charged females also reveals differences in the rate of recorded offending by offenders of different ages. For all age groups, there are fewer female offenders than male offenders, but the gap is smaller for younger age groups. In their examination of Scottish data, Asquith and Samuel (1994) identified a similar relationship between age and incidence of offending for both male and young female offenders, even though the numerical difference was large. This led them to posit that gender differences in the numbers of convictions obscure an age-related pattern of offending amongst young women which 'provides quite convincing evidence that, for females, as with males, crime is very much a youth-related phenomenon in Scotland... To overlook and ignore this pattern...helps sustain the myth of female criminality as individualistic, pathological and essentially non-social' (1994, p.81).

In 1999 in England and Wales, there were 145,700 known male offenders and 35,900 known female offenders between the ages of 10 and 17 years (East and Campbell 2000). Juvenile male offenders outnumber juvenile females by a ratio of 4:1. The largest proportions of juvenile offenders (both male and female) are involved in summary and property offences, especially theft and handling stolen goods (Home Office 2000a). Two-thirds of all males and three-quarters of all females were cautioned or sentenced for these offences. Over the past two decades, the overall number of known juvenile offenders has decreased, but the number of female juvenile offenders has increased. In 1981 there were 7000 male offenders per 100,000 of the population. This dropped to 5400 per 100,000 in 1999. Over the same period, the proportion of female offenders in the population increased from 1300 per 100,000 to 1400 per 100,000 (East and Campbell 2000, pp.21–22). So, although there was a substantial decrease in the proportion of male juvenile offenders (23%) and consequently in known offenders overall, there was an 8 per cent rise in the proportion of females found guilty or cautioned.

The figures from Northern Ireland are another good example of the ways in which slight increases in small base numbers can have a dramatic effect. Over the decade 1990 to 1999, there were 10,565 juveniles prosecuted at all courts, of which females accounted for 10 per cent (Northern Ireland Office 2002, p.44). However, over this period, the number of female juvenile prosecutions steadily increased by 49 per cent from 75 in 1990 to 112 in 1999 whilst the number of male juvenile prose-cutions fluctuated throughout the decade but overall showed a fall of 12 per cent from 1026 to 906. Numbers of female prosecutions rose from a decade low of 61 in 1992 to a decade high of 131 in 1996 (an increase of 84%). In the same period, male prosecutions showed an increase of 17 per cent. The rate of increase in female juvenile prosecutions in the seven years from 1992 to 1999 was almost five times that of males.

Changes in the patterns of female juvenile offending are most marked in relation to violent offences. In 1981 in England and Wales violence against the person accounted for 6 per cent of all indictable offending by females aged between 10 and 17 years; yet by 1999 this had risen to 12 per cent. For males of the same age the rise was much smaller, from 8 to 9 per cent (East and Campbell 2000). Setting this against the general background of an overall decrease in the number of juvenile offenders, violence represents an increasing proportion of all offences for which young females are cautioned or convicted. However, it is still very much the case that, compared to young men, the number of young women who commit violent offences remains very low. For example, in 1999 females (of all age groups) accounted for 8 per cent of non-sexual crimes of violence in Scotland. In terms of actual numbers, 348 women had a charge proven against them and of this group just over a quarter (92 or 26%) were under the age of 21 years (Scottish Executive 2000). This compares to 3817 men who had a charge of non-sexual violence proven against them, of which 39 per cent (1489) were aged under 21 (Scottish Executive 2000). Furthermore, the majority of violent offences that women (of all age groups) are charged with are comprised of less serious offences (such as common assault) and it is in those offence categories that there has been the most increase, rather than in the more serious assault offences.

There is evidence also from North America that female crime and violence patterns are changing. Over ten years from 1991 to 2000, women consistently increased as a percentage of all arrestees. A ten-year trend comparison of arrest data indicates that total arrests for females climbed almost 18 per cent, although total male arrests declined by 45 per cent (Federal Bureau of Investigation 2001). A larger proportional increase was evident for violent crimes, where female arrests jumped 33 per cent, whilst total male violent crime arrests fell 17 per cent (Federal Bureau of Investigation 2001, p.216). For some commentators, these changes in percentages of arrestees appear to reflect not just a change in police behaviours, but an actual increase in female violent offending (Jordan and Jinian 2000). Others are more cautious, arguing that they are more reflective of policing and other institutional practices.

Writing about Canada, Chunn (2000) reports that, despite predictions about violent, liberated female criminals during the 1980s, women are still nowhere near equal with men with respect to crimes against the person. Once again, closer scrutiny of the figures shows that the much-publicised drop in the Canadian male:female charge ratio for violent offences from 21:1 in 1968 to 6.5:1 in 1997 mainly reflects an increase in the number of women charged with minor, non-sexual assault.

'Fessing-up': self-reported offending by females

The media has, somewhat unsurprisingly, drawn much attention to the apparent increases in serious crime by women in recent years and it is this fascination that has generated the newspaper headlines cited at the beginning of this chapter. Several writers have indicated how the 'moral panics' generated about 'new' violent female offenders have drawn on particular interpretations of official data, making much of what, compared to males, are essentially small increases to low base numbers (Batchelor 2001; Burman, Brown and Batchelor 2003; Chesney-Lind 1997). Yet, as discussed in the remaining section of this chapter, there is evidence from other sources that the gender gap between young men's offending and that of young women is closing.

Given the doubts about the validity of official statistics, criminologists have increasingly turned to other sources of information on the scale of offending behaviour. One such means is that provided by self-report studies in which people are asked directly about their involvement in offending and other forms of rule-breaking behaviour, whether this was detected or not. Self-report studies go some way in documenting some of the omissions in official statistical data. They provide an estimate of offending unaffected by selection and processing by the criminal justice system (Graham and Bowling 1995), and have the benefit of including criminal activity that has not resulted in detection and conviction. Self-report studies have been used not only to gain a 'truer' picture of offending, but also as a means of shedding light on why offending occurs, and the degree to which it correlates with other social factors, particularly gender, race and socio-economic position (Muncie 1999). On the whole, they have tended to focus on less serious law-breaking behaviour, such as acquisitive and expressive property offences (e.g. vandalism, theft) and some violent offences (e.g. threats, fights, use of weapon), and have been used mostly in relation to juvenile populations (e.g. Flood-Page *et al.* 2000; Graham and Bowling 1995; Jamieson *et al.* 1999). Albeit hindered by a different set of methodological and ethical problems than those associated with official statistics, they do provide a somewhat different picture.[7] Most conclude that offending, and especially offending by youth, is more widespread in the population than may be supposed by official statistics, whilst at the same time challenging commonly held conceptions about offender characteristics (Coleman and Moynihan 1996, p.67). So what do such studies reveal about patterns and frequency of offending by females?

On the whole, evidence from self-report studies on criminal behaviour show that fewer females than males admit ever committing an offence (so the gender divide persists), but that the difference between male and female offending rates may be smaller than suggested by official figures. Graham and Bowling (1995) interviewed a national sample of 1721 young people aged 14 to 25 years on their offending behaviour, as well as their family life, school experiences and lifestyles. They found offending to be fairly widespread with over a half of males and a third of females reporting that they had committed an offence at some time. But for the most part, these were limited to no more than one or two minor (mainly property) offences. Looking more closely at male and female involvement in 'traditional' forms of property crime, young males were, respectively, eight, six and four times more likely than young females to have committed burglary, car theft and theft from vehicles (1995, p.13).

That said, Graham and Bowling's (1995) study, in common with others (e.g. Anderson *et al.* 1994; Flood-Page *et al.* 2000; Jamieson *et al.* 1999), casts doubt on the relative lack of offending by young women and suggests that more young women than suggested by official data sources are getting involved in crime. An estimate of the extent, frequency and nature of self-reported offending amongst almost 5000 12 to 30 year olds in England and Wales provided by the Youth Lifestyles Survey backs this up (Flood-Page *et al.* 2000). This survey found that males were more than two and a half times more likely to have offended (in the preceding year) than females (26% as compared to 11%). Offences commonly committed by girls aged under 16 years include criminal damage, shoplifting, buying stolen goods and fighting, although as girls grow older they become increasingly more involved in fraud and buying stolen goods (Flood-Page *et al.* 2000). These studies also suggest that approximately 7 per cent of 14- to 17-year-old females admit to having committed a violent offence within the previous year (Graham and Bowling 1995; Flood-Page *et al.* 2000).

A Scottish study also found that girls were less likely than boys to report committing offences, and they reported doing so less frequently (Jamieson *et al.* 1999). Yet this study found a somewhat narrower gender difference in that 94 per cent of boys and 82 per cent of girls in their sample of young people admitted that they had committed one or more offences, with most claiming to have done so within the previous 12 months (85% of boys and 67% of girls) (Jamieson *et al.* 1999, p.12). Although the types of offending were not very serious, there was a striking similarity in the offences reportedly committed by boys and girls. For example, 56 per cent of girls and 69 per cent of boys reported damaging property, 53 per cent of girls as opposed to 66 per cent of boys reported shoplifting, and 49 per cent of girls reported being involved in a street fight, compared to 68 per cent of boys.

On the whole, self-report studies suggest that girls are just as likely as boys to become involved in offending (around 15 years) but whilst girls have generally grown out of this by their later teens, many young men are still involved as late as their mid-twenties. Up to the age of 17 years, female offending rates are not dissimilar to those of young men; but then there is a steep drop in female offending, whilst male property offending increases. Over the age of 17 years, male offenders outnumber females by a ratio of approximately 3:1 (Flood-Page *et al.* 2000). Graham and Bowling (1995) explain this marked gender difference in desistance from offending by reference to social development factors, pointing out that young women who have completed full-time education, who have left home and attained economic independence, entered into a stable relationship, and had a child are more likely to truncate their offending than young men, who 'tend to lag behind young women in virtually every area of social development' (1995, p.56).

In the study by Flood-Page *et al.* (2000), the peak age for self-reported offending for females was 14 years (18 years for boys). It is estimated that whilst at ages 14 to 17 years the male:female ratio of offending may be just 1.4:1, by the ages of 22 to 25 years, it is a markedly different 11:1 (Muncie 1999). Official crime data broadly confirms this picture; the peak age of known offending (for indictable offences) for females is 15 years (Home Office 2000a). After this age, for girls, offending declines, so that for those young women over 21 years all types of offending and law-breaking behaviour tend to fall. So, women 'grow out' of crime earlier than men in that they are most likely to desist from offending in their late teens, but female offending careers also tend to be more truncated than those of men. Home Office (2001b) figures reveal that more than four-fifths (83%) of female offenders have criminal careers lasting less than a year, compared with 60 per cent of male offenders and that just 3 per cent of female offenders have criminal careers spanning more than ten years, compared to a quarter (25%) of men.

Although they do provide useful alternative measures to official statistical data, self-report studies also contain some inherent limitations. Some of these are methodological, including a singular focus on juvenile populations, an over-concentration on trivial misbehaviour, a heavy reliance on questionnaires with their attendant problems of under-completion, and unsatisfactory samples (Coleman and Moynihan 1996). They also rely to a very large degree on the willingness of respondents to divulge their offending in the first place. Perhaps most importantly however, although they do provide interesting material on young offenders, self-report studies are not very successful in shedding light on serious forms of crime or that involving adults.

Female offending: the big picture?

Clearly, different data sources reveal different sorts of information about the nature and extent of law breaking and also the characteristics of offenders. However, there is very little dispute about the validity of the general picture, as reflected in official statistics and self-report studies, of the relative involvement of males and females in criminal activity. Arguments that official statistics distort the 'true' amount of female crime and that much female crime remains concealed cannot be substantiated. There is no evidence to suggest that women are responsible for more crime or, as Pollak (1950) once claimed, that women are responsible for a disproportionate amount of the 'dark figure' of crime.

Although there has been some increase in what Heidensohn (1997) calls the 'female share' of crime, in that women are committing more offences than in previous decades, it most certainly remains the case that women of all age groups consistently commit far less crime than do males, and their criminal convictions are far less common. Female offending tends to be of a mundane nature and is concentrated in more trivial offences.

This chapter has tried to address what are commonly presented as the 'big' questions about patterns of female offending, such as how women's offending compares with men's, and whether women are becoming more criminal and more violent. Jordan and Jinian (2000) note how the troublesome task of explaining crime is aggravated by divergent patterns of female and male crime rates, and remind us that whilst politicians, criminologists and police offer explanations for the decline in serious crimes during the 1990s, they are hard pressed to factor in trends seen in female criminality at a time when these trends are becoming more noticeable. Yet, the 'big' questions are not necessarily the most interesting or valid, nor the answers they generate the most valuable. Furthermore, as Heidensohn (1985, 1997) has argued, concern with the size of the gender gap is based on assumptions that female offending needs to be compared to male offending. A far more interesting, and challenging question might be not what makes women's crime so low but, rather, what makes male crime so high (Heidensohn 1997). Similarly, a closer and more questioning look at criminal justice responses to and social justice outcomes of women's criminality is likely to be informative.

Finally, in pulling together what is 'known' about female offending from a variety of sources, the chapter has also shown that our information about female offending is dependent on the methods we use to obtain the data. It was stated at the beginning of the chapter that the 'true' facts of the scale and patterning of female offending are unknowable and, despite being better informed today than we were a decade ago, due to the recent proliferation of disaggregated sources of information and the analytical opportunities they afford, this 'fact' about female offending still bears repeating.

Notes

1   The police and court statistics for England and Wales are collected and published annually by the Home Office as the *Criminal Statistics, England and Wales*, with biannual bulletins providing supplementary information. In Scotland, statistics on recorded crime and criminal proceedings in the Scottish courts are published annually by the Scottish Executive in the form of a series of *Statistical Bulletins*. The Northern Ireland Office publish a series of *Research and Statistical Bulletins* on aspects of criminal justice. Many other countries publish broadly equivalent data.

2   These are mainly indictable offences (those triable by a judge and jury at the Crown Court), as well as most 'either way' offences, and a small number of summary offences (those triable at magistrates' court).

3   Except in serious violent offences, such as homicide and those involving fire-arms.

4   Scotland's ethnic minority population is approx. 1.5 per cent of the population, according to the most recent census information.

5   Since 1833 in Scotland (Anderson 1999), since 1810 in England and Wales (Emsley 1997).

6   Index crimes are used to track the overall crime picture in the USA, and include murder, rape, robbery, larceny-theft, aggravated assault, vehicle theft and arson.

7   See Graham and Bowling (1995) for a full description of the relative strengths and weaknesses of self-report methodologies.

References

Adler, F. (1975) *Sisters in Crime.* New York: McGraw-Hill.

Anderson, S. (1999) 'Crime statistics and the "problem of crime" in Scotland.' In P. Duff and N. Hutton (eds) *Criminal Justice in Scotland.* Aldershot: Dartmouth.

Anderson, S., Kinsey, R., Loader, I. and Smith, C. (1994) *Cautionary Tales: Young People, Crime and Policing in Edinburgh.* Aldershot: Avebury.

Asquith, S. and Samuel, E. (1994) *Criminal Justice and Related Services for Young Offenders.* Edinburgh: HMSO.

Batchelor, S. (2001) 'The Myth of Girl Gangs.' *Criminal Justice Matters 43,* 26–27. (Reprinted in Y. Jewkes and G. Letherby (eds) *Criminology: A Reader.* London: Sage.)

Batchelor, S., Burman, M. and Brown, J. (2001) 'Discussing violence: Let's hear it from the girls.' *Probation Journal 48,* 2, 125–134.

Box, S. and Hale, C. (1983) 'Liberation and female criminality in England and Wales.' *British Journal of Criminology 23,* 1, 124–134.

Burman, M., Brown, J. and Batchelor, S. (2003) 'Taking it to heart': Girls and the meanings of violence.' In E.A. Stanko (ed) *The Meanings of Violence.* London: Routledge.

Canadian Center for Justice Statistics (2001) *Women in Canada.* Ottawa: Statistics Canada.

Chesney-Lind, M. (1997) *The Female Offender: Girls, Women and Crime.* Thousand Oaks, CA: Sage.

Chesney-Lind, M. (2001) 'Are girls closing the gender gap in violence?' *Criminal Justice,* spring, 18–23.

Chesney-Lind, M. and Shelden, R.G. (1998) *Girls, Delinquency and Juvenile Justice.* Belmont, CA: Wadsworth.

Chunn, D. (2000) 'Female crime, Canada.' In N.H. Rafter (ed) *Encyclopaedia of Women and Crime.* Phoenix, AZ: Oryx Press.

Coleman, C. and Moynihan, J. (1996) *Understanding Crime Data: Haunted by the Dark Figure.* Buckingham: Open University Press.

Daly, K. (1998) 'Gender, crime and criminology.' In M. Tonry (ed) *The Handbook of Crime and Punishment.* New York: Oxford University Press.

East, K. and Campbell, S. (2000) *Aspects of Crime: Young Offenders, 1999.* London: Home Office.

Emsley, C. (1997) 'The history of crime and crime control institutions.' In M. Maquire, R. Morgan and R. Reiner (eds) *The Oxford Handbook of Criminology*, 2nd edn. Oxford: Oxford University Press.

Federal Bureau of Investigation (2001) *Uniform Crime Reports, Crime in the United States, 2000*. Washington, DC: US Government Printing Office.

Feeley, M. and Little, D. (1991) 'The vanishing female: The decline of women in the criminal process, 1687-1912.' *Law and Society Review 25*, 4, 719–757.

Flood-Page, C., Campbell, S., Harrington, V. and Miller, J. (2000) *Youth Crime: Findings from the Youth Lifestyles Survey*. Home Office Research Study no. 209. London: Home Office.

Graham, J. and Bowling, B. (1995) *Young People and Crime*. Home Office Research Study no. 145. London: Home Office.

Harvey, L., Burnham, R.W., Kendal, K. and Pease, K. (1992) 'Gender differences in criminal justice: An international comparison.' *British Journal of Criminology 32*, 208–217.

Hedderman, C. (1995) 'Gender, crime and the criminal justice system.' In M. Walker (ed) *Interpreting Crime Statistics*. Oxford: Clarendon Press.

Heidensohn, F.M. (1985) *Women and Crime*. London: Macmillan.

Heidensohn, F.M. (1991) 'Women and crime in Europe.' In F. Heidensohn and M. Farrell (eds) *Crime in Europe*. London: Routledge.

Heidensohn, F.M. (1997) 'Gender and crime.' In M. Maguire, R. Morgan and R. Reiner (eds) *The Oxford Handbook of Criminology*, 2nd edn. Oxford: Oxford University Press.

Home Office (2000a) *Criminal Statistics, England and Wales, 1999*. London: The Stationery Office.

Home Office (2000b) *Statistics on Race and the Criminal Justice System: A Home Office Publication under Section 95 of the Criminal Justice Act 1991*. London: Home Office.

Home Office (2001a) *Criminal Statistics, England and Wales, 2000*. London: The Stationery Office.

Home Office (2001b) *Statistics on Women and the Criminal Justice System: A Home Office Publication under Section 95 of the Criminal Justice Act 1991*. London: Home Office.

Jamieson, J., McIvor, G. and Murray, C. (1999) *Understanding Offending Among Young Offenders*. Edinburgh: The Scottish Executive.

Jordan, W.T. and Jinian, J.F. (2000) 'Patterns and trends in female crime, USA.' In N.H. Rafter (ed) *Encyclopaedia of Female Crime*. Phoenix, AZ: Oryx Press.

Maguire, M. (1997) 'Crime statistics, patterns and trends.' In M. Maguire, R. Morgan and R. Reiner (eds) *The Oxford Handbook of Criminology*, 2nd edn. Oxford: Oxford University Press.

Muncie, J. (1999) *Youth and Crime: A Critical Introduction*. London: Sage.

Naylor, B. (1995) 'Women's crime and media coverage: Making explanations.' In R.E. Dobash, R.P. Dobash and L. Noaks (eds) *Gender and Crime*. Cardiff: University of Wales Press.

Naylor, B. (2001) 'Reporting violence in the British print media: Gendered stories.' *The Howard Journal 40*, 2, 180–194.

Northern Ireland Office (2002) *Gender and the Northern Ireland Criminal Justice System.* Belfast: NIO.

NSW Bureau of Crime Statistics and Research (2000) *New South Wales Criminal Courts Statistics, 1999.* Sydney, NSW: Bureau of Crime Statistics and Research.

Pollak, O. (1950) *The Criminality of Women.* New York: Barnes/Perpetua.

Rafter, N.H. (ed) (2000) *Encyclopaedia of Women and Crime.* Phoenix, AZ: Oryx Press.

Scottish Executive (2000) *Criminal Proceedings in Scottish Courts, 1999.* Edinburgh: The Scottish Executive.

Scottish Executive (2001) *Criminal Proceedings in Scottish Courts, 2000.* Statistical Bulletin CrJ/2001/7. Edinburgh: The Scottish Executive.

Scottish Executive (2001b) *Homicide in Scotland, 2000.* Statistical Bulletin CrJ/2001/9. Edinburgh: The Scottish Executive.

Scottish Executive (2002) *Recorded Crime in Scotland, 2001.* Statistical Bulletin CrJ/2002/1. Edinburgh: The Scottish Executive.

Simon, R. (1975) *Women and Crime.* Lexington, MA: Lexington Books.

Walker, M. (ed) (1995) *Interpreting Crime Statistics.* Oxford: Clarendon Press.

Walklate, S. (1995) *Gender and Crime: An Introduction.* London: Prentice Hall/Harvester Wheatsheaf.

Walkowitz, J. (1980) *Prostitution and Victorian Society: Women, Class and the State.* Cambridge: Cambridge University Press.

Worrall, A. (2000) 'Governing bad girls: Changing constructions of female juvenile delinquency.' In J. Bridgeman and D. Monk (eds) *Feminist Perspectives on Child Law.* London: Cavendish.

Worrall, A. (2001) 'Girls at risk? Reflections on changing attitudes to young women's offending.' *Probation Journal 48*, 2, 86–92.

Zedner, L. (1991) *Women, Crime and Custody in Victorian England.* Oxford: Oxford University Press.

CHAPTER 3

From 'A Safer to a Better Way'

Transformations in Penal Policy for Women

Jacqueline Tombs

Introduction

Government policy statements supporting decarceration for female offenders are not new. More than 30 years ago the British government imagined that, by the end of the twentieth century, 'penological progress will result in even fewer or *no women* at all being given prison sentences... other forms of penalty will be devised which will reduce the numbers of women necessarily taken from their homes' (Home Office 1970, p.1). Yet at the beginning of the twenty-first century we are further away from realising that hope than ever. Despite the emergence and use of various community-based penal sanctions, increased knowledge about offending by women, and the publication of various official reports criticising imprisonment as a punishment, the incarceration of women continues to rise, both in absolute and percentage terms. In England and Wales, the number of women in prison has doubled since the mid-1990s (Home Office 2001), and in Scotland, for many years a country noted for its relatively infrequent use of imprisonment for women (Coyle 1991), the average female daily prison population rose by almost 42 per cent in the ten years to 2000 – double the growth of the male prison population. This massive increase in incarceration has been particularly marked for young women under 21 years (Scottish Executive 2002) and these bleak trends are not peculiar to Scotland, but are shared by England and Wales and many other countries.

How penal policy has contributed to this expansionist trend in the incarceration of women is the central concern of this chapter. I have chosen to focus substantively on the Scottish experience for two reasons. First, because, despite the alarming upward trend, Scotland still incarcerates comparatively fewer women than other countries. Second, because the endurance of welfare strategies in Scotland has still left a space for a penal policy of decarceration to be achieved. Before I go further, however, I must emphasise that changing the contours of penal responses to female offenders cannot be accomplished without changing broader social and economic policies. As Carlen has argued:

> Although some excellent non-custodial rehabilitative schemes for women offenders already exist, they are by and large rendered ineffective in reducing women's imprisonment: first, because they are too few and far between; and second, because government legislation in other spheres systematically subverts the welfare, housing, employment and education provision which *must* provide reliable backup to all non-custodial penalties. (Carlen 1990, p.9)

This conclusion – about the fragmented nature of non-custodial rehabilitative schemes for female offenders and about how government legislation in other spheres acts against positive rehabilitative schemes – is just as relevant today as it was over a decade ago. But neither fragmentation nor legislation in other spheres is the main concern of this chapter, though both are of profound significance. The focus here is on the penal policy process itself – on the transformations effected through vocabularies and discourses and the consequences for the incarceration of women.

Any policy is, by definition, a 'plan for action'. In the case of penal policy for female offenders, we are familiar with the lack of action. What we are less familiar with is understanding how it is that penal policy plans themselves contain the seeds of their own inaction. The argument in this chapter is, therefore, not simply about the failure to act; it is about more than this. It aims to illustrate how penal policy is translated in the process of developing plans for action. In focusing on a particular example, an attempt to promote a policy of decarceration for the vast majority of female offenders in Scotland, the chapter is really a narrative about a specific instance of penal policy transformation. My argument looks at some of the processes involved in translating and transforming recommendations made in a penal reform document into official government policy and penal practice for women who offend.

In order to consider the significance of penal policy translations, the chapter is structured as follows:

1   The decarceration policy advocated in a Scottish penal reform document is outlined.

2   The processes involved in transforming its conclusions and recommendations within the policy-making process are discussed.

3   The impact of these transformations on current government policy and penal practice are considered.

4   The chapter concludes by drawing attention to the space within which a penal policy of decarceration could still be achieved.

Women Offenders – A Safer Way

In 1998, a joint report by the Social Work Services and Prisons Inspectorates for Scotland (1998), entitled *Women Offenders – A Safer Way*, was published. The report's origins lay in public outcry following the seventh suicide in 30 months at Scotland's only women's prison, HM Institution Cornton Vale; suicides which took place at a time when the average daily female prison population was around 170. The death of these young women (all were under 30 years old) became the subject of the longest running fatal accident inquiry in Scottish legal history and provoked the first comprehensive *official* review of community disposals and the use of custody for female offenders in Scotland.

It was not, however, the first time that the government in Scotland had been made aware of the circumstances of women who offend and of the meaning of imprisonment as a penal response to these women. That had been done more than 15 years earlier in Pat Carlen's (1983) groundbreaking research on female offending and imprisonment; research officially sponsored by the then Home and Health department of the Scottish Office.

Indeed, as HM Chief Inspector of Prisons for Scotland and the Chief Inspector of Social Work Services for Scotland points out; 'In 1983 when Pat Carlen first researched women's imprisonment in Scotland, the profile of the women going into custody and the nature of the crimes they committed were similar to today, although the incidence of drug abuse is higher now' (Social Work Services and Prisons Inspectorates for Scotland 1998, p.36).

It is outside the scope of this chapter to address the question of why so little happened in these intervening years to develop a penal policy for female offenders based on the evidence available – that is another, though not unrelated, story. What is at issue here is to comprehend how penal policy for women offenders has developed in response to the recommendations made in *Women Offenders – A Safer Way*; and, more importantly, whether the story 15 years after the publication of that report, the first official review of community disposals and the use of custody for women offenders in Scotland, is likely to be any different.

Like many other contemporary penal reform and policy documents on female offenders, *A Safer Way* emphasises the evidence on the factors underlying female offending, recommends a gender-specific approach and raises issues about the effectiveness of penal responses. Where *A Safer Way* makes a distinctive contribution is in its use of evidence, its broad conceptualisation of need, its understanding of effectiveness and its impetus towards decarceration through setting specific targets with dates.

Before looking at how the policy-making process has transformed its decarceration impetus, I would like to concentrate on some of the main conclusions and recommendations made in *A Safer Way*. Many of the conclusions reached in the document are familiar ones – that women's offending and the needs of female offenders are different; that women tend to commit minor, mainly property, offences; that their backgrounds are characterised by emotional, physical and sexual abuse; and that they suffer disproportionately from drug and alcohol misuse. Importantly, the report also stresses that women's offending is 'often rooted in *poverty*' (my emphasis) (Social Work Services and Prisons Inspectorates for Scotland 1998, p.52). I will return to the significance of the report's explicit recognition of poverty as an important factor in offending later.

In relation to the main aim of the review, 'to see whether a significant change in emphasis might help to reduce incidences of suicide in custody, some of which will be by young women' (Social Work Services and Prisons Inspectorates for Scotland 1998, p.2), the report concludes that the 'only relatively sure method of reducing the number of suicide attempts in custody is to make a significant reduction in the number of women being imprisoned, via a twin-track strategy' (Social Work Services and Prisons Inspectorates for Scotland 1998, p.52). The 'twin-track strategy' envisaged would involve 'more options in the community' and 'fewer prison places' and the aim of that strategy 'should be to limit the female population at Cornton Vale from over 170 to 100 or less on a daily basis by the end of the year 2000' (Social Work Services and Prisons Inspectorates for Scotland 1998, p.53). *A Safer Way*'s specification of a limit to the numbers of women to be held in custody and the target date by which this is to be achieved is unambiguous. What is being proposed is decarceration for the vast majority of female offenders.

There are seven recommendations made for action in order to give effect to the decarceration policy. These include increased services to support court decision making in relation to bail, measures to ensure a reduction in the unusually high numbers of women imprisoned for defaulting on the payment of fines – a peculiarly Scottish phenomenon – an inter-agency project under the direction of a high level steering group to resolve the issues raised in the report at a local level, tailoring criminal justice social work services to work with women offenders, improved public information on women offenders by 2000, and a revision by the Scottish Prison Service of its estates strategy for women. Additionally, the report specifically recommends that, again by the year 2000, 'young women under 18 years of age are not held in prison establishments' (Social Work Services and Prisons Inspectorates for Scotland 1998, p.57).

The decarceration policy recommended draws heavily on available research evidence about both the factors associated with, and the nature of, female offending. In particular, the report notes the significance of poverty and drug abuse in offending by women and the minor nature of most of the offences they are incarcerated for. Their offences are typically of dishonesty and other minor offences including TV licence evasion and prostitution –

very few commit violent offences. The aim of the twin-track strategy proposed is, therefore, to limit the female prison population within a philosophical position that views imprisonment as appropriate only in relation to serious offenders. Given the minor nature of most offending by women, incarceration for women should be restricted to 'those who pose a real threat to the community rather than themselves' (Social Work Services and Prisons Inspectorates for Scotland 1998, p.53).

A Safer Way also emphasises the research evidence on what has been found to help female offenders to stay out of prison; in particular, satisfactory housing, the return of children to their care, study or employment, and material and emotional support. It further notes that the criteria for effective programmes to reduce recidivism have been identified on the basis of work with male offenders, but that programmes 'for women in the UK may not meet these criteria and yet be effective. It is also questionable if these same criteria are appropriate for women' (Social Work Services and Prisons Inspectorates for Scotland 1998, p.37). This is an important recognition. It leaves the space not only for the development of gender specific programmes but also for the provision of necessary material and emotional support to women living in poverty.

Having said that, at the time of writing in early 2002, the average daily population in HM Institution Cornton Vale is 213, more than double the targeted limit of 100 by the end of the year 2000. There have been more suicides and 15-year-olds are still being incarcerated. How can this be? As I shall argue, a crucial part of the explanation for how this has been possible lies in policy planning processes and penal transformations.

Transformations

From reduction targets to strategic goals

The first stage in translating and transforming the conclusions and recommendations made in *A Safer Way* can be seen in the Scottish Government's Response, which commits itself to 'wherever possible', adopting a 'comprehensive approach...to ensure that all relevant policies are brought together so that the underlying causes of offending as well as the immediate consequences are dealt with in the most effective manner possible' (Scottish Office

1998, p.1). The stated principle underlying the Response is to make 'clear distinctions between the policies which are the responsibility of Government and the role of the judiciary in reaching sentencing decisions in individual cases' (Scottish Office 1998, p.1). But, as we shall see, herein lies the rub.

The Response accepts the seven recommendations made in *A Safer Way*; recommendations explicitly made to effect action to meet the targets set for decarceration. It accepts the need for increased services to support court decision making in relation to bail, measures to ensure a reduction in the high numbers of women imprisoned for fine default, an inter-agency project under the direction of a high level steering group to resolve the issues raised in *A Safer Way* at a local level, tailoring of criminal justice social work services to work with women offenders, improved public information on women offenders by 2000, a revision by the Scottish Prison Service of its estates strategy for women and the need to consult on 'how to ensure that by the year 2000, young women under 18 years of age are not held in prison establishments' (Social Work Services and Prisons Inspectorates for Scotland 1998, p.57).

The Response is, however, silent on central planks of the decarceration policy proposed in *A Safer Way*. The most significant omission is its failure to engage with and support one side of the 'twin-track strategy'. While 'more options in the community' are endorsed, nothing is said about imposing limits to ensure 'fewer prison places'. Moreover, there is no specific comment on a key aim of the twin-track strategy to limit the female population at Cornton Vale 'to 100 or less on a daily basis by the end of the year 2000' (Social Work Services and Prisons Inspectorates for Scotland 1998, p.53). Instead, under 'Plans for Implementation', the Response commits to monitoring the targets set in *A Safer Way* and to ensuring that 'where targets have been set, these are adhered to' (Scottish Office 1998, p.9). Yet far from meeting the reduction targets set, there are significantly more women held in custody in Scotland today than the number considered unacceptably high by the government at the time of *A Safer Way*. How has this happened?

First, the discourse in the Government's Response on the conclusions and recommendations made in *A Safer Way* is telling. It is here that the seeds of inaction are sown. For example, the Response 'acknowledges' the thrust of *A Safer Way* towards 'extending the provision of options for dealing with women offenders in the community' but notes that there 'will, however, continue to be a demand from the courts for prison places for women' (Scottish Office 1998, p.7). While the use of the word 'acknowledge' indicates 'recognition' of *A Safer Way*'s promotion of decarceration as an appropriate aim of penal policy for women, this is followed immediately by a denial of responsibility for achieving that aim. The penal custody issue is shifted from government policy making to the individualised decision making of the judiciary. This shift of responsibility is not surprising; it echoes the principle stated in the opening paragraphs of the Response, that is, to make 'clear distinctions between the policies which are the responsibility of Government and the role of the judiciary in reaching sentencing decisions in individual cases' (Scottish Office 1998, p.1).

It is also important to note that while the Response refers to the 'wider social and economic factors associated with women's offending', the explicit association with poverty made in *A Safer Way* is no longer made. Indeed, the word 'poverty' never again appears in any subsequent official policy document about female offenders. Thus begins the process of decontextualising the policy solutions to women's offending from the material conditions of its existence; a process that leads to the most recent policy document noting that 'we no longer need to ask why these women offend. Rather we need to do something about breaking the cycle which leads them into criminal behaviour in the first place and frequently into prison even when most pose very little danger to others' (Scottish Executive 2002, p.1).

For now, we move to the next stage in policy translations, reflected in the implementation of Recommendation 3 in *A Safer Way* that:

> An inter-agency project should be set up in Glasgow under the direction of a high level Steering Group to bring together all the main partners in the criminal justice system, both in the public and independent sector, to resolve at a local level the issues identified in the report. Participants should include social work, housing providers, the Procurator Fiscal service, sentencers (including the Stipendiary magistrate), Sheriff Clerks, the police, health services, the SPS and key voluntary sector agencies. (Social Work Services and Prisons Inspectorates for Scotland 1998, p.55)

This recommendation was taken forward through the establishment of the Inter Agency Forum On Women's Offending. The Inter Agency Forum (IAF) first met in Glasgow in August 1998 with the intention of working over a three-year period to 'resolve at a local level the issues identified in the joint Prisons and Social Work Inspectorates Inquiry into Female Offenders in Scotland' (IAF 2000, p.1). In doing this, however, by the end of its first year the IAF had shifted the parameters of the main penal policy directions set out in *A Safer Way*.

What is missing in *First Year Report* (IAF 2000) tells the tale. In that report, through a process of omission, the IAF had already diluted the strength of *A Safer Way*'s decarceration impetus. First, look at how the understanding of the factors associated with female offending differs. Where *A Safer Way* notes that women's offending is 'often rooted in poverty' (Social Work Services and Prisons Inspectorates for Scotland 1998, p.52), the IAF is silent on this or any other socio-economic factor. Instead women who offend 'share three characteristics, namely Addiction, Abuse and Anxiety or *other forms of psychological distress*; their offending is closely related to these characteristics, directly or indirectly' (IAF 2000, Preamble – my emphasis). Women's offending is thus decontextualised, at the outset, from wider social structural conditions. Instead it is to be explained by addiction, abuse, anxiety and 'other forms of psychological distress'. But this is only the beginning of the policy transformation process.

The next omission is even more glaring. The twin-track strategy of 'more options in the community' and 'fewer prison places' envisaged in *A Safer Way*, which aimed to 'limit the female population at Cornton Vale from over 170 to 100 or less on a daily basis by the end of the year 2000' (Social Work Services and Prisons Inspectorates for Scotland 1998, p.53), is simply not mentioned in either of the two IAF reports. Instead of this twin-track strategy we are presented with '5 strategic goals'. These are: 'a decrease in women becoming involved in offending; a decrease in the severity of women's offending; a decrease in the number of women in custody; evidence of women being helped to desist from criminal activity; and the development of alternative methods for dealing with female offenders' (IAF 2000, p.2).

These *five strategic goals*, however commendable, are translated into *the targets* – not the specific time and number targets set in *A Safer Way* to be reached using the twin-track strategy of fewer prison places and more options in the community. Indeed, the only time targets set by the IAF are in relation to information (within the first year) and communication (within the first six months). Where have all the 'outcome focused targets' recommended in *A Safer Way* gone? Where are the limits on numbers to be held in penal custody?

The IAF *Second Year Report* (2001), like the one for the first year, notes: 'Unfortunately, the number of women in custody has continued to rise in the last year' (IAF 2001, p.2). Not only is it unfortunate but it is entirely predictable when nothing has happened to change the incarceration momentum. It is, therefore, all the more surprising to read that, although originally planned as a three-year project, the *Second Year Report* states that 'We now believe that the IAF has completed its allocated task...we are of the view that the proposals which we have developed in just over 2 years represent the best way forward' (IAF 2001, p.8). Yes – the task of setting up the Inter Agency Forum On Women's Offending has been accomplished and the recommendations made in *A Safer Way* have been considered – but to what end?

In concluding its work, the IAF put forward 13 recommendations in the second report, all aimed at reducing the use of imprisonment for female offenders. These recommendations include the creation of 'time out' centres to provide a wide range of residentially or non-residentially based support services. However commendable this and other specific recommendations are, not one of them mentions any time or numbers targets.

All the recommendations made by the IAF are about processes; not targeted, time specific outcomes. The language used is indicative – '*monitoring* of the possibility of establishing a single daily court for women', '*building upon* existing diversion strategies', '*establishment* of a database of services', '*consideration* of the value of Arrest Referral Schemes', and so on (IAF 2001 – my emphasis). Even the unambiguous and detailed recommendations in relation to the 'decriminalisation of non-payment of television licences' and the 'implementation of s 235 of the Criminal Proceedings

(Scotland) Act 1995' (IAF 2001) to reduce the numbers of women imprisoned because of fine default have no time targets.

The next significant stage in policy translation is illustrated through the evidence taken by the Justice 2 Committee of the Scottish Parliament on 12 September 2001. On that occasion, the Deputy Minister for Justice informed the Committee about the work of the Ministerial Group On Women Offenders, an inter-agency group set up in December 2000 in response to both *A Safer Way*, 'a milestone in our understanding of the problem of women offenders' (Scottish Parliament 2001, Col.357), and the subsequent establishment of the Inter Agency Forum On Women's Offending. The Minister restates the IAF's transformation of *A Safer Way*'s understanding of offending by women. He notes that 'the root causes of a great deal of women's crime are 'addiction, abuse and anxiety' and that 'the Executive felt that...rather than asking why women offend, we should be doing something about breaking the *cycle of despair* that leads them into criminal behaviour' (Scottish Parliament 2001, Col.358 – my emphasis). Here we see further decontextualising of the policy solutions to women's offending from the material conditions of its existence. The focus is not on the social circumstances of women but on their psychological state.

As Carlen (2002) argues, in her analysis of *The Government's Strategy for Female Offenders* (Home Office 2000) in England and Wales, a 'New Official Criminology for Women in Prison' has been created where the solution is to 'Change their *beliefs* about the world; the problem is in their heads, not their social circumstances' (Carlen 2002).

The Minister also notes that, despite a number of measures such as increased accommodation facilities for women on bail and the introduction of Drug Treatment and Testing Orders, the Ministerial Group 'must consider why, given all that work, the number of women in prison has not declined' (Scottish Parliament 2001, Col.359). He goes on to tell the Justice 2 Committee that the goal of the Ministerial Group's forthcoming proposal to open a day centre is to help women 'to deal with the problems of addiction, abuse and anxiety' (Scottish Parliament 2001, Col.359). Where is poverty? Deprivation? Is there not a link between these structural conditions and the fact that '50 per cent of the women who find themselves in Cornton Vale do so because of fine default' (Scottish Parliament 2001, Col.360), and that of those women many are in default because of failure to pay TV licences? Only at the end of the debate is there any reference to social circumstances under the rubric of social exclusion, and then in relation to women leaving prison where 'getting back into the benefits system is one part of what prison throughcare is meant to cover' (Scottish Parliament 2001, Col.375).

But the silence is unqualified on the 'fewer prison places' track of the twin-track strategy recommended in *A Safer Way* and there is no comment on the decarceration targets set out in that document. On the other hand, the Convener emphasises that 'there will always be a need for a women's prison' (Scottish Parliament 2001, Col.367); a point made again in the next sentence that 'some particular issues are better addressed in time-out centres, but there will still be a need for a women's prison' (Scottish Parliament 2001, Col.367). There is, however, neither any discussion about the women this prison will always need to be for nor about the number of places likely to be required. Which women will always need to go to prison? What crimes will they need to go to prison for? How many women commit these crimes? We are left in the dark on all these questions.

In relation to the other track of the twin-track strategy, that is 'more options in the community', the Minister reinforces the point made in the Government's Response in 1998 that 'We can provide alternatives to custody but it is the sentencers who will decide whether those alternatives are used generally, and in specific cases' (Scottish Parliament 2001, Col.373). Once again the responsibility for limiting the incarceration of women is shifted from government policy to the exercise of judicial discretion in individual cases.

A Better Way

From reduction targets to estimated reductions

At the time of writing in early 2002, almost four years have passed since the publication of *A Safer Way* and the Ministerial Group on Women's Offending has just published its report, *A Better Way* (Scottish Executive 2002). *A Better Way* reviews progress made by the IAF since the publication of *A Safer Way* and uses statistics to 'suggest where action should be focused if overall numbers are to be reduced' (Scottish Executive 2002, p.8). The report identifies specific action points and estimates how reductions in the numbers of women imprisoned could be achieved.

The first action point surrounds the high numbers of women in Scotland received into custody for short prison sentences. In relation to this point, the report suggests that *if the courts* used prison only for women who commit violent and supply of drug offences 'the annual reception of adult women in prison for minor offences for short periods of time (up to 6 months) could be 150 less than it might otherwise be. This translates to a reduction of up to 11 in the average daily population of these women' (Scottish Executive 2002, p.9).

The second action point relates to the high number of female remand prisoners. In this context, *if the courts* made greater use of bail beds and other support systems available and being extended, remands could be significantly reduced. The report estimates that if '25% of those currently held on remand were given bail, the future annual level of reception of women on remand could be up to 250 lower than it might otherwise be. This translates to a reduction in the average daily population of these women of up to 11 people' (Scottish Executive 2002, p.14).

The number of women imprisoned for defaulting in the payment of fines imposed by the courts is the third action point. Courts that impose high levels of custody for fine default are identified. The argument here is that if supervised attendance orders were used more consistently in these courts 'up to another 300 women could be removed from the prison system each year. This would translate to a reduction of up to two people in the average daily population of these women' (Scottish Executive 2002, p.15).

The fourth action point concerns young women. In this case by 'targetting measures on young women offenders who do not require a custodial environment, including specific action for those aged 16 and 17 years of age, there is the potential to reduce the number of young women in custody by up to 45 receptions. This translates to a reduction of up to 3 people in the average daily population' (Scottish Executive 2002, p.18). In total then, *A Better Way* estimates a potential reduction of 27 in the average female daily population. On today's figures that would mean an average daily population of 186 – still more than the average number of 170 in prison at the time *A Safer Way* was published and a long way from the target set in that document of no more than 100 by the end of the year 2000.

Undoubtedly *A Better Way*'s return to setting some kind of decarceration targets is to be welcomed, as is its emphasis on the need for action to be taken 'to alleviate the social circumstances which confront some women and which lead them to offend' (Scottish Executive 2002, p.23). However, the continued silence on the 'fewer prison places' track of the twin-track strategy proposed in *A Safer Way* means that the likelihood of achieving even the estimated reductions in *A Better Way* is highly questionable. As with all the policy transformations since *A Safer Way*, the other track of 'more options in the community' and the courts making more use of them is relied on as the decarceration strategy.

Towards decarceration: a question of morality

In early 2002, the Scottish government's policy or 'plan of action' takes us nowhere near reaching the target of limiting the number of women in prison to no more than 100 and, despite the recommendation in *A Safer Way* that no young women under 18 should be imprisoned, yet another 15-year-old has just been admitted to HM Institution Cornton Vale. Most tragically, despite all the changes introduced at Cornton Vale (HMCIP [Scotland] 2002), there have been further suicides.

My account of how policy transformations have contributed to why things are as they are should not, however, be read as suggesting that this is how they must be. The continued endurance of welfare strategies in Scotland, together with an explicit government policy arguing for reductions in the use of imprisonment for female offenders has still left a space for a penal policy of decarceration to be achieved. But this cannot be achieved without deliberate and principled policy action to decrease the number of prison places for female offenders.

Effecting a policy of decarceration for women who offend cannot and should not be left solely to the courts. The courts can and should be presented with information about the availability and effectiveness of community penalties. Just as it is desirable that penal policy be informed by evidence, so too it is desirable that decision making in individual cases be so informed. But evidence itself carries no particular moral imperative. Penal policy must explicitly recognise and engage with the moral questions that provide the irreducible context of punishment. Yet, while the vocabularies used and discourses surrounding penal policy documents and debates on female offenders in Scotland repeatedly argue that it is *unnecessary* and *ineffective* to incarcerate women whose crimes and offences are not serious, the *language of morality* is rarely used in relation to these same policies.

From my account of some of the recent transformations that have occurred in Scottish penal policy on female offenders, it is clear that the stated aim of decarceration will remain unrealised unless action is taken to reduce the number of prison places. But it is not possible for that action to take place in a moral vacuum. The morality, quite separately from the effectiveness, of punishing women by incarceration for minor property offences and problematic drug use, is central to penal policy. Yet, 'questions about moral penal practice have seldom surfaced as such in the directives of the politicians and civil servants who direct and fund prison policies' (Carlen 2001, p.468). It is time that they did.

References

Carlen, P. (1983) *Women's Imprisonment.* London: Routledge and Kegan Paul.

Carlen, P. (1990) *Alternatives To Women's Imprisonment.* Milton Keynes: Open University Press.

Carlen, P. (2001) 'Death and the triumph of governance? Lessons from the Scottish women's prison.' *Punishment and Society 3,* 4, 459–471.

Carlen, P. (2002) 'New discourses of justification and reform for women's imprisonment in England.' In P. Carlen (ed) *Women and Punishment: The Struggle for Justice.* Cullompton: Willan.

Coyle, A. (1991) *Inside: Rethinking Scotland's Prisons.* Edinburgh: Scottish Child.

HMCIP (Scotland) (2002) *Report on HMP And YOI: Cornton Vale 2001.* Edinburgh: The Scottish Executive.

Home Office (1970) *Treatment of Women and Girls in Custody.* London: HMSO.

Home Office (2000) *The Government's Strategy for Women Offenders.* London: Home Office.

Home Office (2001) *Prison Population Brief, November.* London: Home Office.

Inter Agency Forum On Women's Offending (IAF) (2000) *First Year Report.* Edinburgh: The Scottish Executive.

Inter Agency Forum On Women's Offending (IAF) (2001) *Second Year Report.* Edinburgh: The Scottish Executive.

Scottish Executive (2002) *A Better Way.* Edinburgh: The Stationery Office.

Scottish Office (1998) *A Safer Way: The Government's Response.* Edinburgh: The Scottish Office.

Scottish Parliament (2001) 'Women's offending.' Justice 2 Committee Official Report Meeting 21, 12 September. Scottish Parliament.

Social Work Services and Prisons Inspectorates for Scotland (1998) *Women Offenders – A Safer Way.* Edinburgh: The Stationery Office.

CHAPTER 4

Why Are More Women Being Sentenced to Custody?

Carol Hedderman

Introduction

In 1992, women comprised 3.5 per cent of the prison population in England and Wales. By 2000 they were 5.2 per cent. This may sound like a small change but it reflects a 115 per cent increase in the female prison population. During the same period, the male population went up by 42 per cent. The number of women received into prison rose even more sharply than the population, more than tripling from 2200 in 1992 to 7000 in 2000. Over the same period male receptions rose by only 58 per cent.

Some of the rise in the female prison population is attributable to the increase in the numbers on remand and young offenders under sentence. However, about 80 per cent of female prisoners have been sentenced; and over 80 per cent of those are adults (aged 21 and over). These proportions have remained static, so it is reasonable to assume that the population is largely determined by the frequency with which custody is used and the length of the sentences imposed.

The rise in the female prison population has provoked a great deal of comment. Somewhat predictably, the Director General of the Prison Service has speculated that at least some of the increase reflects changes in the nature and extent of female offending. Equally predictably, the Howard League for Penal Reform has suggested that women are now subject to harsher sentencing (BBC Online, 26 November 2001). Thus far, official publications about the treatment of women in the criminal justice system have noted the increase but have said little about its cause (e.g. Home Office 2001a, 2001b). Surprisingly, trawling through other sentencing literature indicates that no one seems to have examined the available evidence to establish what is causing the rise. There are a number of ways in which the change might have been brought about:

- a change in legislation or sentencing guidelines

- a rise in the number of women being convicted

- an increase in the proportion convicted of more serious offences

- an increase in the proportion of convicted women who are repeat offenders

- a rise in the proportion of women offenders being sentenced at the Crown Court

- tougher sentencing.

This chapter explores the available evidence in order to distinguish what *did* cause the rise from what *might* have done. It begins by examining how the sentencing of women changed between 1992 and 2000 and then looks at what may have brought this about. It concludes by considering how the trend towards the greater use of custody for women might be reversed.

The discussion is limited to a consideration of the sentencing of women in England and Wales. The focus is mainly on adult women, reflecting the fact that the sentences available for juveniles and young offenders, and changes in their sentencing patterns, merit separate and lengthy discussion. The limited geographic focus reflects the general absence of sufficiently detailed statistics about sentencing in Scotland,[1] Northern Ireland or other countries and the difficulties of comparing sentencing across jurisdictions with differing legal codes and legal systems.

How have sentencing patterns changed?

So how exactly has the sentencing of women changed during this period and in comparison to men? The most obvious change, shown in Table 4.1, is that the number of women being sentenced for indictable offences has gone up by 5100 while the number of men has gone down by 5400.

In terms of the types of sentences awarded, both men and women have seen a reduction in the use of discharges, fines and suspended sentences. For men this was largely offset by a doubling in the use of custody, whereas for women the use of custody tripled but the use of probation also increased. Combined with the increase in the number of women being sentenced and the decline in the number of men, the net effect of the changes between 1992 and 2000 is that whereas one woman was previously imprisoned for every 20 men, the ratio is now 1 in 10.

Table 4.1 The sentencing of adult women and men (over 21) for indictable offences 1992 and 2000[2]

	Women		Men	
Sentence	1992	2000	1992	2000
	%	%	%	%
Absolute or conditional discharge	36	24	17	13
Fine	27	22	37	28
Probation order	16	22	9	11
Community service order	5	8	9	9
Combination order	0	3	0	3
Suspended sentence	7	2	8	1
Immediate custody	6	16	18	30
Other[3]	2	3	3	3
Numbers	28,500	33,600	190,100	184,700

Legislative changes

The Criminal Justice Act (CJA) 1991 which was enacted in 1992 enshrined the main principles of the current sentencing framework, including:

- an insistence that sentence severity should be determined mainly by the seriousness of the current offence(s)

- custody should be reserved for the most serious offences or to protect the public from serious (violent or sexual) harm

- community sentences (probation, community service, etc.) were not just to be seen as alternatives to custody but as sentences in their own right

- an expansion of non-custodial options by offering a mix of probation and community service in a new 'Combination Order'.

It is difficult to make sense of the fact that the female prison population began to rise at about the time this legislation was enacted. The Act was intended to reserve the use of custody for those who posed a danger to society, partly by offering sentencers a wider choice of other sentencing options. The greater use of probation and smaller increases in community service and combination orders for women shown in Table 4.1 suggests that it may have had some of the expected effects for women. However, this seems to have been at the expense of discharges, fines and suspended sentences rather than immediate custody. The same is true of men although, with the exception of suspended sentences, the changes are less marked.

The Criminal Justice Act 1993 amended the provisions of the CJA 1991 to allow sentencers to take previous convictions into account when assessing seriousness. However, as women generally have far fewer previous convictions, it is difficult to see how this might have led to more women being sentenced to custody – especially as the 1993 Act essentially reified common practice.

Another important change in the sentencing context between the early 1990s and 2000 that might have contributed to the greater use of custody for women was the Court of Appeal guidance, issued after the CJA 1991 came into effect in October 1992. In defining seriousness of offence, judges and magistrates were advised to discount sentences for offenders who entered guilty pleas; and to ensure that those who pled guilty early were given more credit than those who entered late guilty pleas. Unfortunately, Home Office statistics only provide information on the link between plea and sentencing for adult men sentenced at the Crown Court,[4] so the question of how far the guidance has affected the sentencing of women remains a matter for future research.

How has the mix of cases changed?

Changes in the underlying nature or extent of offending by women are only relevant to a consideration of sentencing practice insofar as they result in more or different women being sentenced. Nevertheless, it is worth examining because it is something commentators pick up on. Fortunately, the first large-scale British self-reported offending survey roughly coincided with the start of the prison population increase (1992 to 1993) and the second occurred in 1998 to 1999. The second round report (Flood-Page *et al.* 2000) confirms the findings of the first Youth Lifestyle Survey (YLS) by Graham and Bowling (1995) that twice as many boys and young men admitting to offending as girls and young women (26% vs 11%). Under 17 the ratio is 2:1, over the age of 17 it is 3:1. The only noteworthy change in the nature of female offending was that there was a small but statistically significant *reduction* of 2 per cent in the proportion admitting violence in 1998 to 1999 than 1992 to 1993, while male violence increased by 4.5 per cent. On the basis of this, admittedly limited, evidence there is little to suggest that female offending (at least among those aged under 30) has become more prevalent or more serious.

During the same period, the official statistics show that the number of men and women cautioned or convicted for indictable offences both dropped by about 12 percentage points. Thus the increase in the number of women being sentenced is not a consequence of more being picked up by the criminal justice system. Table 4.2 shows that a considerable difference has emerged in the way they are dealt with, however, in that the number of women being taken to court and found guilty has gone up by 7700 whereas the number of men has declined by 6300.[5]

Table 4.2 Changes in cautions and convictions for indictable offences (all ages) 1992 and 2000

	Females			Males		
	1992	2000	Change	1992	2000	Change
			%			%
Cautioned	61,000	41,200	-33	155,000	109,700	-29
Found guilty	40,000	47,700	+19	282,800	276,500	-2
Cautioned/ found guilty	101,100	88,900	-12	437,900	386,200	-12

The next obvious question is whether the number of women being convicted and sentenced has increased across all types of offences. As Table 4.3 shows:

- Of the extra women dealt with in 2000, 2900 were convicted of theft and handling or fraud and forgery.

- The number of women found guilty of drugs offences went up by 2500 which meant that this became the index offence for 10 per cent rather than 5 per cent as in 1992.

- There was a large rise in the number of women found guilty of 'other' offences. This change is difficult to interpret as the category is described as a 'miscellaneous' in the published statistics and appears to cover offences as varied as assisting suicide, rioting and failing to surrender to bail. A separate male/female breakdown of the figures is not available.

- The *proportion* of women found guilty of violent crime declined, although the *underlying numbers* remained about the same.

Table 4.3 Number and percentage of women (all ages)
convicted of indictable offences[6]

Offence	1992		2000	
	Thousands	%	Thousands	%
Violence	3.8	9.5	3.7	7.8
Sexual offences	0.1	0.3	0.0	0.0
Burglary	1.2	3.0	1.0	2.1
Robbery	0.3	0.8	0.5	1.0
Theft and handling	24.0	60.0	25.8	54.3
Fraud and forgery	4.4	11.0	5.4	11.3
Criminal damage	0.8	2.0	1.0	2.1
Drugs	2.1	5.3	4.6	9.6
Other (non-motoring)	2.9	7.3	5.3	11.1
Motoring	0.4	1.0	0.4	0.8
Total	40.0	100.0	47.7	100.0

Seriousness, court venue and sentence length

While Criminal Statistics show annual changes in the types of offences for
which women are sentenced, they contain little information about changes
in the seriousness of offending. For example, drug possession and supply
cases are not shown separately.[7] Some sense of changes in seriousness can be
obtained by examining whether the proportion of women dealt with at
magistrates' courts and the Crown Court altered between 1992 and 2000,
as the maximum sentence a magistrates' court can impose for a single offence
is six months in custody. These differences should be interpreted cautiously,
however, as other factors such as plea vary by venue, and these also affect
sentence length. Also, it is not possible to break the figures down by offence

or age. Nevertheless, Table 4.4 shows that although the number of women being dealt with by the courts has increased, the proportion being dealt with at the Crown Court has remained relatively stable. This suggests that the greater use of custody is not being driven by an overall increase in the seriousness of women's offending.

Table 4.4 also shows that over 40 per cent of the women sentenced in the Crown Court are now being given custodial sentences compared to under a quarter eight years ago. Although the proportion given custody at the magistrates' court remains much lower, the *rate of increase* has been higher in that custody is now used five times more frequently than in 1992.

If the numbers being sentenced had risen but the proportions being sentenced to custody had remained the same between 1992 and 2000, there would have been an increase of about 21 per cent in the number of women being sent to prison by magistrates.[8] The numbers being sent to prison by judges would have risen by 8 per cent, leading to an overall increase of 20 per cent in the number sent to prison. However, there was a five-fold increase in the proportion of cases in which magistrates awarded women custody and close to a two-fold increase at the Crown Court. The net effect of these changes is that receptions have tripled and that whereas magistrates' sentencing accounted for less than a third of receptions in 1992, they are now responsible for nearly 60 per cent.

	Magistrates' Courts		Crown Court	
Table 4.4 The use of custody for females (all ages) by type of court				
	1992	2000	1992	2000
No. sentenced to custody	635	3971	1510	2928
Percentage sentenced to custody	2%	10%	23%	42%
No. sentenced for indictable offences	33,454	40,739	6,536	7,059
Percentage of female offenders sentenced at Crown Court			16%	15%

The average length of custodial sentences awarded in magistrates' courts has remained about the same (2.2 to 2.3 months), whereas at the Crown Court it has risen from 18 months in 1992 to 21 months in 2000. Given that the proportion of cases going to the Crown Court has remained stable it is difficult to believe that this increase has been fuelled mainly by an increase in case seriousness.

The figures in Table 4.5 also contradict this idea. First, the increased use of custody has occurred at both venues for all offences, bar robbery at the magistrates' court, indicating the sentencing in general has simply got more severe. Second, the rise in the number of women convicted of theft and handling, and the greater than average increase in the use of custody for this group, lends further support for the idea that the rise in sentenced prison receptions is being driven by a *more severe* response to *less serious* offences.

Table 4.5 Proportion of adult women (over 21) convicted
of indictable offences who were sentenced to custody

	Magistrates' Courts		Crown Court	
Offence	1992	2000	1992	2000
	% custody	% custody	% custody	% custody
Violence	2	11	22	33
Sexual offences	0	(13)	(41)	(67)
Burglary	9	32	27	53
Robbery	0	0	58	75
Theft and handling	2	14	21	41
Fraud and forgery	2	8	22	32
Criminal damage	4	5	19	25
Drugs	1	4	39	55
Other (non-motoring)	2	6	22	30
Motoring	0	3	(22)	(32)
All indictable offences	2	11	24	42

( ) based on less than 100 women sentenced

Unfortunately, published statistics do not provide enough detailed information to be able to say exactly how the increase in prison receptions is related to a generally tougher sentencing climate, more severe sentencing for specific offences or more women being convicted (especially for drug offences). They simply note that '*drugs*' and '*theft and handling stolen goods*' offences explained 53 per cent and 14 per cent of the increase in the female Implied Prison Population (IPP)[9] respectively (Home Office 2001a, p.22).

The impact of previous convictions

The chance of being sentenced to custody goes up for men and women as the number of their previous convictions increases. It therefore follows that if the number of women being sentenced who have previous convictions has increased during the 1990s, one would expect to see their chances of custody increasing. Published statistics on this are not available for 1992, but the percentage of women who had no previous convictions was 47 per cent in 1993 and 54 per cent in 2000. If anything, this change should work to reduce the numbers going to prison (Home Office 2001b).

Why are sentencers making greater use of custodial sentences?

The lack of recent research into sex differences in sentencing, combined with gaps in the picture provided by official statistics, make it difficult to provide a clear answer to this question. However, an examination of the statistics which are available suggests that the increase in the female sentenced prison population has been fuelled by an increase in the number of women being convicted. If that was all that had happened prison receptions would have gone up by about 20 per cent. They would not have tripled. There has also been a general move away from lower tariff sentences which does not appear to be explained by courts dealing with more serious cases. The percentage of women imprisoned for virtually every type of offence has increased. Moreover, a third of the extra women are convicted of theft and handling; and the proportionate use of custody for this group by magistrates has risen more than for other offences.

Convictions for drug offences have risen disproportionately, but there is nothing to suggest that courts are now dealing with more serious women offenders than eight years ago. Indeed, self-report results and official statistics both suggest that, for example, women are no more violent now than they were in 1992; and the proportion of cases dealt with at the Crown Court is the same although the number of women sentenced there has risen. Despite this the average length of the custodial sentences being given out at the Crown Court has increased by three months. The idea that this is because the courts are dealing with more women recidivists can also be discounted.

Overall, the evidence suggests that sentencing has simply got more severe since 1992.

Regardless of whether they are concerned about the financial or social costs of imprisonment, few people relish the idea of a general increase in the use of custody for women or men. Most believe that it should be reserved for serious or persistent offenders and this idea inspired the sentencing framework introduced under the CJA 1991. Nevertheless the last eight years has seen a dramatic increase in the use of this sentence of last resort for both men and women. This is difficult to justify for either sex, but given that women's offending continues to be characterised by being infrequent, rarely repeated and of limited seriousness, it is hard to argue that sending more women to prison serves any useful purpose. It may be the result of a generally harsher sentencing climate, but it offers no benefits in terms of public protection because most women offenders are not dangerous. It offers no benefits in terms of deterrence because most women do not commit crime. There are no benefits in terms of rehabilitation because most women receive sentences of less than a year and are therefore ineligible for rehabilitative programmes in prison and unsupervised on release. Even those serving two years cannot access programmes inside and accredited community-based programmes for women are only just being developed (see Hedderman, Chapter 11 this volume).

Meanwhile, the cost to society is enormous. Research for the Prison Reform Trust suggested that in 1998 the financial cost of supporting a female prison population of 3100 was £118 million (Wolfe 1999). In 2001, the population was 3350 and it is continuing to rise at such a rate that one male prison (Downview) has been converted to hold women. At least one further conversion is planned. The cost of this work can only be guessed at, along with the other less obvious social costs of imprisoning women measured in terms of family disruption, lost employment and earnings, and subsequent mental health problems (Morris *et al.* 1995; Wolfe 1999). Reversing the trend towards the greater use of custody for women will be difficult but worthwhile as the increased use of prison for women seems to offer few advantages at enormous social and financial cost.

How can the use of custody for women be reduced?

A blueprint for reducing the female prison population has been produced by the Prison Reform Trust (2000). Their recommendations include setting up new centres for women and reintroducing unit fines. These may indeed be useful reforms which will bring added social benefits in terms of reducing social exclusion, but it is not clear that additional sentencing options are what is needed or that their availability will bring about a change in sentencing practice. The aspiration to reserve the use of custody for more serious offenders underlay the introduction of the CJA 1991, yet what has happened in practice since could not have been more different. At the very least, any new options need to be accompanied by a very strong drive to make sentencers better informed about women offenders, stressing their low reconviction rates, scotching the myth that they are becoming more violent, and reminding them of the generally non-serious nature of the majority of their offending. The social costs of imprisoning women also need to be more widely publicised.

Other proposals such as the recent Sentencing Review's (Home Office 2001c) idea of mixing a brief taste of custody with supervision in the community may easily increase the use of custody for women still further, although they are intended to reduce the use of short prison sentences. This is because sentencers retain considerable discretion about the sentencing of individual cases. Clearly current sentencing guidelines are not enough to ensure that the use of custody is reserved for persistent or serious offenders. That is not because the guidance is inappropriate or unclear but because it is neither monitored nor enforced. The greater prescription proposed by the Sentencing Review is likely to be ineffective for the same reasons (see Wilkinson, Chapter 8 this volume). The alternatives are to limit sentencers' discretion or to police their compliance with existing guidance. The least tenable but most likely option seems to be to leave their discretion unchecked and to look forward to the female prison population in England and Wales exceeding 5000 by 2008 as the latest projections suggest it will (Gray and Rogers 2001).

Acknowledgements

The author would like to thank Professor Michael Hough for his comments on a previous draft of the chapter and David Elliot for checking the calculations.

Notes

1   The statistics available for Scotland suggest that the rise in the number of adult women being sentenced to custody in England and Wales has not been mirrored there. After reaching a peak of 835 in 1994, the trend has been downwards. In 2000, 584 women over 21 were sentenced to custody. However, the number of women under 21 sentenced to custody has risen steeply over the same period (Scottish Executive 2001).

2   All tables are derived from *Criminal Statistics, England and Wales, 2000* (Home Office 2001b).

3   Includes drug treatment and testing orders and curfew orders.

4   Of men who pleaded not guilty 76 per cent were sentenced to imprisonment compared to 64 per cent who pled guilty (Home Office 2001b).

5   The number of offenders sentenced differs slightly from the number found guilty for a number of reasons including data shortfalls, proceedings being terminated and cases being written off.

6   Percentages in tables may not add to 100 due to rounding.

7   These could be calculated from supplementary volumes for previous years, but they are difficult to obtain.

8   $40,739/33,454$ = a 21% increase.

9   IPP = 'Implied Prison Population' = Numbered sentenced × Custody rate × (Average sentence length/2). The formula assumes that a person will remain in prison for exactly half their sentence.

References

Flood-Page, C., Campbell, S., Harrington, V. and Miller, J. (2000) *Youth Crime: Findings from the 1998/99 Youth Lifestyles Survey.* Home Office Research Study no. 209. London: Home Office.

Graham, J. and Bowling, B. (1995) *Young People and Crime.* Home Office Research Study no. 145. London: Home Office.

Gray, C. and Rogers, K. (2001) *Prison Population Brief. England and Wales: December 2001*. London: Home Office.

Home Office (2001a) *Statistics on Women and the Criminal Justice System: A Home Office Publication under Section 95 of the Criminal Justice Act 1991*. London: Home Office.

Home Office (2001b) *Criminal Statistics, England and Wales, 2000*. London: Home Office.

Home Office (2001c) *Report of a Review of the Sentencing Framework for England and Wales*. London: Home Office.

Morris, A., Wilkinson, C., Tisi, A., Woodrow, J. and Rockley, A. (1995) *Managing the Needs of Female Prisoners*. London: Home Office.

Prison Reform Trust (2000) *Justice for Women: The Need for Reform. Report of the Wedderburn Committee on Women's Imprisonment*. London: Prison Reform Trust.

Scottish Executive (2001) *Criminal Proceedings in Scottish Courts, 2000*. Statistical Bulletin CrJ/2001/7. Edinburgh: The Scottish Executive.

Wolfe, T. (1999) 'Counting the cost: The social and financial consequences of women's imprisonment. Report prepared for the Wedderburn Committee on Women's Imprisonment.' Unpublished research for the Prison Reform Trust.

PART II

Women in the Criminal Justice System

CHAPTER 5

Living with Paradox

Community Supervision of Women Offenders

Judith Rumgay

Introduction

This chapter explores the statutory supervision of convicted women offenders as a sentence of the court. It is concerned with those community sentences known in Scotland and Northern Ireland as Probation Orders, which were also so known in England and Wales until they were renamed in the Criminal Justice and Courts Services Act 2000 as Community Rehabilitation Orders. The term community supervision has been adopted to refer collectively to these orders, since, following those changes in England and Wales, we lack a common terminology.

Nomenclature was not the only difficulty presented by this topic. As we shall see, there have been many and passionate opinions expressed, both as to the merits, or otherwise, of community supervision programmes for women in comparison with other penal sanctions, and as to the ideal forms that these should take. Unfortunately, the number of well-documented programmes available for our examination does not match the strength of these convictions. We have remarkably few examples upon which to draw for more dispassionate appraisal. For example, only two out of the total 12 chapters in a recent edited collection on the topic of women and punishment concern community-based programmes, despite the book's oppositional stance on imprisonment (Carlen 2002). McMahon concisely sums up the problem: 'In any given country, there tends to be far more literature available about prisons than about community alternatives. Moreover, such literature as does exist tends to be overwhelmingly focused on programs for males' (2000, p.295; also Chesney-Lind 2000).

This chapter aims to avoid the temptation to respond to the dearth of documented practice by merely adding to the mounting pile of prescriptive models. Instead, it explores the underpinnings of this unsatisfactory state of affairs. The effort will expose a battery of contradictions in perspectives, which will surely continue to thwart implementation of good practice ideals, unless and until they are confronted and resolved. It begins by studying the 'invisible woman' in community supervision, moving to the debate as to its appropriate use and thence to an examination of practice examples, focusing on the challenges to their development, sustainment and replication.

Some measures have been taken to address the shortcomings in the literature. Although the chapter is primarily concerned with adult women, reference will be made to young female offenders where it illuminates the discussion. While the British policy and legislative environment will form the backdrop to the discussion, liberal use is made of North American research and commentary concerning female offenders and their treatment, which complements and compensates for the fragmented UK literature. Attention has also been paid to other relevant forms of community-based social intervention such as drug, alcohol, mental health and family support services.

Cherchez la femme

Raynor and Vanstone describe the evaluation of a programme 'designed to affect the thinking and behaviour of men who persistently offend' (1997, p.1). They offer three passing reminders of the gender exclusivity of the programme (pp.9, 24, 33) during their analysis, elsewhere preferring gender-neutral terms such as 'offenders', 'participants' and 'completers'. No rationale is offered for a gender-specific programme; no quest is declared for 'man-wise' (after Carlen 1989) provision. The authors conclude that 'the programme can have a reductive impact on *people's* offending' (1997, p.39, emphasis added), although it was tested solely on *men*.

Perhaps it is small wonder that feminists have persistently complained of the invisibility of women in criminological writing and the unquestioning application to women of principles derived entirely or predominantly from studies of men (e.g. Morris 1987; Smart 1977). Equally, perhaps the bewilderment of others, who consider themselves with some justification to be demonstrably committed to fairness and equality, on finding themselves thus accused, is less surprising when we consider the rich gender-neutral vocabulary available to obscure their masculine focus. Men, it seems, are 'people' and thus speak for us all; women are unnecessary to that conversation.

Women also impede the smoothness of the dialogue. McGuire and Hatcher's (2001) evaluation of a cognitive skills programme studied a group of 220 individuals, of whom only 19 (8.6%) were female. Describing the participants, the authors tell us that they had, on average, 12 previous convictions and 2.61 previous prison sentences. Data from a table to which they do not refer in the text, however, suggests that the relevant averages for the women were 8 and 0.4 respectively. McGuire and Hatcher do not disaggregate their promising results according to the sex of the participants. It is not intended to suggest here that the programme had a different impact on males and females, but rather that we cannot tell from the findings as reported how it affected the women participants. The point is simply that suspicion as to the results might be aroused among many feminist critics by the prior overlooking of sex differences in the demographic data. Indeed, one re-evaluation of a programme for drug-involved offenders that claimed overall effectiveness in reducing relapse and recidivism found that its results for women were quite poor (Farrell 2000).

Curiously, women even disappear at times when scrutiny would reveal them as the primary targets of social intervention. For example, Schaffner's (1997) study of a parenting-skills course for parents of delinquent teenagers reveals that the majority of these 'parents' were mothers. Yet, this does not seem to reflect a view that, as people, women may speak for all. Indeed, Schaffner's observations suggest that the input of the male group leaders often denigrated typically maternal contributions to family support, such as cooking, cleaning and mending, as pandering inappropriately to delinquents in need of firm control.

Rather, the cloaking of gender frequently obscures professionals' failure to confront men's crucial contributions to the predicaments of the women under their gaze. In the literature on statutory interventions implicating male abuse of children, the tendency for women to become the primary foci of concern and effort has been acknowledged. Studies have found that at each stage of the investigation and intervention processes, professional attention is systematically refocused away from males onto mothers, whose pleas for support are often treated with suspicion, while their partners remain uninvolved (Farmer and Owen 1998; O'Hagan 1997). Describing these endeavours in such terms as 'family support' or 'child protection' obscures professional collusion with assumptions of men's marginality in parenting and avoidance of recalcitrant, possibly threatening, male abusers. Thus, women subject to the attentions of agencies such as social work and probation may find themselves co-opted as tools in the attempt to regulate the behaviour of men (see also Walker and Beaumont 1981; Worrall 1990).

These observations on women's invisibility in accounts of social and penal interventions raise questions, not only about the neglect of females as subjects in their own right, but also about the perspectives on the causes, nature, treatment and *prioritisation* of male problems that may underpin that neglect. The present inadequacy of the latter analysis serves to perpetuate interventions with male offenders which fragment their complex, often disordered lives, prioritising issues with which professionals themselves prefer to deal. Thus, Morran (1995) insightfully observes probation officers' reluctance to engage with evidence of domestic violence perpetrated by males under their supervision, exploring techniques for encouraging female partners to disclose their victimisation and challenging male rationalisations. Underlying this discussion, however, is an apparent assumption that probation officers are hampered only by lack of skills to tackle the problem. Their *motivation* to deal with the problem of domestic violence by men on their caseload receives little attention.

How many women?

Explicit recognition of female subjects in discussions of the interventions that importantly regulate their lives and behaviours has led, unfortunately, to further contention. While there seems to be no clear consensus as to the number of women who should be subject to community supervision, discussions of the probation service's extant female caseload might well lead the observer to conclude that there are, in fact, far too many.

A preliminary glance at recent statistics for England and Wales suggests that community supervision is currently a popular disposal for women. The numbers of women sentenced to community supervision have increased over the past decade from 9435 in 1990 to 11,767 in 2000 (Home Office 2002). It is currently the most common community sentence passed on women, who are proportionately more likely to attract it than males (Home Office 2001a).

Many critics, however, have not greeted this popularity with gratification. Rather, a marked scepticism has permeated many responses to the apparent enthusiasm for this disposal. The view that there were simply too many women on the probation service's caseload gained strength during the 1980s, when the drive to represent community supervision as a tough option for relatively serious and recidivist offenders effectively 'masculinised' the order. Critiques of community supervision of females during this time are notable for its portrayal as 'penological regulation' (Webb 1984, p.367) of deviance sinisterly disguised as sympathetic concern for personal troubles. The marked tendency for women, in comparison with men made subject to community supervision, to have no previous convictions or prior custodial experience (Home Office 2001a) was often interpreted as a systemic failure to ensure the proper application of high tariff targeting procedures. That failure was in itself frequently attributed to social attitudinal influences, which were, however, far more widely assumed than proven (Sagatun 1989). For example, in one study, magistrates, although not asked for their views, were attributed with low intervention thresholds for female drug users, arising from their assumptions of poor parenting (Buchanan, Collett and McMullan 1991). This study followed others in also accusing probation officers of colluding with 'a gender stereotype which stresses both traditional roles (as wife, mother, carer) and assumed feminine attributes (passivity, irrationality, emotionality) as the components of "normal" womanhood' (Buchanan *et al.* 1991, p.61; also Allen 1987; Carlen 1989; Walker 1985; Worrall 1990).

Allen's (1987) condemnation of psychiatric assessments of women that neutralised their criminal culpability was rooted in a study that revealed that seriously mentally disturbed men were callously rejected from treatment. Despite this indication of the potential results, Allen insisted that 'the struggle for women's equality will never be furthered by the attempt to retain either the privileges or the disabilities of femininity' (1987, p.120). From this perspective, then, the superfluity of women on the community supervision caseload arose out of professional preoccupation with their social and personal distress, obscuring an appropriate focus on their criminality (also, e.g. Webb 1984). In similar vein, Orme complained that 'the criminal justice system reflects the patriarchal attitudes of the rest of British society and such attitudes...are mediated through a paternalism which considers that women offenders need, at best care, and at worst treatment' (1992, p.79). The persistence of this line of argument is reflected in its invocation to explain disparities in probation officers' and sentencers' responses to males and females in two articles published by the *Howard Journal of Criminal Justice*, in 1988 (Mair and Brockington) and again in 2000 (Horn and Evans). Moreover, the possibility that female offenders present more complex practical sentencing problems than such attitudinal inferences imply has been inadequately explored (but see Ablitt and Durrance 2000; Daly 1994; Rumgay 2000a). These attacks on 'sentencing by stereotype' (Walker 1985, p.70) tend to be offered as if all sentencing of males were unquestionably based solidly in reality – an inference which would be rapidly undermined by a short excursion into relevant research (e.g. Mileski 1969; Rumgay 1998a).

Yet, stripped of the 'privileges' and 'disabilities' of their femininity, what remained to justify the inclusion of female offenders in supervision opportunities? Unfortunately, women's failure to respond to this challenge by becoming more serious offenders meant that denial of care and treatment was easier than development of high tariff opportunities. Revisiting the Home Office's Probation Statistics, for a closer and longer term inspection, this perspective appears initially to have borne fruit in reducing the superfluity of women. From the 1960s, numbers of women made subject to community supervision increased steadily, as did their proportionate representation on the caseload. By 1980, women comprised 35 per cent of those sentenced to community supervision. The following decade, however, witnessed a reversal of this trend: numbers of women placed on community supervision fell steadily from 11,604 in 1980 to 7104 in 1993, in which year they comprised 16.5 per cent of those so sentenced (Home Office Probation Statistics 1967–2000). The Probation Inspectorate by then had been moved to observe that the 'single most important finding of the inspection in regard to probation orders was that the relative scarcity of serious female offenders militated against their satisfactory inclusion in (intensive programmes)' (HM Inspectorate of Probation 1991, p.24).

It has been suggested that the prioritisation of public protection during the 1990s increased 'pressure to reject females as candidates for probation, because of their tendency to commit non-violent offences with a relatively low risk of recidivism and almost none at all of serious injury to members of the public' (Rumgay 2000a, p.194; also McMahon 2000; Roberts 2002). On this view, the reasons for the re-expansion of the female supervision caseload during that decade would lie outside any putative revision of the probation service's enthusiasm for engaging with women. Rather, part of the explanation for the dearth of programme development, despite the increase in numbers, would implicate a negative focus on excluding 'unsuitable' women from community supervision, with little attention to the qualities of positive practice (see also Roberts 2002). Indeed, the Probation Inspectorate observed derisive attitudes towards those female-specific programmes that were operating, which were 'viewed as "tea and sympathy" groups by other officers because of the economic and gender content of the discussions' (HM Inspectorate of Probation 1991, p.25; also Rumgay 2000a). The failure of the probation service's enterprise to purge its caseload of unsuitable women thus requires an alternative explanation (also Worrall 1997).

The numbers of women sentenced to terms of imprisonment have been rising since the mid-1970s (Home Office 2000, 2001b; also Chapter 4 this volume) and at an unprecedented rate since 1991, necessitating urgent accommodation solutions including re-roling of male establishments and new prison building specifically for women. The simultaneous expansion of the female community supervision caseload, therefore, appears to have contributed little, if anything, to stemming the tide of women entering the prisons. Indeed, relatively early in this spate of imprisonment, the Home

Office opined that the increasing proportion of women on the community supervision caseload reflected a decline in the use of financial penalties (Home Office 1996). Similarly, a study of one probation area's experience supported the conclusion that women offenders' 'treatment locally reflects national trends for rising imprisonment in tandem with the more intense forms of supervision, increasingly visited upon a less criminally experienced population of offenders' (Rumgay 2000a, p.211).

Gender-specific programming

Recent perspectives on programme development for females have been less concerned with controlling disproportionate intervention in the lives of criminally unsophisticated women. These ideas focus instead on the qualitative content of practice development. Notably, the emergent models, rather than condemning it as an unhealthy feature of a patriarchal society, promote an active concern with women offenders' social and personal distress. At stake here, is the argument, is not that women offenders are excessively subjected to the scrutiny of the state, but that they are excluded from provision appropriate for their needs. Where previous perspectives railed against the 'double jeopardy of being judged as offenders and as women' (Orme 1992, p.80), proponents of 'gender-specific programming' complain that insufficient attention has been paid to particular problems which offenders experience by virtue of their femininity.

This perspective has been most fully articulated by a number of North American writers (e.g. Bloom and Covington 1998, 2001; Chesney-Lind 2000; Chesney-Lind, Artz and Nicholson 2001; Community Research Associates 1998; Covington 1998, 1999; Greene, Peters and Associates 1998; Loper 2000; Morash, Bynum and Koons 1998; Owen, Bloom and Covington 2001). Notwithstanding their variations, there is strong consensus among them that programme development for females should be directed at resolving their problems relating to poor self-esteem, histories of trauma and abuse, pregnancy and parenting, physical and mental health, and substance abuse (also Rumgay 1996). A particular feature of the approach is its appeal to 'relational theory' in feminist psychology (Covington 1998; Covington and Surrey 1997; Miller 1986; Miller and Stiver 1997) to justify its emphasis on the quality of women's interpersonal relationships, both as a target and as a vehicle for change. There is also unanimous agreement that programmes for women should aim for their empowerment, which is variously defined as improvements in their intrapsychic, social, economic or political conditions (McIvor 2001).

While there may be sympathy for women offenders' distressed circumstances, and while a holistic response to their social and personal needs may have intuitive appeal for many (see e.g. Home Office 2001b), attempts to fashion practice on these principles do not seem to thrive. As noted earlier, the paucity of women offenders under supervision at local level plays a role in this. However, much of the explanation also lies in perspectives on the causes of crime and recidivism, with their implications for treatment, which are currently persuasive at policy-making level. Programmes of the type mentioned earlier in the evaluations of Raynor and Vanstone (1997) and McGuire and Hatcher (2001) derive from a theoretical understanding of offending as caused by individual 'criminogenic needs', which 'include patterns of social interaction, skill deficits in problem solving or self-management, and anti-social attitudes' (McGuire and Hatcher 2001, p.565). This perspective has encouraged the development of cognitive- behavioural treatment programmes designed to rectify the problematic thinking styles attributed to offenders.

This is not the place for a thorough review and critique of this 'effective practice' enterprise (for which see e.g. Andrews and Bonta 1994; Gorman 2001; Kendall 2002; McGuire 1995; Mair 2000; Merrington and Stanley 2000). However, the contemporary drive towards practice development based on these principles poses special problems for gender-specific programming initiatives (McIvor 1999). First, the foci of intervention recommended by its proponents do not conform to the criminogenic needs targeted by cognitive-behavioural treatment. Second, the relational thrust of gender-specific programmes conflicts with cognitive-behavioural treatment goals of promoting individual autonomy in thinking and behaviour. Third, the emphasis on empowerment contradicts a medical model in which individual 'deficits' are defined as pathogenic disorders requiring clinical correction. In short, as McMahon observes, 'the journey down a more pluralistic and humanistic route seem(s) to reach an impasse when the junction with positivism (is) encountered' (2000, p.304).

Responses to the charge that gender-specific programmes as advocated are poorly targeted on the factors underpinning offending have been somewhat confused. Some critics (e.g. Kendall 2002) view cognitive-behavioural treatment itself with considerable scepticism. Principled refusal to expose women to treatments for which confidence derives only from male-dominated studies, however, produces the perverse effect of excluding women from the most prestigious and well-resourced programmes available (Hirst 2002). Moreover, another approach posits that research, through its predominantly masculine focus, has thus far failed to identify criminogenic needs that are specific to females (McMahon 2000; Hedderman, Chapter 11 this volume). Underlying this argument is the apparent expectation that discovery of female-specific criminogenic needs would justify the types of programmes advocated. The Home Office has countered this line of defence by commissioning research which, it is claimed, 'shows that women and men share many of the factors linked with re-offending, although their signifi-cance may differ' (2000, p.6). This broad conclusion would potentially support programme development for women mirroring that for men, with minor modifications such as altering pronouns and examples to the female type (Kendall 2002). 'Gender-specific' provision based merely on adaptations of male cognitive-behavioural treatment programmes falls far short, however, of aspirations for holistic needs-based services.

Moreover, government policy appears deeply ambivalent about the appropriate response to needs that fail to achieve endorsement as 'criminogenic'. For example, *The Government's Strategy for Women Offenders* concludes its brief review of factors underlying women's recidivism with the unsettling observation:

> In many cases the link with re-offending is unclear. For example, women prisoners record high levels of mental illness and personality disorders. It is not clear whether this is a criminogenic factor, or a response to incarcer-ation, or both. There is also no clear evidence that a history of abuse makes women more likely to re-offend. (Home Office 2000, p.6)

What, precisely, are the policy implications of a lack of proven causal relationship between women's mental disturbance and crime supposed to be? Does it follow that no response is required? Are we being invited to view mental disorder incurred as a 'response to incarceration' as an acceptable outcome of punishment (Rumgay 2001)? Certainly, the Strategy does not contain any unequivocal commitment to reducing the numbers of women incarcerated. Does a failure to demonstrate that a history of abuse is criminogenic imply that women offenders are disqualified from benefiting from current government policy that the victims of violence should receive help (Home Office 1999; Kelly and Humphreys 2000; Walby and Myhill 2000; Women's Unit, Cabinet Office and Home Office 1999)? In this uncertain policy environment, the quest for female-specific criminogenic needs risks participating in the exclusion of women from provision for needs that fail that test.

That the limitations of cognitive-behavioural treatments themselves as responses to the identified criminogenic needs has escaped critical attention testifies to the reductive power of 'solutions' that blend with overarching policy interests (Kendall 2002). The needs targeted by those programmes, as defined by McGuire above, represent a small subset of the 'promising targets for change' (Andrews and Bonta 1994, p.233) posited by exponents in this field. For example, the list offered by Andrews and Bonta extends beyond individual problem-solving competence to include the following:

> Promoting familial affection/communication; promoting familial monitoring and supervision; promoting child protection; promoting identification/association with anticriminal role models; reducing chemical dependencies; shifting the density of the personal, interpersonal, and other rewards and costs for criminal and noncriminal activities in familial, academic, vocational, recreational and other behavioral settings, so that the noncriminal alternatives are favored; providing the chronically psychiatrically troubled with low-pressure, sheltered living arrangements; confronting the personal and circumstantial barriers to service; and *changing other attributes of clients and their circumstances that, through individualized assessments of risk and need, have been linked reasonably with criminal conduct.* (Andrews and Bonta 1994, p.233, emphasis added)

Not only is it inconceivable that intervention in such a catalogue of criminogenic needs is reducible to cognitive-behavioural therapies aimed at individual thinking deficits, but also neither is it obvious that any of the interventions advocated for gender-specific programming would be excluded. Even interventions targeting women's experiences of victimisation might be justified under the category of 'ensuring that the client is able to recognize risky situations, and has a concrete and well-rehearsed plan for dealing with those situations' (Andrews and Bonta 1994, p.233). Reviewing this inventory of multiple and complex needs, implicating not only individual, but also relational and organisational change, should serve to remind that multi-modal programmes repeatedly emerge as effective strategies for reducing recidivism in the same literature which is often used to advance specifically cognitive-behavioural methods (Chapman and Hough 1998; Lipsey 1995; Lösel 1995; Palmer 1992, 1995).

Programmes in practice

Notwithstanding theoretical and ethical controversies about the appropriate focus of interventions for female offenders, an examination of documented programmes rapidly reveals a strong tendency towards multi-modality (see also Morash *et al.* 1998). Reasons for this seemingly inherent inclination towards diversification of methods may include difficulties in separating women's criminal involvement from their personal and social problems (Clarke 2002; Rumgay 1996, 2000a; Westmarland and McIvor 2002). This may be more than merely poor differentiation on the part of probation officers. For example, some research suggests that drinking problems impact more pervasively on other aspects of women's lives than is the case for men (Fillmore *et al.* 1997). One evaluation of a 'single issue' programme found that the women themselves, while appreciative of the opportunity, were unsatisfied by its narrow perspective and desirous of broader coverage (Deakin, Spencer and Littler 2000).

Certain themes recurrently appear in accounts of programmes for women offenders. These commonly concern access, service integration, mutual help and programme sustainment.

Access

A wide literature suggests that women offenders fail to access community-based services relevant to their criminal involvement. Partly, this may reflect difficulties of access experienced by women generally. For example, several studies report under-representation of women in alcoholism treatment services (reviewed in Walitzer and Connors 1997); a comparison of homeless women and men showed particularly poor access to substance misuse treatment on the part of the women, despite a high level of reported problems (Geissler *et al.* 1995).

It also seems that women who offend experience particular isolation from services. Studies of female offenders show low levels of access to mainstream provision including substance misuse, social welfare, employment and education, accommodation and mental health services (Klausner and Smith 1991; Lewis 1982; Pearl 1998; Wellisch, Prendergast and Anglin 1996). One of these found a positive relationship between increased use of such services and reduced recidivism (Pearl 1998). One comparison of women using domestic violence services as victims and women entering the criminal justice system as 'batterers' found similar victimisation histories but lower contact with helping agencies on the part of the offenders, the discrepancy being particularly pronounced among black women (Abel 2001).

Some critiques implicate feminist perspectives themselves in this exclusion from mainstream provision, alleging reluctance to prejudice a cause by drawing attention to deviant women (e.g. Fitzroy 2001; Lewis 1982). The strong appreciation of group programmes expressed by women, even while voicing criticisms of content, may reflect their isolation from alternative support networks (Buchanan *et al.* 1991; Clarke 2002; Deakin *et al.* 2000; Durrance and Ablitt 2001; Hirst 1996; HM Inspectorate of Probation 1995; Rumgay 2000a; also Schaffner 1997 on parenting programmes). However, a number of studies also report that females are excluded from offender programme opportunities, that their needs and family responsibilities interfere with their prospects of programme compliance and that follow-up support is inadequate following programme completion (Clarke 2002; Deakin *et al.* 2000; Durrance and Ablitt 2001; Hay 1998; Hirst 1996; Poteat 2002). Negative professional attitudes towards female offenders and female-specific programmes, as observed above, may exacerbate the effects of poor provision (Baines and Alder 1996; HM Inspectorate of Probation 1995). Yet, low referral rates to mainstream programmes may also reflect probation officers' intuitive recognition that inclusion of women who differ in important respects from the general male profile would merely increase their discomfort (Rumgay 1998b).

Practical strategies for enhancing women's access to and ability to comply with programmes show considerable consistency across projects. They most commonly include sex segregation, transport, crèche and childcare facilities, scheduling at appropriate points in the day/week/ school term, and provision of food, since programmes tend to run through the middle of the day (Bloom and Covington 2001; Deakin *et al.* 2000; Hay 1998; Hirst 1996; Mistry 1993; Roberts 2001; Rumgay 2000a; Wright and Kemshall 1994). Implicit in these arrangements is the acquisition of suitable accommodation; programmes tend to be based in premises separate from mainstream probation provision, often in alternative community resources (also Clarke 2002; Durrance and Ablitt 2001). Additional reasons underlying this are the safety implications of children's presence, the vulnerability to disruption on male-dominated mainstream probation premises and the reassurance which sex segregation offers to women who have suffered abuse by males. High attendance and completion rates have been attributed in great part to these design modifications to create 'woman- friendly' conditions (Deakin *et al.* 2000; Hirst 1996; Poteat 2002; Roberts 2002). Completion in itself has been linked to reduced reconviction, and found to be unaffected by voluntary, as opposed to coerced attendance (Clarke 2002; Klausner and Smith 1991; Probation Studies Unit 2000). Nevertheless, HM Inspectorate of Probation (1996) commented on the service's failure to apprise probation officers at local level of resources intended to improve access to child care, resulting in unnecessary exclusion from programmes.

While sex segregation in itself has been a focus of controversy, often meeting with resistance where it has been introduced (e.g. Roberts 2002), elsewhere it has been noted that in practice female staff undertake the majority of work with women offenders (McIvor 2001; Rumgay 1998b). Studies of group therapy indicate that women fare poorly in mixed-sex programmes (Coker 1997, reviewed in Jarvis 1992; Nelson-Zlupko,

Kauffman and Dore 1995). One comparison of specialist and mixed-sex substance misuse services found that women accessing the former displayed considerably more complex problems (Copeland and Hall 1992), suggesting the ability to reach more difficult populations through sex-segregated provision. A study concerned with drug-abusing offenders found that 'programs that treated women only were more likely to offer services specific to the needs of women, to offer a wider range of services, and to offer continued counseling and referral of clients to support groups following discharge' (Wellisch *et al.*1996, p.46).

Service integration

In part, the intrinsic push towards multi-modality of female-specific programmes can be understood as a natural extension of the practical measures outlined above for increasing women's access to supervision opportunities. Moreover, observers of female offenders' exclusion from mainstream services and the requirement for long-term support implied by the severity of some of their problems, urge the development of strategies to facilitate their transition from penal to wider social and health provision as a means to reducing recidivism (Abel 2001; Fitzroy 2001; Lewis 1982; Pearl 1998; Wellisch *et al.* 1996; Westmarland and McIvor 2002). Elsewhere, the enhancement of female offenders' access to community-based support agencies is defended in terms of normalisation (Rumgay 2000a) and empowerment (Clarke 2002; Roberts 2002).

Nevertheless, female offender programmes repeatedly report that women's progress is hampered by a shortage of follow-up opportunities on exit (Deakin *et al.* 2000; Durrance and Ablitt 2001; Mistry 1993). Indeed, one study observed women voluntarily repeating the programme in the absence of alternative support (Deakin *et al.* 2000). The transition to mainstream services is not easily made by marginalised and stigmatised women. Merely basing offender programmes in community centres may not automatically result in onward movement to additional resources (Mistry 1993; but see Clarke 2002). Yet HM Inspectorate of Probation (1996) has criticised the poor prioritisation of women's services in probation partnership strategies.

Service integration thus demands proactive collaboration with allied services. Successful programmes have developed strong partnerships with statutory and voluntary agencies providing opportunities relevant to women offenders' problems. The potential for clustering opportunities for access to a variety of women's services presented by the separate location of female programmes has been exploited to good effect to ameliorate the difficulties associated with transition (Rumgay 2000a). One partnership has established an active multi-faceted criminal justice programme for female drug users (Turning Point 1999, 2000). While such projects appear to develop opportunistically, as intuitively creative practice, a human service model of integrated individualised service, as articulated in the 'wraparound' approach to child and family support (Malysiak 1997, 1998), offers a theoretical foundation for systemic development relevant to women offenders' needs (Glover Reed and Leavitt 2000; Zaplin 1998a, 1998b).

Mutual help

The theoretical tensions between clinical and empowerment or relational approaches have been noted. Feminist perspectives have placed great value in basing services on assumptions of women's competence as problem solvers (Fitzroy 2001; see also Roberts 2001). Whether or not it is explicitly theoretical in origin, programmes for women offenders often display a strong quality of mutual help through sharing problems and solutions, to which participants ascribe considerable benefits (Clarke 2002; Deakin *et al.* 2000; Durrance and Ablitt 2001; Jones *et al.* 1993; Rumgay 2000a) and also report satisfaction in assisting other women in similar difficulties (Rumgay 2000a).

Some criminological research has suggested the importance of social ties between women as an important element in local informal mechanisms of crime prevention (Rountree and Warner 1999). Research in other fields has pointed to a positive connection between women's experiences of effective social support and their ability to cope with problems associated with social and personal stress (Carten 1996; Farrell 2000; Green and Rodgers 2001; Thompson *et al.* 2000). Interestingly, therefore, one community-based programme for female offenders incorporates elements of voluntary service

(Ravoira 1998), in striking contrast with the emphasis in male programmes on self-sufficiency.

Programme sustainment

The elements of enhanced access through 'woman friendly' conditions, service integration strategies and mutual help combine to make women's programmes burdensome. Compounding the low prioritisation of female offenders are differences in perspectives, organisational arrangements and physical resources from 'standard fare' in mainstream probation provision. Increasing pressure on the service to meet specific performance targets which do not reflect this approach exacerbate the disincentives to invest in it (Hirst 2002; Pakula 2002). Moreover, present emphasis on cognitive-behavioural treatments in the 'effective practice' enterprise inhibits recognition of multi-modal initiatives (Roberts 2002), despite the noted tendency for women's programmes to develop in this way. It is not surprising, therefore, that initiatives perish.

Programmes that have stood the test of time testify to the crucial importance of a supportive agency environment to their survival (Durrance and Ablitt 2001; Hirst 1996, 2002; Pakula 2002; Roberts 2002; Rumgay 2000a). Favourable policy conditions may help in this. While ambiguities in Home Office policy for women offenders in England and Wales have been marked, policy in Scotland is explicit about its ambitions both to reduce female incarceration and to foster broad-based community provision (Social Work Services and Prisons Inspectorates for Scotland 1998). Nevertheless, well-intentioned, female-specific government policies have been criticised for their vulnerability to distortion and counterproductivity in implementation (Hannah-Moffat 2001).

Despite the disincentives, several local areas seized the opportunity of a critical HM Inspectorate of Probation (1991) report to justify improvements to their provision for women. However, the inspectorate later found that a minority of probation areas had developed specific policy for women offenders, while broad equal opportunities statements failed to provide adequate practice guidelines (HM Inspectorate of Probation 1996). One area, enterprisingly, sought to protect its threatened women's services by developing not only a specific overarching policy, but also a community re-integration strategy for females that defends a multi-modal approach and attributes to the service a crucial role as a gateway to wider local provision (National Probation Service Merseyside 2001, 2002). Successful sustainment strategies designate specific individual responsibility for females at all levels in the agency to counteract tendencies towards neglect and/or override (National Probation Service Merseyside 2001, 2002; Rumgay 2000a).

Notably, those programmes that currently survive within a policy environment that is at best ambivalent have an extensive history that has fostered allegiance to them. Of more interest, however, is that, while local implementation may vary, each has arrived at a broadly similar solution in principle of placing offender programmes at the heart of multi-agency provision for socially excluded women (Ablitt 2001; Clarke 2002; National Probation Service Merseyside 2002; Roberts 2001). Within this framework, moreover, local scarcities of women under supervision can be ameliorated by integrated access to community-based services (Deakin *et al.* 2000; Hirst 2002; Rumgay 2000a).

Conclusion

With the exception of some isolated examples of practice excellence, this exploration of community supervision of women does not reflect well on those upon whom its development largely depends. In the face of escalating incarceration, the probation service's prolonged wrangling about the prolif-eration of 'unsuitable' women on its supervision caseload conveys an unfortunate impression of an agency standing idly by, preoccupied with narrow priorities, while another inappropriate population of lightly convicted, low-risk female prisoners burgeons. Moreover, the weaknesses in service quality for women implicate the misdirection of aspects of feminist theory as well as the dominant masculine ethos to which the finger of blame is more often pointed. Despite the contemporary reliance on particular per-spectives on effective practice, in which 'responsivity' is a key principle (Andrews and Bonta 1994), programmes that attempt to honour this requirement in gender-relevant ways have been rejected (Roberts 2002).

Commentators have remarked many times on the counterproductivity of practices that purport to maintain women in the community while impeding their ability to comply with supervision requirements, to keep families together while forcing women to choose between programme compliance and domestic responsibilities, and to manage risk while enforcing constraints that may obstruct women's escape routes from abuse (Ansay and Benveneste 1999; Poteat 2002; Robinson 1992). It is a heavy irony of such poorly designed approaches that they impact upon women offenders, whose characteristics generally make them more likely than men to succeed under community supervision (Olson, Lurigio and Seng 2000; Sims and Jones 1997).

Yet, the features of positive practice, together with their implications for the policy-making and managerial environment of the agency, strike at the heart of broader debates about the probation service's role in the community. Impassioned pleas have been made for correctional agencies to involve themselves in practice that emphasises community support over individual surveillance, is proactive rather than reactive in its approach to offenders' problems and advocates for local services which improve the quality of life of all residents (Byrne 1989; Clear and Karp 1999; Rumgay 2001). Such arguments identify, coincidentally, the direction that surviving women's programmes seem to have chosen. Indeed, it has been observed that the service performs at its best in multi-agency partnerships, which emerge as crucial to women's programming, when it clearly perceives a contribution to the wider health of its local community (Rumgay 2000b).

Placed in this broader context of debates about the future directions of community supervision, it is small wonder that many of the issues raised by this review of provision for women have pointed to the need for critical analysis of the assumptions and priorities underpinning the treatment of males. While there is a clear need for female offenders to be visible in research and commentary, debates about women's treatment suffer in the longer term when they continue to be 'quarantined' as gender-specific controversies. What happens to women should be permitted to contribute to the mainstream of criminal justice debate. There is no validity in the persistent assumption that, unlike men, they cannot speak for all.

Acknowledgements

I am grateful to Loraine Gelsthorpe and Eileen Munro for their comments on earlier drafts of this chapter.

I am grateful to a number of individuals who went out of their way to assist me in collecting information about particular programmes: Rebecca Clarke, Jo Deakin, Pauline Durrance, Gill Hirst, Anne Pakula, Sally Poteat, Jenny Roberts, Adrian Smith and Sophia Young.

References

Abel, E.M. (2001) 'Comparing the social service utilization, exposure to violence and trauma symptomology of domestic violence female "victims" and female "batterers".' *Journal of Family Violence 16*, 4, 401–420.

Ablitt, F. (2001) 'The Women's Probation Centre – an approach that Works.' Paper presented at the Gender and Justice Policy Network Seminar, Fawcett Society, London, 26 November.

Ablitt, F. and Durrance, P. (2000) 'Effective practice with serious women offenders.' Paper presented at the 'What Works?' Conference, Manchester, 20–22 September.

Allen, H. (1987) *Justice Unbalanced: Gender, Psychiatry and Judicial Decisions.* Milton Keynes: Open University Press.

Andrews, D. and Bonta, J. (1994) *The Psychology of Criminal Conduct.* Cincinnati, OH: Anderson.

Ansay, S.J. and Benveneste, D. (1999) 'Equal application or unequal treatment: Practical outcomes for women on community control in Florida.' *Women and Criminal Justice 10*, 3, 121–135.

Baines, M. and Alder, C. (1996) 'Are girls more difficult to work with? Youth workers' perspectives in juvenile justice and related areas.' *Crime and Delinquency 42*, 3, 467–485.

Bloom, B. and Covington, S. (1998) 'Gender-specific programming for female offenders: What is it and why is it important?' Paper presented at the American Society of Criminology Annual Meeting, Washington, DC, 11–14 November.

Bloom, B. and Covington, S. (2001) 'Effective gender-responsive interventions in juvenile justice: Addressing the lives of delinquent girls.' Paper presented at the American Society of Criminology Annual Meeting, Atlanta, GA, 7–10 November.

Buchanan, J., Collett, S. and McMullan, P. (1991) 'Challenging practice or challenging women? Female offenders and illicit drug use.' *Probation Journal 38*, 2, 56–62.

Byrne, J.M. (1989) 'Reintegrating the concept of community into community-based corrections.' *Crime and Delinquency 35*, 3, 471–499.

Carlen, P. (1989) 'Feminist jurisprudence – or women-wise penology?' *Probation Journal 36*, 3, 110–114.

Carlen, P. (ed) (2002) *Women and Punishment: The Struggle for Justice.* Cullompton: Willan.

Carten, A.J. (1996) 'Mothers in recovery: Rebuilding families in the aftermath of addiction.' *Social Work 41*, 214–223.

Chapman, T. and Hough, M. (1998) *Evidence Based Practice: A Guide to Effective Practice.* London: Home Office.

Chesney-Lind, M. (2000) 'What to do about young girls? Thinking about programs for young women.' In M. McMahon (ed) *Assessment to Assistance: Programs for Women in Community Corrections.* Lanham, MD: American Correctional Association, pp.139–170.

Chesney-Lind, M., Artz, S. and Nicholson, D. (2001) 'Girls' delinquency and violence: Making the case for gender-responsive programming.' Paper presented at the American Society of Criminology Annual Meeting, Atlanta, GA, 7–10 November.

Clarke, R. (2002) *Evaluation of the Think First for Women Programme.* Manchester: National Probation Service Greater Manchester, Research and Evaluation Team.

Clear, T.R. and Karp, D.K. (1999) *The Community Justice Ideal: Preventing Crime and Achieving Justice.* Boulder, CO: Westview Press.

Coker, M. (1997) 'Overcoming sexism in AA: How women cope.' In S.L.A. Straussner and E. Zelvin (eds) *Gender and Addictions: Men and Women in Treatment.* Northvale, NJ: Jason Aronson, pp.263–281.

Community Research Associates (1998) *Juvenile Offenders: A Status of the States Report.* Washington, DC: Office of Juvenile Justice and Delinquency Prevention.

Copeland, J. and Hall, W. (1992) 'A comparison of women seeking drug and alcohol treatment in a specialist women's and two traditional mixed-sex treatment services.' *British Journal of Addiction 87*, 1293–1302.

Covington, S. (1998) 'The relational theory of women's psychological development: Implications for the criminal justice system.' In R.T. Zaplin (ed) *Female Offenders: Critical Perspectives and Effective Interventions.* Gaithersburg, MD: Aspen, pp.113–131.

Covington, S. (1999) *Helping Women Recover: A Program for Treating Addiction.* San Francisco: Jossey-Bass.

Covington, S. and Surrey, J. L. (1997) 'The relational model of women's psychological development: Implications for substance abuse.' In R.W. Wilsnack and S.C. Wilsnack (eds) *Gender and Alcohol: Individual and Social Perspectives.* New Brunswick, NJ: Rutgers Center of Alcohol Studies, pp.335–351.

Daly, K. (1994) *Gender, Crime, and Punishment.* New Haven: Yale University Press.

Deakin, J., Spencer, J. and Littler, L. (2000) *Evaluation of the Freedom Programme: Report to Merseyside Probation Service.* Manchester: University of Manchester, Department of Applied Social Science.

Durrance, P. and Ablitt, F. (2001) '"Creative solutions" to women's offending: An evaluation of the Women's Probation Centre.' *Probation Journal 28*, 4, 247–259.

Farmer, E. and Owen, M. (1998) 'Gender and the child protection process.' *British Journal of Social Work 28*, 4, 545–564.

Farrell, A. (2000) 'Women, crime and drugs: Testing the effect of therapeutic communities.' *Women and Criminal Justice 11*, 1, 21–48.

Fillmore, K.M., Golding, J.M., Leino, E.V., Motoyoshi, M., Shoemaker, C., Terry, H., Ager, C.R. and Ferrer, H.P. (1997) 'Patterns and trends in women's and men's drinking.' In R.W. Wilsnack and S.C. Wilsnack (eds) *Gender and Alcohol: Individual and Social Perspectives*. New Brunswick, NJ: Rutgers Center of Alcohol Studies, pp.21–48.

Fitzroy, L. (2001) 'Violent women: Questions for feminist theory, practice and policy.' *Critical Social Policy 21*, 1, 7–34.

Geissler, L.J., Bormann, C.A., Kwiatowski, C.F., Braucht, G.N. and Reichardt, C.S. (1995) 'Women, homelessness, and substance abuse.' *Psychology of Women Quarterly 19*, 65–83.

Glover Reed, B. and Leavitt, M.E. (2000) 'Modified Wraparound and women offenders in community corrections: Strategies, opportunities and tensions.' In M. McMahon (ed) *Assessment to Assistance: Programs for Women in Community Corrections*. Lanham, MD: American Correctional Association, pp.1–106.

Gorman, K. (2001) 'Cognitive behaviourism and the holy grail: The quest for a universal means of managing offenders risk.' *Probation Journal 48*, 1, 3–9.

Greene, Peters and Associates (1998) *Guiding Principles for Promising Female Programming: An Inventory of Best Practices*. Report. Washington, DC: US Department of Justice, Office of Justice Programs, Office of Juvenile Justice and Delinquency Prevention.

Green, B. L. and Rodgers, A. (2001) 'Determinants of social support among low-income mothers: A longitudinal analysis.' *American Journal of Community Psychology 29*, 3, 419–441.

Hannah-Moffat, K. (2001) *Punishment in Disguise: Penal Governance and Federal Imprisonment of Women in Canada*. Toronto: University of Toronto Press.

Hay, A. (1998) 'Women need women.' *Probation Journal 45*, 1, 36–38.

Hirst, G. (1996) '"Moving forward": How did we do that?' *Probation Journal 43*, 2, 58–63.

Hirst, G. (2002) Personal communication.

HM Inspectorate of Probation (1991) *Report on Women Offenders and Probation Service Provision: Report of a Thematic Inspection*. London: HM Inspectorate of Probation.

HM Inspectorate of Probation (1995) *Probation Orders with Additional Requirements: Report of a Thematic Inspection*. London: HM Inspectorate of Probation.

HM Inspectorate of Probation (1996) *A Review of Probation Service Provision for Women Offenders*. London: HM Inspectorate of Probation.

Home Office (1996) *Probation Statistics England and Wales 1995.* London: Home Office.

Home Office (1999) *Domestic Violence: Break the Chain.* London: Home Office.

Home Office (2000) *The Government's Strategy for Women Offenders.* London: Home Office.

Home Office (2001a) *Statistics on Women and the Criminal Justice System.* London: Home Office.

Home Office (2001b) *The Government's Strategy for Women Offenders: Consultation Report.* London: Home Office.

Home Office (2002) *Probation Statistics England and Wales 2000.* London: Home Office.

Horn, R. and Evans, M. (2000) 'The effect of gender on pre-sentence reports.' *Howard Journal of Criminal Justice 39,* 2, 184–197.

Jarvis, T.J. (1992) 'Implications of gender for alcohol treatment research: A quantitative and qualitative review.' *British Journal of Addiction 87,* 1249–1261.

Jones, M., Mordecai, M., Rutter, F. and Thomas, L. (1993) 'The Miskin model of groupwork with women offenders.' In A. Brown and B. Caddick (eds) *Groupwork with Offenders.* London: Whiting and Birch, pp.169–196.

Kelly, L. and Humphreys, C. (2000) *Reducing Domestic Violence...What Works? Outreach and Advocacy Approaches.* London: Home Office, Policing and Reducing Crime Unit.

Kendall, K. (2002) 'Time to think again about cognitive behavioral programmes.' In P. Carlen (ed) *Women and Punishment: The Struggle for Justice.* Cullompton: Willan, pp.182–198.

Klausner, M.L. and Smith, B. (1991) *Opening Doors for Change: Alternatives to Incarceration. A Report on Alternative Sentencing for Women.* Boston, MA: Social Justice for Women.

Lewis, D.K. (1982) 'Female exoffenders and community programs: Barriers to service.' *Crime and Delinquency 28,* 1, 40-51.

Lipsey, M.W. (1995) 'What do we learn from 400 research studies on the effectiveness of treatment with juvenile delinquents?' In J. McGuire (ed) *What Works: Reducing Offending. Guidelines from Practice and Research.* Chichester: Wiley, pp.63–78.

Loper, A.B. (2000) *Female Juvenile Delinquency: Risk Factors and Promising Interventions.* Juvenile Justice Fact Sheet. Charlottesville, VA: Institute of Law, Psychiatry and Public Policy, University of Virginia.

Lösel, F. (1995) 'The efficacy of correctional treatment: A review and synthesis of meta-evaluations.' In J. McGuire (ed) *What Works: Reducing Offending. Guidelines from Practice and Research.* Chichester: Wiley, pp.79–111.

McGuire, J. (ed) (1995) *What Works: Reducing Offending. Guidelines from Practice and Research.* Chichester: Wiley.

McGuire, J. and Hatcher, R. (2001) 'Offense-focused problem solving: Preliminary evaluation of a cognitive skills program.' *Criminal Justice and Behavior 28*, 5, 564–587.

McIvor, G. (1999) 'Women, crime and criminal justice in Scotland.' *Scottish Journal of Criminal Justice Studies 5*, 1, 67–74.

McIvor, G. (2001) 'Community supervision of female offenders: Client and staff perspectives.' Paper presented at the Australian and New Zealand Criminology Conference, Melbourne, 21–23 February.

McMahon, M. (2000) 'Assisting female offenders: Art or science? – Chairman's Commentary.' In M. McMahon (ed) *Assessment to Assistance: Programs for Women in Community Corrections*. Lanham, MD: American Correctional Association, pp.279–328.

Mair, G. (2000) 'Credible accreditation?' *Probation Journal 47*, 4, 268–271.

Mair, G. and Brockington, N. (1988) 'Female offenders and the probation service.' *Howard Journal of Criminal Justice 27*, 2, 117–126.

Malysiak, R. (1997) 'Exploring the theory and paradigm base for Wraparound.' *Journal of Child and Family Studies 6*, 4, 399–408.

Malysiak, R. (1998) 'Deciphering the Tower of Babel: Examining the theory Base for Wraparound Fidelity.' *Journal of Child and Family Studies 7*, 1, 11–25.

Merrington, S. and Stanley, S. (2000) 'Doubts about the what works initiative.' *Probation Journal 47*, 4, 272–275.

Mileski, M. (1969) *Courtroom Encounters: An Observation Study of a Lower Criminal Court*. Yale: Yale Law School.

Miller, J.B. (1986) *Toward a New Psychology of Women*, 2nd ed. Boston, MA: Beacon Press.

Miller, J.B. and Stiver, I.P. (1997) *The Healing Connection: How Women Form Relationships in Therapy and in Life*. Boston, MA: Beacon Press.

Mistry, T. (1993) 'Establishing a feminist model of groupwork in the probation service.' In A. Brown and B. Caddick (eds) *Groupwork with Offenders*. London: Whiting and Birch, pp.155–168.

Morash, M., Bynum, T.S. and Koons, B.A. (1998) *Women Offenders: Programming Needs and Promising Approaches*. Washington, DC: US Department of Justice, Office of Justice Programs.

Morran, D. (1995) 'Male offenders' violence against women: Suggestions for practice.' *Probation Journal 42*, 4, 215–219.

Morris, A. (1987) *Women, Crime and Criminal Justice*. Oxford: Blackwell.

National Probation Service Merseyside (2001) *Policy and Practice in Relation to Women Offenders SDPP*. Liverpool: National Probation Service Merseyside.

National Probation Service Merseyside (2002) *Strategy for Reintegration of Women Offenders*. Liverpool: National Probation Service Merseyside.

Nelson-Zlupko, L., Kauffman, E. and Dore, M.M. (1995) 'Gender differences in drug addiction and treatment: Implications for social work intervention with substance-abusing women.' *Social Work 40*, 1, 45–54.

O'Hagan, K. (1997) 'The problem of engaging men in child protection work.' *British Journal of Social Work 27*, 1, 25–42.

Olson, D.E., Lurigio, A.J. and Seng, M. (2000) 'A comparison of female and male probationers: Characteristics and case outcomes.' *Women and Criminal Justice 11*, 4, 65–79.

Orme, J. (1992) 'Women and the Criminal Justice Act 1991.' *Probation Journal 39*, 2, 78–81.

Owen, B., Bloom, B. and Covington, S. (2001) 'Distinctions with a difference: Developing gender-appropriate policy for women in the criminal justice system.' Paper presented at the American Society of Criminology Annual Meeting, Atlanta, GA, 7–10 November.

Pakula, A. (2002) Personal communication.

Palmer, T. (1992) *The Re-emergence of Correctional Intervention*. Newbury Park, CA: Sage.

Palmer, T. (1995) 'Programmatic and nonprogrammatic aspects of successful intervention: New directions for research.' *Crime and Delinquency 41*, 1, 100–131.

Pearl, N.R. (1998) 'Use of community-based social services to reduce recidivism in female parolees.' *Women and Criminal Justice 10*, 1, 27–52.

Poteat, S. (2002) 'The Women at Risk Programme.' In P. Carlen (ed) *Women and Punishment: The Struggle for Justice*. Cullompton: Willan, pp.125–137.

Probation Studies Unit (2000) *Report on the Retrospective Study of the Hereford and Worcester Probation Service Women's Programme*. Oxford: University of Oxford, Centre for Criminological Research, Probation Studies Unit.

Ravoira, L. (1998) 'The PACE program: Giving young women a positive start.' In J.B. Morton (ed) *Complex Challenges, Collaborative Solutions: Programming for Adult and Juvenile Female Offenders*. Lanham, MD: American Correctional Association, pp.199–208.

Raynor, P. and Vanstone, M. (1997) *Straight Thinking on Probation: The Mid Glamorgan Experiment*. Oxford: University of Oxford, Centre for Criminological Research.

Roberts, J. (2001) *West Midlands Crime Reduction and Social Inclusion Unit: Partnership Development Fund Application*. Worcester: Asha Women's Centre.

Roberts, J. (2002) 'Women-centred: The West Mercia community based programmes for women offenders.' In P. Carlen (ed) *Women and Punishment: The Struggle for Justice*. Cullompton: Willan, pp.110–124.

Robinson, R. (1992) 'Intermediate sanctions and the female offender.' In J.M. Byrne, A.J. Lurigio and J. Petersilia (eds) *Smart Sentencing: The Emergence of Intermediate Sanctions*. Newbury Park, CA: pp.245–260.

Rountree, P.W. and Warner, B.D. (1999) 'Social ties and crime: Is the relationship gendered?' *Criminology 37*, 4, 789–814.

Rumgay, J. (1996) 'Women offenders: Towards needs-based policy.' *Vista 2*, 2, 104–115.

Rumgay, J. (1998a) *Crime, Punishment and the Drinking Offender.* Basingstoke: Macmillan.

Rumgay, J. (1998b) *Analysis of Pre-sentence Reports on Female Offenders Undertaken in 1997 and Survey of User Satisfaction in 1998: A Report Commissioned by West Sussex Probation Service.* Chichester: West Sussex Probation Service.

Rumgay, J. (2000a) 'Policies of neglect: Female offenders and the probation service.' In H. Kemshall and R. Littlechild (eds) *User Involvement and Participation in Social Care.* London: Jessica Kingsley Publishers, pp.193–213.

Rumgay, J. (2000b) *The Addicted Offender: Developments in British Policy and Practice.* Basingstoke: Palgrave.

Rumgay, J. (2001) 'Accountability in the delivery of community penalties: To whom, for what and why?' In A. Bottoms, L. Gelsthorpe and S. Rex (eds) *Community Penalties: Change and Challenges.* Cullompton: Willan, pp.126–145.

Sagatun, I.J. (1989) 'Gender biases in probation officers' attributions of juvenile delinquency.' *International Journal of Offender Therapy and Comparative Criminology 33*, 2, 131–140.

Schaffner, L. (1997) 'Families on probation: Court-ordered parenting skills classes for parents of juvenile offenders.' *Crime and Delinquency 43*, 4, 412–437.

Sims, B. and Jones, M. (1997) 'Predicting success or failure on probation: Factors associated with felony probation outcomes.' *Crime and Delinquency 43*, 3, 314–327.

Smart, C. (1977) *Women, Crime and Criminology.* London: Routledge and Kegan Paul.

Social Work Services and Prisons Inspectorates for Scotland (1998) *Women Offenders: A Safer Way. A Review of Community Disposals and the Use of Custody for Women Offenders.* Glasgow: The Scottish Executive.

Thompson, M.P., Kaslow, N.J., Kingree, J.B., Rashid, A., Puett, R., Jacobs, D. and Matthews, A. (2000) 'Partner violence, social support, and distress among inner-city African American women.' *American Journal of Community Psychology 28*, 1, 127–143.

Turning Point (1999) *A Very Good Year for Turnaround.* Glasgow: The Drugs Crisis Centre, Turning Point Scotland.

Turning Point (2000) *Turnaround: Year 2000.* Glasgow: The Drugs Crisis Centre, Turning Point Scotland.

Walby, S. and Myhill, A. (2000) *Reducing Domestic Violence...What Works? Assessing and Managing the Risk of Domestic Violence.* London: Home Office, Policing and Reducing Crime Unit.

Walitzer, K.S. and Connors, G.J. (1997) 'Gender and treatment of alcohol-related problems.' In R.W. Wilsnack and S.C. Wilsnack (eds) *Gender and Alcohol:*

Individual and Social Perspectives. New Brunswick, NJ: Rutgers Center of Alcohol Studies, pp.445–461.

Walker, H. (1985) 'Women's issues in probation.' In H. Walker and B. Beaumont (eds) *Working with Offenders.* Basingstoke: Macmillan.

Walker, H. and Beaumont, B. (1981) *Probation Work: Critical Theory and Socialist Practice.* Oxford: Blackwell.

Webb, D. (1984) 'More on gender and justice: Girl offenders on supervision.' *Sociology 18,* 367–381.

Wellisch, J., Prendergast, M.L. and Anglin, M.D. (1996) 'Needs assessment and services for drug-abusing women offenders: Results from a national survey of community-based treatment programmes.' *Women and Criminal Justice 8,* 1, 27–60.

Westmarland, N. and McIvor, G. (2002) 'What works with women on probation? Key findings from research with women in Scotland.' Paper presented at the British Criminology Conference, Keele, 17–20 July.

Women's Unit, Cabinet Office and Home Office (1999) *Living without Fear: An Integrated Approach to Tackling Violence against Women.* London: Cabinet Office.

Worrall, A. (1990) *Offending Women: Female Lawbreakers and the Criminal Justice System.* London: Routledge.

Worrall, A. (1997) *Punishment in the Community: The Future of Criminal Justice.* Harlow: Addison-Wesley Longman.

Wright, L. and Kemshall, H. (1994) 'Feminist probation practice: Making supervision meaningful.' *Probation Journal 41,* 2, 73–80.

Zaplin, R.T. (1998a) 'Female Offenders: A systems Perspective.' In R.T. Zaplin (ed) *Female Offenders: Critical Perspectives and Effective Interventions.* Gaithersburg, MD: Aspen, pp.65–79.

Zaplin, R.T. (1998b) 'A systems approach to the design and implementation of a day program for women offenders.' In J.B. Morton (ed) *Complex Challenges, Collaborative Solutions: Programming for Adult and Juvenile Female Offenders.* Lanham, MD: American Correctional Association, pp.129–140.

CHAPTER 6

Service with a Smile?

Women and Community 'Punishment'

Gill McIvor

Introduction

Community service orders (now community punishment orders in England and Wales) require convicted offenders to undertake a specified number of hours of unpaid work for the community. Offenders who are made subject to community service orders carry out a variety of tasks – which would not otherwise be completed by paid employees – ranging from environmental improvements to painting and decorating and care duties in voluntary or statutory agencies. Confusion has existed from the outset regarding the philosophy underlying community service (Pease *et al.* 1975). Although it may be most appropriately conceptualised as a fine on the offender's time, increasing interest is now being paid to the rehabilitative potential of the sentence (e.g. McIvor 1998a; Rex and Gelsthorpe 2002).

Community service by offenders has proved to be a popular sentencing option since its introduction in England and Wales 30 years ago and its subsequent introduction in Scotland 5 years later. Despite this, its use with women who offend has been somewhat controversial. For example, McIvor (1998b) has argued that women have been consistently under-represented on community service schemes and Worrall (1995) concluded that community service is permeated by the ideology that is it a 'young man's punishment' and, as such, is a highly gendered disposal.

This chapter focuses upon the use made of community service with women who offend. It begins by reviewing the use made of community service with female offenders before examining some of the issues that have arisen in relation to its use with women. The chapter concludes by describing recent developments in community service in the UK and considering the implications for women ordered to undertake unpaid work by the courts.

Use of community service with women who offend

As McIvor (1998b) has argued, access to community service is influenced by decisions reached at a variety of stages in the sentencing process and gender differences may be introduced at any of these stages. Since community service was first introduced, there has been considerable debate as to whether women are under-represented on community service schemes. For example, there is some evidence that when age, current offence and criminal history are controlled for, women are as likely to receive community service as men (Mair and Brockington 1988). Scottish data have also indicated that women who are referred for community service assessments are as likely to receive a community service order as men (Scottish Office 1995).

There is also evidence that courts have traditionally been reluctant to impose community service orders in respect of women. This can be attributed to some extent to the practices of probation officers and social workers. For example, a thematic inspection of women offenders and probation service provision in England and Wales suggested that probation officers were sometimes not referring women with domestic responsibilities for community service assessments despite the availability of childcare provision (HM Inspectorate of Probation 1991). A more recent inspection (HM Inspectorate of Probation 1996) made a similar point, suggesting that probation officers were unaware of childcare arrangements for women offenders or did not make them clear to sentencers.

Dominelli (1984) found in interviews with magistrates, probation officers and community service staff that women with domestic responsibilities were considered poor risks for community service with respect to the organisational objective of getting offenders through their orders. Jackson and Smith (1987) found that community service had been presented as an option in only 54 per cent of social inquiry reports relating to women who subsequently received a custodial sentence. Many women in their custody sample had a social inquiry report which contained arguments against community service, with the domestic responsibility of the women as carer being the reason most frequently given. Similarly Barker (1993) suggested that in the majority of pre-sentence reports prepared upon a sample of women on community service a stronger case could have been made for the imposition of a community service order. For instance, 31 of the 48 women in the sample were mothers, yet almost all reports failed to make reference to the fact that assistance could, if necessary, be given with childcare provision if the woman was made subject to community service.

A Scottish study which focused upon social enquiry reports prepared in respect of 72 women who were subsequently sentenced to probation, community service or imprisonment (Dickie 1995) adjudged 18 reports as containing material which inappropriately militated against the making of a community service order. On a more positive note, each of the 21 recommendations for community service resulted in the imposition of a community-based social work disposal (community service orders were imposed in 17 cases and probation orders in 4) and none of the women for whom community service was recommended received a custodial sentence. This suggests that the active promotion of community service in reports to the court may persuade sentencers to make greater use of community service with women.

Data on social inquiry reports prepared for Scottish courts in 2001 to 2002, however, reveal that social workers were much less likely to recomend community service orders for women than for men (Scottish Executive 2002a). Seven per cent of reports on women had community service put forward as a preferred sentencing option, compared to 12 per cent of reports on men. Probation, by comparison, was equally likely to be recommended for men and for women (in 18 per cent of cases). Turning to the sentences imposed, although women were the subjects of 15 per cent of all reports prepared for the courts, they accounted for only 10 per cent of community service orders and probation orders with a requirement to undertake unpaid work. Overall, 12 per cent of men in respect of whom social inquiry reports were prepared received a community service order compared with 8 per cent of women, suggesting that sentencer decisions were broadly congruent with social worker recommendations. Interestingly, women were more likely than men to receive a probation order (including additional requirements but excluding unpaid work), with 17 per cent of the former but only 11 per cent of the latter receiving this disposal. This suggests that there is still a tendency for women to be perceived by sentencers as 'troubled' and therefore in need of measures of support (Gelsthorpe and Loucks 1997).

The same statistical bulletin reveals, however, that despite less often being considered suitable for a community service order, women were more likely than men to complete their orders or to have them terminated following a review. Men, on the other hand, were more likely to have their orders terminated as a consequence of breach (Scottish Executive 2002a). A similar pattern of results was found by Barker (1993) in her study of community service in three probation services in England and Wales.

There has been an increase in the proportionate use of community service with women who offend over the last decade, both in Scotland and in England and Wales. For example, Home Office data suggest that 12 per cent of those starting community punishment orders in England and Wales in 2001 were women, compared with 6 per cent of those starting community service in 1991 (Home Office 2002a, 2002b). In Scotland the increase in the proportionate use of community service with women has been less marked. In 1999 (the last year for which statistics on the use of community service by Scottish courts are presented separately) it accounted for only 3 per cent of all disposals made in respect of women (Scottish Executive 2000). Worrall (2000) has suggested that the under-utilisation of community service for women is partly a result of practical problems and partly due to ideological ones. She suggests that sentencers have never been fully convinced about the appropriateness of community service for women, perceiving it as a punishment for 'fit young men' (p.2). This, she suggests, is a more fundamental barrier to the use of community service with women than any perceived inadequacies in provision for women which stems, in turn, from their low numbers on orders.

Dowds and Hedderman (1997) have suggested that women may receive community service orders at an earlier point in their offending histories than men, through the imposition of these orders instead of a fine. This proposal was supported by a study of community service assessments carried out for three Scottish courts. It found that women who were referred had fewer previous convictions, were facing sentence for less serious offences and were less likely than men to be considered by the social worker preparing their social inquiry report to be at risk of attracting a custodial sentence (McIvor 1998b). McIvor and Tulle-Winton (1993) found that courts often impose community service orders in lieu of other non-custodial sanctions, even though in Scotland the legislation stipulates that community service should only be used as a direct alternative to imprisonment. The reluctance of courts to fine women and to use community service with women who are at risk of custody removes important steps from the penalogical ladder, making it likely that woman will move up quickly through the range of 'appropriate' sentences towards imprisonment (Scottish Executive 2002b).

Whether women are treated more or less leniently than men by the courts is difficult to determine. It is clear, however, that they are treated differently. In 1999, for example, women in Scotland were three times more likely to receive probation than community service, even though these disposals were used almost equally with men (Scottish Executive 2000). Hine (1993) found that women on community service in England and Wales were more likely to be first offenders and suggested that there was less consistency, in terms of criminal history and current offence, in the sentencing of women to community service (see also Hine and Thomas 1995). This, she argued, suggested that factors other than offence and previous history played a greater part in the sentencing of women who offend.

Effectiveness of community service

The apparent under-use of community service with women is unfortunate not least because offenders on community service consistently have lower reconviction rates than would be predicted by their criminal history, age and other relevant characteristics (Lloyd, Mair and Hough 1995). For example, May (1999) found that reconviction rates among offenders given community service were better than predicted, even when social factors such as unemployment and drug use were taken into account. In a Swiss study,

Killias, Aebi and Ribeaud (2000) found lower reconviction rates among offenders sentenced to community service than among those given short prison sentences. A Scottish comparison of reconviction rates following different sentences suggested that when factors such as sex, age and previous criminal history were controlled for, reconviction rates tended to be similar following prison sentences and a range of non-custodial disposals including community service (Scottish Executive 2003). However, if the custodial sample had been restricted to offenders serving shorter prison sentences (for example, up to 12 months) and if allowance had been made for the effect of pseudo-reconvictions community service would have outperformed imprisonment in this respect.

There is also evidence that women given community service may do better, in terms of subsequent reconviction, than men who are similarly sentenced. For example, the Home Office found that 51 per cent of men given community service were reconvicted within two years compared to 35 per cent of women, though women who were heavily convicted (that is who had seven or more previous convictions) tended to do worse than men (Home Office 2002a). A recent analysis of reconviction data by the Justice Statistics Unit of the Scottish Executive found that women were less often reconvicted than men, regardless of previous criminal history (Scottish Executive 2003). These data (see Table 6.1) indicate that community service may, therefore, be a particularly effective and appropriate disposal for women and would tend to justify its increased use with women who offend.

Table 6.1 Percentage reconvicted within two years by sex and number of previous convictions

No. of previous convictions	Women %	Men %
none	17	30
1 or 2	29	43
3–10	37	61
11 or more	62	77

Almost two-thirds of women received into custody under direct sentence in Scotland in 2001 were given prison sentences of less than six months and the offences for which women were most commonly imprisoned that year were thefts (primarily shoplifting) and drug offences (Scottish Executive 2002c). Most women who are imprisoned cannot therefore be deemed to pose a significant risk to society and would be more appropriately dealt with by means of a non-custodial disposal such as community service. As the Ministerial Group on Women's Offending (Scottish Executive 2002b) observed:

> When considering the option of a community sentence against the option of a prison sentence each time, we suggest a simple test. It should be whether the offender presents any threat to the community and whether prison is more likely than a community sentence to be successful in reducing the likelihood of their re-offending. On that basis, we believe that many more women could be given a community sentence whilst still safeguarding the safety of communities, thereby improving the efficiency of the system, with better results for the women. (Scottish Executive 2002b, p.29)

The Ministerial Group noted with some concern that in 2000 there had been a 5 per cent decrease from the previous year in the use of community sentences (probation and community service) for women offenders aged over 21 and a 10 per cent decrease for women offenders aged under 21. The proportionate use in Scotland of custody relative to community sentences has fallen for women aged 21 years and over since the mid-1990s. However it has almost doubled among young women under 21 years of age, from 22 per cent in 1997 to 40 per cent in 2001 (Scottish Executive 2002d). Across the UK, the increase over recent years in the use of community sentences with women has been matched by an increase in the use of imprisonment.

Women's experiences of community service

Given that women comprise a small percentage of offenders made subject to community service orders it is perhaps not surprising that relatively little attention has been paid to their experiences of undertaking court-mandated unpaid work. The extent of the neglect of women's experiences is highlighted in an editorial introduction to an article on women and community service orders in a North American journal: 'As far as we know, there has been no research whatsoever in the United States that assesses the impact of community service sentences on women' (Immarigeon 2000, p.35).

Rex and Gelsthorpe (2002) similarly point to the relative invisibility of women's experiences in studies of community service. While acknowledging that there is much more to learn about the experiences of women and members of ethnic minority groups who are made subject to community service, they anticipate having a relatively small proportion of women in their own sample and observe that 'their individual experiences are likely to be lost among those of white males who predominate in the sample' (Rex and Gelsthorpe 2002, p.323).

Studies focused specifically upon women given community service are therefore necessary in order adequately to capture women's experiences and views of this disposal. That is not to say, however, that comparisons of men and women given community service cannot in themselves be instructive. For example, such comparisons can, as we have seen, point to the tendency for women and men to be given community service at different points in their offending 'careers'. They can also reveal interesting differences in the types of community service placement to which men and women are allocated. McIvor (1992), for instance, found that women were more likely than men to be allocated to individual agency placements and were more likely than men to be engaged in work of a caring, personalised type. This pattern appears still to pertain and despite attempts on the part of probation services to avoid allocating women to work of a stereotypically feminine nature, some services singled out projects requiring caring skills as being particularly appropriate for women (Howard League 1999).

Several studies have directly documented the experiences of women given community service orders or have examined policy and practice with respect to women and community service. In general they have shown that women find their experiences of community service to be positive (e.g. Barker 1993; Goodwin and McIvor 2000, 2001; Queensland Department of Families, Youth and Community Care 1999), though they have also identified aspects of community service that appear particularly problematic for women.

In one of the earlier studies of women on community service, Barker (1993) found that most women considered their experience of community service to have been reasonably rewarding and ascribed equal value to group and individual placements. As in the research by the Queensland Department of Families, Youth and Community Care (1999) and by Goodwin and McIvor (2001), women found the interpersonal aspects of their placements more significant than the activities they were required to carry out. How women are treated by agency staff and other personnel appears to be central to their experience of community service. As Goodwin and McIvor (2001, p.16) commented: 'the women said that what they liked most was being treated as a person, not being judged by other people, meeting people who knew that had committed an offence but did not judge them for it and being treated equally and fairly'.

Despite their preferences for community service rather than a prison sentence, the public nature of community service was disliked by a number of women in Goodwin and McIvor's (2001) study, with the perception of public shaming being particularly acutely felt among those living in rural areas. Some women, it seems, experience a degree of stigma as a result of being placed on a community service order.

Perhaps in some cases to protect 'vulnerable' women, there is a tendency for women to be placed in individual agency placements where they can make use of their existing skills rather than in group placements where they might have an opportunity to acquire new ones (Barker 1993; Goodwin and McIvor 2001). In Barker's (1993) study the comparatively limited use of group placements for women offenders reflected the absence of women-only group provision and, as a consequence, attempts to ensure that group placements were used only if women could be 'clustered' in mixed sex groups. The Howard League (1999) found that women were often perceived by probation services to be an asset in mixed groups because they helped to facilitate the smooth running of the placement.

Barker (1993) suggested that a policy of clustering women in mixed sex groups appeared to ameliorate the effects of sexual or racial harassment since such incidents were rarely reported. However this relatively positive picture of mixed sex placements may have resulted from the study's focus on women who were successfully completing their orders, since Armstrong (1990, cited in Worrall 1995) found that the harassment of women on orders was more widespread. Most of the women in Goodwin and McIvor's (2001) study reported not having been made to feel uncomfortable on account of their gender, but four indicated that they had and one reported having been sexually harassed by other team members. The study by the Howard League (1999) suggested that levels of reported harassment of women in mixed sex groups were low, but that actual levels might be higher as a result of some staff members overlooking such incidents to avoid upsetting the 'smooth running of the group' (p.11).

The difficulty of providing women-only groups has been well documented both in the UK and elsewhere (e.g. Althorp 1996; Barker 1993; Howard League 1999). The low numbers of women given community service at any one time can make it difficult to bring together sufficient women for a single-sex team. The study by the Howard League (1999) pointed to the potential benefits of single-sex provision for women in raising the profile of women on community service among probation staff and sentencers and offering a more flexible approach to issues such as reporting times and childcare provision. All-women teams can additionally provide women with support in a non-threatening environment. However the Howard League report also identified difficulties experienced by probation services in recruiting female supervisors for women-only teams. Goodwin and McIvor (2001) found that women allocated to individual agency placements were more often supervised by women but that those who spent all or part of their orders in a team placement were supervised by men.

Resource constraints may mean that the provision of women-only teams is not possible in most areas, but that should not mean that women are rendered vulnerable by being isolated in what is otherwise male-only provision. Goodwin and McIvor (2001) found that half of the 18 women who had been allocated to a workshop or to a team placement were the only women in the group, while two others found themselves in a group in which the women were heavily outnumbered by men. Where single-sex teams are impractical, agency placements are preferable if they prevent women from being allocated to male-dominated teams. Agency placements may also be more suitable for women because they are able to offer greater flexibility with respect to working hours (Howard League 1999).

Those studies that have explored the reasons for the allocation of women to community service placements have usually found that the women felt involved in the decision making process (e.g. Goodwin and McIvor 2001; Queensland Department of Families, Youth and Community Care 1999). However it also appears that placement choice is often constrained, to a greater degree than is the case with for men, by a lack of transport and childcare facilities (Barker 1993; Goodwin and McIvor 2001).

Several studies have highlighted the difficulties encountered by women on community service in making appropriate arrangements for the care of their children (e.g. Althorp 1996; Barker 1993; Goodwin and McIvor 2001). As the Howard League report found, childcare provision was patchy and haphazard, partly as a result of limited resources but also because 'many community service units are not yet culturally prepared for women' (Howard League 1999, p.17). Only 12 of the probation services surveyed had crèche facilities available for women on community service and while all would pay for the costs of a registered childminder, only six services would make a payment to someone other than a registered childminder. Yet Barker (1993) and Goodwin and McIvor (2001) found that women were usually reluctant to leave their children with strangers, preferring instead to make their own informal arrangements with family members, partners or friends and, if necessary, paying for a childminder themselves. Goodwin and McIvor also suggested that few women in their study may have exercised their right to financial entitlement for childcare and travel to placement because they had not been provided with clear information as to what their rights were. Even when women did avail themselves of the financial support to which they were entitled, this was by no means unproblematic. One woman, for example, reported having been so embarrassed by the conspicuous bus pass that was issued by the social work department that she opted to pay for her bus fare herself.

Punishment in the community?

Most of the women who participated in Goodwin and McIvor's (2001) study perceived their order to be first and foremost a punishment for their offence: only a quarter thought that they had been placed on community service to give something back to the community and fewer still believed that the purpose of their sentence was to help them stop offending. In April 2001 the Criminal Justice and Court Services Act 2000 came into force, resulting in the community service order in England and Wales being renamed the community punishment order. (It is somewhat ironic that legislation enacted to emphasise the punitive nature of community service should be accompanied by a government initiative aimed at enhancing the rehabilitative potential of community punishment orders.) Community Punishment Pathfinders were established in 2000 under the Home Office's Crime Reduction Programme. A total of seven pathfinders were set up across ten probation areas and, like the other Home Office Pathfinders, they have been subject to evaluation (Rex and Gelsthorpe 2002). The projects have focused in various combinations upon the use of pro-social modelling (Rex 1999; Trotter 1999), skills accreditation and addressing the problems underlying offending behaviour. In some projects attempts were also made to improve the quality of work placements and hence their perceived value to offenders. One project focused specifically upon enhancing the integration of the community service and probation elements of combination orders through improved induction and supervision planning.

Rex and Gelsthorpe found that short-term outcomes were encouraging, with offenders showing reductions in perceived problems and pro-criminal attitudes. Two-thirds of offenders on orders were viewed by staff as having undergone positive change and as having good prospects of future change while (no doubt because they were relatively low risk in the first place) three-quarters were thought by staff to be unlikely to reoffend. A similar proportion of offenders considered that their experience of community service had made them less likely to reoffend. Importantly, the features of community service that were most strongly linked with changes in offenders' attitudes were whether they perceived the work to have been of value to themselves and to the beneficiaries. The next phase of the pathfinder evaluation will examine whether these positive attitudinal changes are translated into reduced rates of reconviction.

As we have already noted, Rex and Gelsthorpe (2002) have cautioned that the relatively small number of women in their sample will make it likely that women's experiences are 'lost' in their analyses. This is unfortunate since little is known about how skills accreditation and pro-social modelling might impact differently upon men and women. The Howard League's (1999) study of women and community service recognises the potential for training and accreditation to enhance women's employment prospects and in so doing increase the possibility of living a crime-free life. Goodwin and McIvor (2000, 2001) have similarly argued that the potential to engage women in the workforce could be harnessed more effectively and more investment made in this aspect of community service.

Pro-social modelling – the way in which those responsible for supervising offenders model and reinforce pro-social attitudes and values in their clients – has been found to be associated with reductions in offending among men (e.g. Trotter 1999) but its relevance to and effectiveness with women has not yet been explored. McIvor (1998a) has suggested that community service may offer many opportunities for the modelling of pro-social behaviour by community service supervisors. However the allocation of women to agency placements and the relative paucity of female supervisors (Howard League 1999) means that the potential for pro-social modelling with women on community service is unlikely to be fully exploited.

Conclusion

Community service is now a well-established sentencing option in many western jurisdictions but its use with women who offend continues to be problematic. Even if women in the UK are now more likely to receive community service sentences than they were in the past, it appears that many community service schemes are still unable to recognise their needs and make suitable provision for women. How the redefinition of community service as 'community punishment' will impact upon its use with women remains to be seen, but it does not seem unrealistic to suggest that it will further confirm the sentence as being particularly suited to young men. Although the aim of the Community Punishment Pathfinders in England and Wales is to enhance the rehabilitative potential of unpaid work for the community (and this is an aim that it could be argued may be setting community service up to fail), the research base upon which the Pathfinders are premised is itself highly gendered and the significance of these developments to women who offend remains unclear.

References

Althorp, G. (1996) 'Young women and community service orders.' In C. Alder and M. Baines (eds) *...And When She Was Bad? Working with Young Women in Juvenile Justice and Related Areas.* Hobart, Tasmania: National Clearinghouse for Youth Studies.

Armstrong, S. (1990) *Alternatives to Custody? Day Centre and Community Service Provision for Women.* Occasional Paper no. 4. Keele: University of Keele Centre for Criminology.

Barker, M. (1993) *Community Service for Women Offenders.* London: Association of Chief Officers of Probation.

Dickie, D. (1995) 'Women offenders and social enquiry reports: A study of women and social work practice in Lothian.' Unpublished MSc thesis, Department of Applied Social Science, University of Stirling.

Dominelli, L. (1984) 'Differential justice: Domestic labour, community service and female offenders.' *Probation Journal 31*, 3, 100–103.

Dowds, L. and Hedderman, C. (1997) 'The sentencing of men and women.' In C. Hedderman and L. Gelsthorpe (eds) *Understanding the Sentencing of Women.* Home Office Research Study no. 170. London: Home Office.

Gelsthorpe, L. and Loucks, N. (1997) 'Magistrates' explanations of sentencing decisions.' In C. Hedderman and L. Gelsthorpe (eds) *Understanding the Sentencing of Women.* Home Office Research Study no. 170, London: Home Office.

Goodwin, K. and McIvor, G. (2000) 'Women and community service orders.' *Women, Girls and Criminal Justice 1*, 3, 35–36, 42–44.

Goodwin, K. and McIvor, G. (2001) *Women's Experience of Community Service Orders.* Stirling: Social Work Research Centre, University of Stirling.

Hine, J. (1993) 'Access for women: Flexible and friendly?' In D. Whitfield and D. Scott (eds) *Paying Back: Twenty Years of Community Service.* Winchester: Waterside Press.

Hine, J. and Thomas, N. (1995) 'Evaluating work with offenders: Community Service orders.' In G. McIvor (ed) *Working with Offenders: Research Highlights in Social Work 26.* London: Jessica Kingsley Publishers.

HM Inspectorate of Probation (1991) *Report on Women Offenders and Probation Service Provision: Report of a Thematic Inspection.* London: HM Inspectorate of Probation.

HM Inspectorate of Probation (1996) *Women Offenders and Probation Service Provision: Report of a Thematic Inspection.* London: HM Inspectorate of Probation.

Home Office (2002a) *Probation Statistics England and Wales 2001.* London: Home Office.

Home Office (2002b) *Statistics on Women and the Criminal Justice System.* London: Home Office.

Howard League (1999) *Do Women Paint Fences Too? Women's Experiences of Community Service.* London: The Howard League.

Immarigeon, R. (2000) 'Editor's note.' *Women, Girls and Criminal Justice 1*, 3, 35.

Jackson, H. and Smith, L. (1987) 'Female offenders: An analysis of social inquiry reports.' *Home Office Research Bulletin 23.* London: HMSO.

Killias, M., Aebi, M. and Ribeaud, D. (2000) 'Does community service rehabilitate better than short-term imprisonment? Results of a controlled experiment.' *The Howard Journal 39*, 1, 40–57.

Lloyd, C., Mair, G. and Hough, M. (1995) *Explaining Reconviction Rates: A Critical Analysis.* Home Office Research Study no. 136. London: Home Office.

McIvor, G. (1992) *Sentenced to Serve: The Operation and Impact of Community Service by Offenders.* Aldershot: Avebury.

McIvor, G. (1998a) 'Prosocial modeling and legitimacy: Lessons from a study of community service.' In A. Matravers and S. Rex (eds) *Prosocial Modeling and Legitimacy: The Clarke Hall Day Conference.* Cambridge: University of Cambridge Institute of Criminology.

McIvor, G. (1998b) 'Jobs for the boys?: Gender differences in referral for community service.' *The Howard Journal 37*, 3, 280–291.

McIvor, G. and Tulle-Winton, E. (1993) *The Use of Community Service by Scottish Courts.* Stirling: Social Work Research Centre, University of Stirling.

Mair, G. and Brockington, N. (1988) 'Female offenders and the probation service.' *The Howard Journal 27*, 2, 117–126.

May, C. (1999) *Explaining Reconviction Following Community Sentences: The Role of Social Factors.* Home Office Research Study no. 192. London: Home Office.

Pease, K., Durkin, P., Earnshaw, I., Payne, D. and Thorpe, J. (1975) *Community Service Orders.* Home Office Research Study no. 29. London: HMSO.

Queensland Department of Families, Youth and Community Care (1999) *What About the Girls! Young Women's Perceptions of Juvenile Justice Programs and Services.* Brisbane, Queensland: Department of Families, Youth and Community Care.

Rex, S. (1999) 'Desistance from offending: Experiences of Probation.' *The Howard Journal 38*, 4, 366–383.

Rex, S. and Gelsthorpe, L. (2002) 'The role of community service in reducing offending: Evaluating Pathfinder projects in the UK.' *The Howard Journal 41*, 4, 311–325.

Scottish Executive (2000) *Criminal Proceedings in Scottish Courts, 1999* Edinburgh: Scottish Executive Statistical Services.

Scottish Executive (2002a) *Criminal Justice Social Work Statistics 2001–02*. Edinburgh: Scottish Executive Statistical Services.

Scottish Executive (2002b) *A Better Way: The Report on the Ministerial Group On Women's Offending*. Edinburgh: The Scottish Executive.

Scottish Executive (2002c) *Prison Statistics Scotland, 2001*. Edinburgh: Scottish Executive Statistical Services.

Scottish Executive (2002d) *Criminal Proceedings in Scottish Courts, 2001*. Edinburgh: Scottish Executive Statistical Services.

Scottish Executive (2003) *Reconvictions of Offenders Discharged from Custody or Given Non-custodial Sentences in 1997*. Edinburgh: Scottish Executive Statistical Services.

Scottish Office (1995) *Statistical Bulletin: Community Service by Offenders in 1992 and 1993*. Edinburgh: The Scottish Office.

Trotter, C. (1999) *Working with Involuntary Clients*. London: Sage.

Worrall, A. (1995) 'Gender, criminal justice and probation.' In G. McIvor (ed) *Working with Offenders: Research Highlights in Social Work 26*. London: Jessica Kingsley Publishers.

Worrall, A. (2000) 'Community sentences for women: Where have they gone?' Paper presented at the Probation and Community Corrections Officers Conference, Brisbane, Australia.

CHAPTER 7

Women in Prison

Nancy Loucks

Introduction

When I first started conducting research in prisons, I confess I had little interest in women as a subject group. Since women make up about 5 per cent of prison populations worldwide (Stern 1998), it seemed appropriate to focus instead on the majority. However, it is precisely this minority status and marginalisation that increases the need to recognise women in prison as a distinct group with distinctive needs. When I finally conducted a project on women in custody, the differences between women and men in prison stood out much more starkly than I had ever imagined. Throughout the research on women, a consistent picture of poverty, deprivation, victimisation and marginalisation made up the basis of every female population in every jurisdiction. The 'career' criminals and thrill-seekers common amongst male prisoners were virtually absent in women's prisons, replaced instead by people in custody often through desperate circumstances or lives so chaotic that they failed to comply with community penalties or bail.

This chapter outlines the backgrounds, characteristics and issues surrounding women who end up in custody. Much of the information is based on my own research in Scotland (Loucks 1998), but an international context is included where appropriate.

Backgrounds of women in custody

Women who end up in custody are distinctive for a number of reasons. Features such as addiction, psychological distress, abuse, poverty and unemployment, while not exclusive to women in custody, characterise the vast majority.

Drugs

Drug use is amongst the most common features of women in custody in many countries. In Scotland, 87.7 per cent of women in prison reported having used illicit drugs at some time in their lives. This rate is higher than in some countries (e.g. research in prisons in England by Fraser 1994; Johnson and Farren 1996; Morris *et al.* 1995; Singleton *et al.* 1998). As a comparison, recent work by the Prison Service in HMP Holloway, London (King 1998) reported 31 per cent previous use of drugs. However, the higher rate is comparable to that found in other countries. One US study (Birecree *et al.* 1994), for example, recorded rates of 90 per cent. A later project on young offenders in Scotland (Loucks *et al.* 2000) found the rate of prior drug use to be about 95 per cent, with no significant difference in reported experience of drug use between young men and women prior to custody.

Backgrounds of drug use among female prisoners tend to be heavy. In Scotland, a third had injected drugs at some stage and over half the women (50.7%) said they were addicted to drugs (based on self-assessment, medical interviews at reception and clinical scales). The rate of addiction in the Scottish sample was double that found in research in women's prisons in England and Wales, which showed rates of about a quarter (Gunn, Maden and Swinton 1991; Maden, Swinton and Gunn 1991), but even the lower estimates suggest that addiction is a significant problem. A national survey of prisoners in the USA (Snell and Morton 1994) showed that women in prison used more drugs and used them more frequently than did male prisoners. Prior to custody, 41.5 per cent of female prisoners used drugs daily, compared to 35.7 per cent of male prisoners, and were more likely to be under the influence of drugs when they committed their offence (36.3% compared to 30.6%).

The available research suggests that few women begin their drug use in prison. Only three women in the Scottish research did so, and more often than not they simply tried drugs once or twice, usually cannabis. Others began using different drugs in prison; for example, where their normal drug of choice was not available, or where they chose to experiment. Drug use most commonly began for the women as teenagers.

Alcohol

Though not as common a problem as illicit drug use amongst female prisoners, a significant proportion of women in prison show evidence of alcoholism or alcohol-related problems. For example, 22.5 per cent of female prisoners in Scotland said they never drink, but 18.8 per cent said they drink daily outside custody. Based on the AUDIT scale (Fleming, Barry and MacDonald 1991), 10 to 15 per cent were addicted to alcohol. This is similar to rates of alcoholism amongst female prisoners in much of the past research, but a lower rate to that most recently reported in Singleton *et al.* (1998), which found a rate of 36 per cent amongst female prisoners in England. In the Scottish sample, binge drinking was more common than regular heavy drinking. Female binge drinkers tended to combine drink and drugs, and a third had been drinking at the time of their offence, almost all of whom thought this contributed to their offence. These behaviours would not necessarily show up as addiction on clinical scales, nor did most of these women believe they had a problem with alcohol.

In contrast to the findings of previous research amongst female prisoners (e.g. Kendall 1993 in Canada), few women in Scottish prisons were cross-addicted to drugs and alcohol. Only one women in the research in Scotland was found to be cross-addicted. Her story was important in other ways too in that it exemplified the dire situation of many women when they enter custody. This woman had a substantial history of all forms of abuse: she grew up in an alcoholic family, ran away from physical and sexual abuse at home and was taken into care, where she was sexually abused by her foster father. She then entered a series of abusive relationships from which she had yet to escape. The following section shows that this woman's story was more often the norm than the exception amongst women in prison.

Backgrounds of abuse

Another recurring theme throughout the research into women in custody is the fact that so many of the women are victims as well as offenders. The research in Scotland showed that the vast majority of women in prison had been direct or indirect victims of physical, sexual or emotional abuse, and often a combination of these: 82.2 per cent had suffered some form of abuse during their lives, and 66.7 per cent were directly aware of the abuse of others close to them. The rate of abuse in Scotland is similar to rates found in other female prison populations, such as in Canadian research by Lightfoot and Lambert (1992). A survey of 13,986 male and female prisoners in the USA (Snell and Morton 1994; also Morash, Bynum and Koons 1998) showed lower reported rates of abuse amongst women. However, the reported rates for female prisoners in their research (43%) were almost four times higher than the comparable figure for men (12.2%).

In the Scottish research, most women who reported being victims of abuse said this had taken place throughout their lives (as children, teenagers and adults), usually on a daily or virtually daily basis. Many were going back out to violent families or partners, and for some prison was the first 'safe' place they had been.

Suicidal behaviour and emotional distress

Suicide and self-injury are common experiences for a significant proportion of female prisoners. In Scotland, over a third (37.7%) had attempted suicide at some time in the past. Suicide attempts were more common outside custody than in prison; only 7 of the 29 women who said they had tried to kill themselves had done so while in prison. A notable proportion (16%) had a history of deliberately injuring themselves, separate from what they considered to be a suicide attempt. None of the women did this for the first time in prison.

A history of treatment for mental health or emotional problems is also a common feature amongst this group. Research in England and Wales (Singleton *et al.* 1998), for example, showed that 40 per cent of women in custody had received help or treatment for a mental health or emotional problem in the year before they entered custody – double the proportion for male prisoners. Women in prison prior to conviction or sentence (i.e. remand prisoners) contained the highest proportion of prisoners ever admitted to a psychiatric hospital: 22 per cent, including 6 per cent admitted for 6 months or more and 11 per cent admitted to a secure ward. This compares to 8 per cent of sentenced male prisoners, with 2 per cent admitted for 6 months or more and 3 per cent in a secure facility.

Education, employment and economic circumstances

Education amongst women in prison is generally limited. The research in Scotland found that over 90 per cent had left school at age 16 or under. Roughly three-quarters had a history of truancy, half had been suspended at some stage, and a third had been expelled. A subsequent study (Henderson 2001) largely supported these findings, showing that only 14 per cent of women in prison had stayed in school beyond the statutory minimum age (16 in Scotland), and 61 per cent left school with no qualifications.

Most of the women in prison in Scotland (80%) were unemployed at the time of their imprisonment (Loucks 1998). Henderson (2001) found that of those who had been employed most were employed in unskilled manual work. For those who had held a job at any stage, the longest period of employment was usually less than a year. Because of these features, the main source of income for women in prison tends to be from social welfare services. In Scotland, two-thirds of the women in custody depended on state benefits (income support, incapacity benefit, job seekers' allowance, and so on) for their main income (Henderson 2001). Almost half of the 179 respondents believed their offence was related to financial need, with a similar proportion saying past offences were the result of a shortage of money.

Characteristics

The backgrounds of women in prison outlined above make them a distinctive population once in prison as well. Even a brief glance at offence types, sentences, demographics and mental health sets female prisoners aside as a distinctive group with very different needs from the vast majority of the population in prison.

Offences and sentences

As stated at the outset, women make up a very small proportion of the offending population (14% of those convicted in Scottish courts) and an even smaller percentage of the prison population. The patterns of women's offending also differ quite substantially to those for men. Offending by women is disproportionately for relatively minor or non-violent offences, such as soliciting and shoplifting, and financial crimes such as fraud, forgery and embezzlement. In the USA, a national survey of almost 14,000 male and female prisoners (Snell and Morton 1994) found that nearly half of all women in prison were serving sentences for non-violent offences and had past convictions only for other non-violent offences. One in three women in US prisons is there for a violent crime, compared to roughly one in every two male prisoners (Chesney-Lind 1997).

Not surprisingly then, a higher proportion of women are in prison for very short sentences. In Scotland, 17 per cent of women in custody are serving sentences of less than three months, compared to less than 5 per cent of men. Over half of women received into prison in Scotland are there for non-payment of a fine – 54 per cent, compared to 38 per cent of male receptions. Further, a higher proportion of the female prison population is made up of people not yet convicted or sentenced (28% vs 17% of male prisoners). In Scotland, many of these unconvicted and unsentenced women end up without a custodial sentence. In 1998, for example, 525 convicted females were held in custody prior to sentencing. Of these, less than half (222 women, or 42.3%) eventually received a custodial sentence (Scottish Court Services 2000).

Demographics

In general, imprisonment begins early for women (in Scotland, by age 16). Female prison populations are therefore generally young. Again in Scotland, roughly two-thirds are under the age of 30, and a fifth are under age 21. Many have been to courts or even to prison several times. However, two-thirds of those serving sentences at any given time will have never spent time in custody before. Almost half of this group are first offenders. The majority of women in prison are parents, though in Scotland only about two-thirds currently had custody of their children (some of whom had adult children).

A disproportionate number of women in many countries (e.g. England and the USA) are from ethnic minorities. Indeed, recent surges in female prison populations in many countries have included an even greater proportion of women from ethnic minorities (Chesney-Lind 1997). In the USA, a higher prevalence of drug use amongst ethnic minorities is likely to be responsible for much of this, as increasingly harsh punishments for the use and sales of drugs such as crack cocaine have been imposed (see Huling 1995). In a number of countries, ethnic minorities and foreign nationals who have been used as drug couriers or 'mules', with and without their knowledge or consent, make up a substantial number of women in prison. The types of problems that women in prison face (see Issues for women in custody, below) are even more extreme for foreign nationals, who are even further away from children, family and social and community supports than are the other women.

Psychological distress

Psychological distress was clearly a common feature of women in custody, perhaps unsurprisingly in light of their extensive histories of suicidal behaviour, mental health problems, addiction and abuse. Levels of hopelessness, based on the Beck Hopelessness Scale (Beck *et al.* 1974), showed clinical levels of hopelessness for a high proportion of women. Prisoners often score highly for hopelessness using this scale. Zamble and Porporino (1988) found, for example, that a third of their subjects scored six or higher (where higher scores indicate higher levels of hopelessness). In Scotland, the average score amongst women in prison was 6.3.

Distress was also evident from the results of the Hospital Anxiety and Depression Scale (HADS, Zigmond and Snaith 1983). Only just over half of the women in prison in Scotland had scores for depression within the 'normal' range, and only a third had 'normal' scores for anxiety. Over a quarter of women were recorded as having moderate or severe depression, and over a third had such scores for depression. Research in prisons in England and Wales showed similar patterns. According to Singleton and colleagues (1998), female prisoners were significantly more likely than male prisoners to suffer from a neurotic disorder. While 59 per cent of remand and 40 per cent of sentenced male prisoners in their sample were assessed as having a neurotic disorder, the proportions for women were 76 per cent and 63 per cent respectively. These were most commonly mixed anxiety and depressive disorders. Their research also suggested that psychotic disorders may be more common amongst female prisoners on remand (those held in custody prior to conviction or sentence: 21%, as assessed by lay interviews, compared to 9% of male remand prisoners, 4% of male sentenced prisoners, and 10% of female sentenced prisoners).

Issues for women in custody

Issues that women face while in prison are in most cases similar to those of men. For example, both groups have difficulty finding housing and employment upon release; both are separated from children and family; both may be struggling with addiction and the stress of imprisonment; both may be faced with intimidation and violence while in prison. However, the proportion of male and female prisoners dealing with these issues differs, as does the impact on the two groups. This section outlines such issues in more detail.

Childcare

As noted above, a high proportion of female prisoners have dependent children. Custody of children is generally of more concern for women in prison than for men. Research in Scotland (Inspectorates of Prisons and Social Work Services 1998) found that only 17 per cent of fathers looked after their children while the mother was in custody. This compares to 87 per cent of mothers who care for the children when the father is in prison. Comparable US figures showed that 25 per cent of the women's children, compared to 90 per cent of children of male prisoners, lived with the other parent during imprisonment (Morash *et al.* 1998). The picture in England and Wales was even more extreme, where only 5 per cent of the 8100 children affected each year by their mother's imprisonment remained in their homes and were looked after by the other parent (Wolfe 1999).

Potential loss of custody of a child is therefore of very real concern for women who end up in prison.

Visits to women in prison can also be problematic. The small number of women held in custody means that few prisons or young offender institutions exist which hold women. By definition this means that many women will be located at a great distance from their families. Statistics from the Prison Reform Trust in London note that nearly a fifth of female prisoners in England and Wales are held over 100 miles away from their committal court town. In such circumstances, women in prison are less likely than male prisoners to have contact with their children. Research in the USA (Snell and Morton 1994) reported that over half of women with children under age 18 had never received a visit from their children while in prison. This is particularly the case where the women are foreign nationals. One study in England found that only 11 per cent of female foreign nationals had received a visit from their children while in prison (Caddle and Crisp 1997).

The research by Caddle and Crisp also noted a range of psychological effects on children whose mothers are imprisoned. This included problems with behaviour, sleeping, eating, bedwetting, overall health and making and keeping friends. These issues were particularly acute when the children had to move home or go into care. While these problems may occur when the father is imprisoned, problematic behaviour amongst children has been found to be more common when the mother is taken into custody (Richards and McWilliams 1996).

Housing

As with childcare, housing is another issue that differs for female prisoners. Again, statistics in Scotland show that women are more likely to lose their housing while in custody than are men (Inspectorates of Prisons and Social Work Services 1998). Research in England and Wales noted that a third of female prisoners lose their homes while in prison (Wolfe 1999). Women are more often single parents and have tenancy agreements in their own names; men, in contrast, are more likely to have a partner at home to maintain the tenancy.

Addiction

Some women use custody as an opportunity to withdraw from drugs. However, others continue to abuse licit and illicit drugs. Drug use amongst women tends to differ from their use outside, usually because drugs are less readily available and, similarly, because their drug of choice may not be accessible. Because addiction is such a common feature of female prisoners prior to custody, withdrawal from addiction and its consequences pose tremendous problems for many women in prison. The difficulty of withdrawal for women in prison is usually more than the physical consequences. Rather, withdrawal forces many women to face issues they had blocked out with drugs, often for the first time, such as experiences of abuse and social realities such as poverty and loss of housing or custody of children. Issues around drug use and women who offend are discussed further by Malloch (Chapter 12 this volume).

Victimisation and custody

Victimisation has many implications for women in general, but perhaps particularly for those in custody. Increased substance abuse was one possible consequence, where people tried to block out memories of abuse (or, as one woman mentioned, violence from her partner hurt less if she was drunk). A small-scale US study (Chiavaroli 1992) noted that treatment for drug abuse amongst victims of sexual abuse appeared to be more effective when it addressed both types of abuse. Increased vulnerability during withdrawal from drugs or alcohol was therefore an important problem for victims.

People in custody often have feelings of shame, isolation, or self-blame as a result of their imprisonment, which in turn reduces their self-esteem. This is particularly the case for women who have been victims of abuse, where even standard prison procedures such as body searches or cell searches, and the loss of autonomy which is a basic part of prison life, can trigger feelings of helplessness and frustration common to the experience of abuse itself. In a sense prison 'retraumatises' them, albeit unintentionally, forcing them to relive past abuse.

Finally, prison staff are placed in a difficult position with victim/offenders; to what extent should professional staff in prisons 'open cans of worms' and help women address their past or ongoing abuse? This question is controversial, especially because the majority of the female prison population are short-term prisoners; whether it is safe or even responsible for a prison to start addressing issues which may take years to deal with is a question as yet unresolved. Some women are forced to address past abuse while they are in custody, for example, if it is directly relevant to their offence or addiction, but these would primarily be longer term prisoners who are more likely to have access to ongoing support while in custody.

Bullying

More direct victimisation can also take place in prisons; violence and bullying are not unusual amongst female prisoners. In Scotland, a quarter of prisoners said they had been bullied at some stage, though not necessarily during their current sentence. Physical assaults were also surprisingly common, with 15.1 per cent of prisoners saying they had been assaulted in a prison. These figures can however be misleading, as definitions of bullying and assaults are generally problematic. Bullying in women's prisons is often in the form of 'taxing' (where prisoners who are more dominant take things from those who are more vulnerable), intimidation, ostracism and extortion. Physical bullying (assaults, etc.), in contrast, is generally more common amongst male prisoners. Bullying amongst female prisoners is more subtle and therefore more difficult for staff to detect. As a result, some women complained during the research in Scotland that bullying often took place in front of staff, but that staff did nothing about it. Often, however, the behaviour was too ambiguous for staff to act upon it.

Bullying amongst female prisoners in Scotland was often related to competition for medication. The prison's detoxification programme meant that the vast majority of women were receiving prescription drugs, usually diazepam and dihydrocodeine. Prescriptions were also common for other problems such as mental disorder or poor health, with the result that about 97 per cent of the women were receiving some form of medication in the prison. With the relative shortage of illicit drugs coming into prison, the women would go to extreme measures to get prescription drugs from others. This included threats for people to give others their medication or telling people what to say to the medical staff to get extra. Measures designed to keep people from retaining their medication were being abused. Women taking liquid medication would put cotton wool in their mouths to absorb it, or alternatively people would regurgitate their medication to pass on to other people. Despite the problems associated with medication, however, the physical and psychological distress of the vast majority of the women made it a necessary part of prison life.

Suicidal behaviour

Rates of suicide amongst women in custody are higher than amongst women in the population at large. One reason is that withdrawal from drugs and the stresses of imprisonment increase the risk of suicide and self-harm amongst a group already vulnerable to such behaviour (see, for example, Liebling 1996). Further, women use more lethal methods of suicide in custody than they do outside of prison; outside, women are most likely to resort to overdoses or cutting up, but inside prison methods are generally limited to hanging, which is much more lethal. Men tend to resort to more lethal forms of suicide both in and out of custody (firearms or hanging outside prison, and again hanging inside custody). Amongst female prisoners in Scotland, suicide attempts were more often associated with addiction to alcohol than to drugs. The reason for this is less clear, though it may be because drug use was a feature of such a large proportion of the population. Finally, clinical levels of hopelessness, anxiety, depression and poor problem solving were notably high amongst the women in prison in Scotland – characteristics often related to suicidal behaviour.

What was very clear from the research in Scotland was that prison is unlikely in itself to 'cause' suicidal behaviour. It can however be the 'last straw' in combination with problems outside. Such problems include the fact that many women will be withdrawing from drugs and will therefore be facing reality, perhaps for the first time in years. This reality can be intolerable, especially where extreme physical and sexual abuse are involved. In prison, women are away from their usual social supports. They may feel a sense of failure or shame, perhaps combined with bullying in custody and the loss of autonomy and (for victims of abuse) the retraumatisation that imprisonment can bring.

One question is whether the higher levels of distress amongst women in prison are all that surprising. Psychometric tests are designed to look at people's response to 'everyday' problems. However, the 'everyday' problems amongst women in prison are unusually severe compared to the 'average' population outside. If women are wrestling with daily drug use and addiction, daily physical, sexual and emotional abuse, daily financial crises and housing problems, etc., their distress will understandably be high. This is not to say that women or even female offenders outside prison do not experience similar problems. What is clear, however, is that an 'alarmingly high' proportion of women in prison show characteristics (such as the above) associated with risk of suicide (Liebling 1994).

Life events

Previous research has shown a consistent relationship between the number of stressful events in a person's life and that person's emotional and physical health (Holmes and Rahe 1967). That research measured the number of stressful events with a Life Change Scale (also known as the Holmes and Rahe Social Readjustment Rating Scale). With this in mind, I designed a short Prisoner Life Events Scale (PLES, Loucks 1999), developed specially for women in custody, during some research I conducted in two women's prisons in England (Loucks 2001). The PLES is a 19-point scale, with an option for additional responses, designed to measure types of events other than custody itself which may influence a person's behaviour and ability to cope while inside.

The results derived from the use of the scale showed quite dramatically the stressors that affect women in custody, above and beyond the stress of custody itself. Nearly half the women lost possession of their accommodation outside while they were in prison. Lack of visits from family were also common concerns. A high proportion in both prisons (roughly a third) had a close family member seriously ill while they were in custody. Having a close friend or family member go to prison during their time in custody and formal separation from partners were also common events, as were death or victimisation of family and friends. In total, the women reported an average of 3.0 to 4.8 such events during their current period of custody.

A man's world

The small proportion of women in custody inevitably means that custodial culture is dominated by the needs of men. Programmes and activities in prisons are often designed with the needs and interests of male prisoners in mind (see Carlen 1983; Stern 1998). Stephanie Covington cites an example of the situation in the USA, but arguably the same situation exists in most jurisdictions:

> Despite this growing information on best practices for treating females, male-based programming remains the norm in many settings. Even female-only programs are often merely copies of men's programs, not based on research or clinical experience with women and girls. This problem is especially acute for juveniles. Boys far outnumber girls in the juvenile justice system, so programs are designed with the needs of males in mind, and services for female adolescents simply replicate the male model (Pepi 1998). (Covington 1998, pp.12–13)

Overall, female offenders are a vastly different group with different needs and problems to male offenders. The Criminal Justice System seems to have a very different effect on them, so policies and programmes directed towards men will often not be particularly useful.

Conclusion

Two inquiries into women's offending were conducted in Scotland (Inspectorates of Prisons and Social Work Services 1998) and in England (Wedderburn Committee 2000) specifically to understand and address the needs of women who end up in prison. The main emphasis of the recommendations from the two reports was on ensuring appropriate alternatives to custody for female offenders and on increasing the information available about the women and their needs. Importantly in Scotland, the recommendations secured a commitment by the government to halving the female prison population within two years and to keeping young women under the age of 18 out of Prison Service custody. The logic behind this was that the problems these women are dealing with are best identified and addressed outside of custody, without complicating already difficult circumstances by the fact of imprisonment. This is not to say that serious offending should be ignored, rather that it be prevented through more appropriate targeting of resources for female offenders. Unfortunately the goals in both countries to reduce the population of female prisoners have failed to meet their targets, and the number of women who enter custody continues to rise.

Much of the information above is based on research in Scotland. However, the evidence available internationally shows an almost identical picture of female prisoners in every country (Lemgruber 2001; McIvor 1999; Stern 1998). Women consistently made up a tiny proportion of prisoners. They consistently come from backgrounds of poverty, unemployment, abuse and addiction. They are consistently young, uneducated and unskilled. Most are mothers of young children and are often single mothers. Most have committed a non-violent offence. An inquiry into female offenders in England and Wales (Wedderburn Committee 2000) described female prisoners as '…overwhelmingly, though not exclusively, drawn from a group who share all the characteristics of "social exclusion"'. Overall, it is clear that the problems which female offenders face are unlikely to be solved by imprisonment, and can in fact be made worse.

References

Beck, A.T., Weissman, A.W., Lester, D. and Trexler, L. (1974) 'The assessment of pessimism: The Hopelessness Scale.' *Journal of Consulting and Clinical Psychology* 42, 861–865.

Birecree, E., Bloom, J., Leverette, M. and Williams, M. (1994) 'Diagnostic efforts regarding women in Oregon's prison system: A preliminary report.' *International Journal of Offender Therapy and Comparative Criminology 38, 3, 217–230.*

Caddle, D. and Crisp, D. (1997) *Imprisoned Women and Mothers.* Home Office Research Study no. 162. London: Home Office.

Carlen, P. (1983) *Women's Imprisonment: A Study in Social Control.* London: Routledge and Keegan Paul.

Chesney-Lind, M. (1997) *The Female Offender: Girls, Women and Crime.* Thousand Oaks, CA: Sage.

Chiavaroli, T. (1992) 'Rehabilitation from substance abuse in individuals with a history of sexual abuse.' *Journal of Substance Abuse Treatment 9, 4, 349–354.*

Covington, S. (1998) *Helping Women Recover, Correctional Journal.* New York: Jossey-Bass.

Fleming, M.F., Barry, K.L. and MacDonald, R. (1991) 'The Alcohol Use Disorders Identification Test (AUDIT) in a college sample.' *International Journal of the Addictions 26,* 11, 1173–1185.

Fraser, J. (1994) *Drugs Survey: An Investigation into Women Prisoners' Attitudes Towards a Proposed Drug-free Zone at Holloway and the Experience of Drug Use.* London: Psychology Department, HMP Holloway.

Gunn, J., Maden, A. and Swinton, M. (1991) *Mentally Disturbed Prisoners.* London: Home Office.

Henderson, S. (2001) *Women Offenders: Effective Management and Intervention.* Scottish Prison Service Occasional Papers no. 2001. Edinburgh: Scottish Prison Service.

HM Inspectorates of Social Work Services and Prisons (1998) *Women Offenders–A Safer Way: A Review of Community Disposals and the Use of Custody for Women Offenders in Scotland.* Edinburgh: Social Work Services and Prisons Inspectorate for Scotland.

Holmes, T.H. and Rahe, R.H. (1967) 'The Social Readjustment Rating Scale.' *Journal of Psychosomatic Research 11,* 213–218.

Huling, R. (1995) 'African American Women and the war on drugs.' Paper presented at the Annual Meeting of the American Society of Criminology Conference, Boston.

Johnson, G. and Farren, E. (1996) 'An evaluation of prisoners' views about substance free zones.' In N. Clark and G. Stephenson (eds) *Psychological Perspectives on Police and Custodial Culture and Organisation. Issues in Criminological and Legal Psychology 25,* 30–38.

Kendall, K. (1993) *Literature Review of Therapeutic Services for Women in Prison: Companion Volume I to Program Evaluation of Therapeutic Services at the Prison for Women.* Toronto: Correctional Services of Canada.

King, R. (1998) 'Females in custody: A profile.' *Prison Research and Development Bulletin 6,* 1.

Lemgruber, J. (2001) 'Women in the criminal justice system.' Keynote speech. In N. Ollus and S. Nevala (eds) *Women in the Criminal Justice System: International Examples and National Responses.* Proceedings of the workshop held at the Tenth United Nations Congress on the Prevention of Crime and the Treatment of Offenders, Vienna, Austria, 10–17 April 2000. Helsinki: HEUNI.

Liebling, A. (1994) 'Suicide amongst women prisoners.' *The Howard Journal of Criminal Justice 33,* 1, 1–9.

Liebling, A. (1996) 'Prison suicide: What progress research?' In A. Liebling (ed) *Deaths in Custody: Caring for People at Risk.* London: Whiting and Birch, pp.41–53.

Lightfoot, L. and Lambert, L. (1992) *Substance Abuse Treatment Needs of Federally Sentenced Women: Technical Report no. 2* (draft). Toronto: Correctional Services Canada.

Loucks, N. (1998) *HMPI Cornton Vale: Research into Drugs and Alcohol, Violence and Bullying, Suicides and Self-Injury, and Backgrounds of Abuse.* Scottish Prison Service Occasional Papers, Report no. 1/98. Edinburgh: Scottish Prison Service.

Loucks, N. (1999) 'The prisoner life events scale.' Unpublished.

Loucks, N. (2001) 'Evaluation of improved regimes for female offenders.' London: HM Prison Service for England and Wales, Women's Policy Group, unpublished.

Loucks, N., Power, K., Swanson, V. and Chambers, J. (2000) *Young People in Custody in Scotland: The Characteristics and Perceptions of Young People Held in Custody.* Occasional Paper no. 3/2000. Edinburgh: Scottish Prison Service.

McIvor, G. (1999) 'Women, crime and criminal justice in Scotland.' *Scottish Journal of Criminal Justice Studies 5*, 1, 67–74.

Maden, A., Swinton, M. and Gunn, J. (1991) 'Drug dependence in prisons.' *British Medical Journal 302*, 6781, 880.

Morash, M., Bynum, T. and Koons, B. (1998) *Women Offenders: Programming Needs and Promising Approaches.* Washington, DC: National Institute of Justice.

Morris, A., Wilkinson, C., Tisi, A., Woodrow, J. and Rockley, A. (1995) *Managing the Needs of Female Prisoners.* London: Home Office Publications Unit.

Pepi, C. (1998) 'Children without childhoods: A feminist intervention strategy utilising systems theory and restorative justice in treating female adolescent offenders.' In J. Harden and M. Hill (eds) *Breaking the Rules: Women in Prison and Feminist Therapy.* New York: Haworth.

Richards, M. and McWilliams, B. (1996) *Imprisonment and Family Ties.* Home Office Research Bulletin no. 38. London: Home Office.

Scottish Court Services (2000) Personal correspondence.

Singleton, N., Meltzer, H. and Gatward, R., with Coid, J. and Deasy, D. (1998) *Psychiatric Morbidity among Prisoners: A Survey Carried Out in 1997 by the Social Survey Division of ONS on behalf of the Department of Health.* London: Office for National Statistics.

Snell, T.L. and Morton, D.C. (1994) *Women in Prison.* Special report. Washington, DC: Bureau of Justice Statistics.

Stern, V. (1998) *A Sin Against the Future: Imprisonment in the World.* London: Penguin Books.

Wedderburn Committee (2000) *Justice for Women: The Need for Reform.* Report of the Committee on Women's Imprisonment. London: Prison Rejerm Trust.

Wolfe, T. (1999) *Counting the Cost: The Social and Financial Consequences of Women's Imprisonment.* Report prepared for the Wedderburn Committee on Women's Imprisonment. London: Prison Reform Trust.

Zamble, E. and Porporino, F.J. (1988) *Coping, Behaviour, and Adaptation in Prison Inmates.* New York: Springer-Verlag.

Zigmond, A.S. and Snaith, R.P. (1983) 'Hospital anxiety and depression scale.' *Acta Psychiatrica Scandinavica 67*, 361–370.

CHAPTER 8

Women's Release from Prison
The Case for Change
Christine Wilkinson

Introduction

Two decades of research on women in prison has done little to alleviate their plight. Over and over again policies designed for men have been applied to women without due recognition of their needs. A number of recent government initiatives indicate, however, that this should change.[1] At the same time, more recent penal critique in relation to women has pointed to the barriers and obstacles that prevent effective reform (Lothian 2002) and to the factors that contribute to the gap between penal reformers' intentions and outcomes (Hannah-Moffat 2002).

Currently, the government is engaged in an overhaul of the criminal justice system. The latest proposals for reform are contained in the White Paper *Justice for All* (Home Office 2002). This takes account of the review of the criminal courts of Sir Robin Auld (2001) and the review of sentencing policy of John Halliday (2001). One of the principal concerns in the White Paper is with sentencing, but its proposals in this respect involve a radical change to procedures for release from prison. The aim in this chapter, therefore, is to examine these proposals for change to release procedures in order to assess the extent to which account is taken of women's needs and the likely impact on women. The chapter is divided into three sections: the first focuses on release policy and practice as it currently operates; the second section outlines and discusses women's experiences of release from prison;

the third section considers the proposed changes. Overall, it is argued that there is a considerable amount of consensus about the need for change and the form that some of these changes might take but there are some crucial points of difference that result from differences in underlying philosophy.

Release policy and practice

The Criminal Justice Act 1991 (CJA 1991) provided for three types of release from prison and, at the time of writing, this system of release is still operative. For prisoners serving sentences of less than 12 months, release operates automatically at the halfway point, the prisoner is not the subject of a licence, and the remaining part of the sentence is not subject to any conditions. Release on licence means that prisoners are required to undergo a compulsory period of supervision. For prisoners serving 12 months but less than 4 years, release operates automatically at the halfway point but the prisoner is on licence and subject to conditions which last to the three-quarters point. A discretionary element to release, for both groups, was introduced in the Crime and Disorder Act (1998) with home detention curfew (HDC). The scheme came into operation in January 1999 and allows for most prisoners serving at least 3 months but less than 4 years to be released up to 60 days early on an electronically monitored curfew (Dodgson *et al.* 2001). Prisoners serving sentences of four years and over are subject to discretionary conditional release that operates at the halfway to two-thirds point on the basis of a decision of the parole board and are also subject to licence and conditions which last to the three-quarters point. Prisoners released under licence are supervised by the Probation Service.[2] All prisoners, irrespective of the operation of a licence and conditions, if convicted of a further offence committed after release but before expiry of the sentence, may have the outstanding part of the sentence from the date of that offence activated by the court.

A large proportion of the adult female prison population serves short sentences (Home Office 2001a).[3] Thus, in practice, this release policy means that the majority of women leaving prison will do so free of licences and conditions. This lack of licence and conditions means that there is no statutory duty to provide any kind of assistance on release. Instead, these women are the subject of 'voluntary' after-care, which means that they are able to contact the Probation Service for help. The difficulty arises because many women do not know of this entitlement or, given their interactions with probation officers at the time of their sentence, do not regard the service as a helping agency (Morris *et al.* 1995). We know, however, that even short periods of imprisonment can have disastrous effects upon women and that such effects can come into play very quickly (Morris *et al.* 1995; NACRO 2001; Prison Reform Trust 2000). The fact that few women leaving prison will be the statutory responsibility of the Probation Service also raises serious questions about the type of provision for women who are their statutory responsibility. Since most service areas will deal with only a handful of such women, few have specialist provision for them (Morris *et al.* 1995).

There is now considerable consensus about the backgrounds of women in prison and this has changed little in recent years (Home Office 1997, 2001b; Morris *et al.* 1995; NACRO 2000a, 2001; Prison Reform Trust 2000; also Loucks, Chapter 7 this volume). The majority are young and criminally unsophisticated, around two-fifths to a half are the mothers of dependent children (a significant proportion will be lone mothers and a significant proportion will have become mothers in their teens); the educational record of many is poor; few have been in paid employment prior to imprisonment and some have never been employed; most have lived on state benefits and by the time of their incarceration may have incurred large debts; the majority will have lived in rented accommodation but around one in ten will have experienced homelessness and some two in five will have experienced the child 'care' system; the majority report drug use at some point in their lives and around half of this group report some form of recent dependence; many have suffered physical and/or sexual abuse; a significant proportion will have self-harmed or attempted suicide; and a large proportion will suffer mental disorders of various kinds. The interrelatedness of women's problems and difficulties is now well recognised and their social exclusion emphasised (Player 2000, p.18). The link between women's life experiences and their offending has also been acknowledged (Home Office 2001c).

The extent to which women continue to experience such problems and difficulties on release from prison and the way in which they cope with these and with their release in the absence of statutory responsibility for the resettlement needs of the majority is examined in the next section.

Women's release experiences

Finding accommodation on release is perhaps the biggest problem facing women. The difficulties are fourfold: housing situations may deteriorate as a result of imprisonment; a significant minority leave prison homeless or face 'hidden' homelessness – that is they have no accommodation of their own and live in other people's homes; few women report receiving any help in finding accommodation; and accommodation after release is both changeable and unstable. Morris *et al.* (1995) reported that half of their sample of 200 women had experienced problems with accommodation, more than two-fifths were homeless at the time of their first prison interview and, at the time of release, more than a third of these homeless women did not have an address to go to. Only about a fifth of the total sample had received any help in sorting out their problems and this help was not always in accordance with their wishes; for example, women were reluctant to be housed in hostels. When interviewed post-release, one-third of the women were not living at the address they expected to be and almost half of the women wanted to move. NACRO (2001), on the basis of a more recent survey of 417 women in 6 prisons, painted a similar picture. Finding accommodation, however, is not the only problem. Some women report problems of obtaining and replacing furniture, cooking facilities and other essential household items which in turn can prevent them living in accommodation even when it is available (Wilkinson, Morris and Woodrow 2001).

Women who manage to retain their homes face a different set of difficulties. Housing benefit, although available to prisoners who are tenants and likely to be in custody for less than 13 weeks, may be operated differently from one local authority to another and not all women are aware of their entitlements. Also, other utilities such as water charges may still need to be paid. But retaining accommodation is not the end of the matter; women continually report vandalism and/or burglary of their properties during which most of their belongings may be lost (Morris *et al.* 1995; NACRO 2001). Wilkinson *et al.* (2001) have pointed to the way in which the majority of the difficulties women face on release are linked to housing.

Families may be one of the key factors in helping women to reintegrate successfully into the community. They may pay off debts, help find jobs and provide somewhere to live (Morris *et al.* 1995), but this is not always the case. Wilkinson *et al.* (2001) highlighted the extent of the prior physical and sexual abuse suffered by women in prison, the regularity with which such abuse featured in women's lives, and stressed that the sites of this abuse were women's families and their abusers were those closest to them. They expressed concern about resettlement where the focus was on encouraging women to return to families even when they had lived independently for many years. Many women had not disclosed their prior victimisation to the professionals with whom they came into contact. Where disclosures had been made, responses had often involved moving the women from their families early in their lives, thus leaving them with no families or support at all. This left some women and girls with no homes to go to on release. The result was going to hostels, sleeping at friends' houses or sleeping rough.

The links between prior victimisation and offending have also been demonstrated (Morris *et al.* 1995; Wilkinson and Morris 2000; Wilkinson *et al.* 2001). When asked why they offend, the most common reasons given by women are related to drug or alcohol use, need for money for these substances, or lack of money generally (Hamlyn and Lewis 2000; Morris and Wilkinson 2000). Women using drugs and/or alcohol report higher levels of physical and sexual abuse and women's own accounts demonstrate the way in which the use of such substances followed the violence in the early part of their lives. A link between prior victimisation and self-harm has also been highlighted (Morris *et al.* 1995; Wilkinson and Morris 2000; Wilkinson *et al.* 2001).

Prior victimisation is becoming a regular feature of discussions of women prisoners (see for example, Home Office 2001b, 2001c; NACRO 2001; Prison Reform Trust 2000). But such recognition and increases in the provision of counselling, support and therapy in prison and on release is not sufficient in itself. Wilkinson *et al.* (2001) point out that there is little point in helping women to begin to understand the violence and abuse they have suffered if they are catapulted back into situations where they cannot manage their own security and where further violence and abuse seem unavoidable.

Employment, clearly, has the potential to help women achieve some degree of autonomy on release and to break free of an enforced dependency upon welfare or other people. Most research (Dodd and Hunter 1992; Hamlyn and Lewis 2000; Home Office 1997; Morris *et al.* 1995; NACRO 1996) has demonstrated that few women have been employed prior to their imprisonment.[4] Morris *et al.* (1995) also demonstrated the tenuous nature of this employment; work was often short term and part time. Also, in around a third of cases, women had never worked. Around half of those with jobs lost them at the time of imprisonment and around half of the women with jobs reported offences related to their employment. Hamlyn and Lewis (2000), in a later study, replicated many of these findings.

There is little evidence of women's employment needs being addressed during sentence. The majority of women work in prison but this is largely menial, unskilled and related to the need to service the institution or outside contracts. Training courses are provided but access may be limited by shortage of places and sentence length and there is a failure to match to need (Hamlyn and Lewis 2000; Morris *et al.* 1995). There are also disincentives to undertaking full-time education where weekly wages are lower than those earned in other parts of the prison (Morris *et al.* 1995). Despite these problems, women report enjoying the work and finding courses helpful. They also seem optimistic of finding employment on release. The reality, however, is somewhat different with only around a fifth (Morris *et al.* 1995) to a third (Hamlyn and Lewis 2000) reporting having obtained work at post-release interviews. Success in this respect was related to informal rather than formal application procedures and the help of family and friends or previous employers and also to pre-sentence work experience and skills. The biggest barrier to success was thought to be criminal records (Hamlyn and Lewis 2000; Morris *et al.* 1995).

There are conflicting views of the state of education, training and employment opportunities in women's prisons.[5] Whatever the position, three important points need to be stressed. First, as shown above, the majority of women spend quite short periods in prison and so opportunities to improve literacy and numeracy and to obtain skills are quite limited and need to be continued into the community in order to have any impact (Prison Reform Trust 2000). There is no indication that this is happening. Hamlyn and Lewis (2000) reported only 10 per cent of prisoners undertaking education or training post-release. Second, one of the principal barriers to obtaining employment is childcare; a significant proportion of released women are the mothers of very young children. Finally, it has to be remembered that women's earnings are significantly less than men's[6] and may not provide sufficient income on which to live (Morris *et al.* 1995). This inability to obtain some autonomy on release through employment enhances women's dependency, both on benefits and on the men with whom they form relationships (Wilkinson *et al.* 2001).

Obtaining money on release is consistently reported as one of the biggest problems faced at that time (Dodd and Hunter 1992; Hamlyn and Lewis 2000; Morris *et al.* 1995). The majority of women return to live on benefits (Hamlyn and Lewis 2000; Morris *et al.* 1995), many report delays in obtaining these, confusion or ignorance about entitlements and discharge grants, and differences between areas in the way in which loans and grants are paid out. In addition, many women have to cope with debts that have worsened during their period of imprisonment (Morris *et al.* 1995). Incomes, whatever their source, are generally low and, in a sample of women released in 1999, more than half of all women and nearly three-quarters of single women reported incomes of less than £100 per week (Hamlyn and Lewis 2000). One of the biggest problems concerns girls who are sometimes too young to claim benefits, have little experience and understanding of the welfare system, and who sometimes report being seen as a financial burden by their families who are expected to support them (Wilkinson and Morris 2000).

In financial terms, women returning to relationships may fare better than single women in that partners may be employed and/or already claiming benefits. But relationships create a whole different set of problems on release. Some relationships break down during the period of imprisonment. Morris *et al.* (1995) reported that around a third of relationships, where women had been living with partners, had broken down. This appeared to have happened regardless of whether the women had reported prior relationship problems. In some cases, women were pleased with the outcome but this was not always the case. The breakdown of relationships raises a whole host of potential problems in terms of developing independent living: finding accommodation, furnishing it and obtaining financial support. Although many women do return to live with partners and the majority report no readjustment difficulties, around a quarter do (Hamlyn and Lewis 2000; Morris *et al.* 1995). Women often attribute these difficulties to depression, learning to cope again and feeling overwhelmed by the different family problems and pressures placed upon them (Morris *et al.* 1994). In some cases, difficulties associated with establishing independent living leave women with little choice but to return to relationships that they had previously left or to move quite quickly into new ones. Such relationships serve to enhance women's dependency and leaving can become very difficult (Wilkinson *et al.* 2001).

Each year an estimated 8000 children are affected by the imprisonment of their mothers (Wedderburn 2000). Whilst male prisoners are able to leave children in the care of partners or ex-partners, women generally have to make special arrangements. Most children are looked after by relatives (often grandparents or other female family members), few children remain with fathers, and around 10 per cent will be placed in local authority or foster care. This substitute care sometimes leads to financial difficulties with which some carers are ill equipped to deal. Not all mothers consider the substitute care arrangements satisfactory and this dissatisfaction increases over time. Also, care arrangements may break down, leading to further change for children, with the likelihood of this happening increasing over time (Caddle and Crisp 1997; Morris *et al.* 1995; Richards and McWilliams 1996).

Children also face difficulties. For many, this period will be their first separation from their mother. Some children, especially young children, will not know where their mother is. Even when children do know of their mother's situation, there will be problems of keeping in touch. A significant minority will have had no contact with their mother since her imprisonment. An even larger number will not have seen their mothers. But mothers of children who have visited report problems with this: for example, children's fears of coming into a prison and their tiredness from sometimes long and difficult journeys. It is hardly surprising then that children have been reported to experience behavioural problems and problems of withdrawal, sleeping, ill-health and eating disorders during the period of separation (Caddle and Crisp 1997; Morris *et al.* 1995; Richards and McWilliams 1996).

The majority of mothers resume the care of their children on their release (Morris *et al.* 1995). Some of these mothers will resume this care as lone parents (Caddle and Crisp 1997). Most mothers report no difficulties in caring for their children. A significant minority, however, do report such difficulties and those who have served longer sentences are more likely to do so. These include problems that their children have experienced but of which they were unaware at the time of their imprisonment and problems experienced by children after their release (Morris *et al.* 1995). Two major factors in mothers not resuming care of their children are the reluctance of social services to allow this and the nature of the women's offences (Morris *et al.* 1994). A minority of these mothers report difficulties in maintaining contact with their children after release.

One final point must be stressed. Women are not an homogeneous group – at the very least they differ by virtue of age and ethnicity. There is little in the research to indicate the extent to which the problems and difficulties faced by women on release are applicable across all groups. Focusing on the 15 girls in their study aged 15 to 17 years of age, Wilkinson and Morris (2000) demonstrated that, whilst overall the girls were similar in profile to adult prisoners, they differed in some important respects: their lives had been more disrupted; levels of self-harm, sexual abuse and use of alcohol and drugs were much higher; and many more reported experience of the 'care' system. Most girls entered prison with a multitude of interrelated problems but it was the recency and immediacy of these problems that distinguished them from adult prisoners. The picture on release was bleak. Most had little or no money on which to live, few job prospects, little or no family support, very limited access to safe accommodation, and limited access to appropriate drug and alcohol services. In 1999, the government made a commitment to remove 15- and 16-year-old children from Prison Service establishments and to house them in new, purpose-built, local authority secure units. To date, however, this commitment has not been met and the situation continues to generate much concern (Home Office 2001c).

NACRO (2000b) focused on the issue of the resettlement of black women. These women were less likely to have received regular visits from spouses, partners and children; were less satisfied with pre-release advice generally; and were less satisfied with advice about money and benefits. NACRO also stressed that this group of women may experience racial discrimination in employment and that their status as ex-offenders would add to the problems they faced.

One other difference, which is rarely mentioned in this context, concerns sexuality. This is not surprising. Feminist scholarship has been heavily criticised for either rendering lesbian women invisible or for rendering lesbians as something 'other' or 'perverse' requiring explanation (Rich 1993). A not insignificant number of women in prison identify as lesbian:[7] many will have done so before their incarceration but some women make such choices in a prison setting. At the very least the latter group may face problems around their sexuality on their release.[8] Despite declarations of recognition of diversity, legislation, policy and practice in a whole range of areas are imbued with a model of heterosexuality. This means that lesbian women, potentially, face a different set of problems on release. One benefit may be that, because rules of cohabitation do not recognise same-sex relationships, lesbian women will not be pushed into an enforced financial dependency. There may, however, be a downside: lesbian women may face additional problems with accommodation – especially where this involves mixed hostels,[9] or where tenancies were in the name of the woman imprisoned and hence were not transferred. Prior relationships may be more precarious, either because keeping in touch was too difficult or because of a general lack of support and understanding. Family support may be less forthcoming or involve conditions about lifestyle. Employment prospects may be hampered and lesbians may face numerous difficulties concerning children – in resuming the care of their children whether the substitute carers be family members or social services, or in claiming parental responsibility, where they are not the biological mother, in order to maintain their role as carer in the community or in order to exercise their rights to keep in touch through, for example, provision of special visits.

A number of changes in practice have taken place in recent years: sentence planning has been further developed; CARATS[10] schemes have been introduced in all prisons as part of the drug strategy, the Prison Service has begun to readdress the issue of resettlement,[11] and a number of resettlement pathfinder projects are being piloted, one of which deals with women (Home Office 2001c). Despite these changes, it is clear that, to date, the release experiences of women have changed little. Two recent documents from the Social Exclusion Unit (2002) and the Inspectorates of Prisons and Probation (Home Office 2001d) provide clear evidence of continuing problems with prisoners' resettlement. In both documents, the links between social exclusion and reoffending were examined and key factors identified, some of the specific problems faced by women highlighted, the lack of support for short-term prisoners stressed, and the lack of any clear strategy for release and resettlement emphasised.

Thus, after two decades of research on women's imprisonment, there is now considerable consensus about the problems and difficulties faced at the time of release. These points are now recognised by government and, as part of its commitment to an overhaul of the criminal justice system, proposals for change to release procedures are contained in the White Paper *Justice for All* (Home Office 2002). These proposals are the focus of the next section. The issue to be addressed is the extent to which these take account of the plight of women.

Proposals for change

Key parts of the penal critique have centred on the way in which services to assist women with resettlement should be organised and delivered. Morris *et al.* (1995) called for a focus on the practical rather than the therapeutic, for a more proactive approach and for women to be encouraged to take responsibility for themselves. The introduction of resource centres in women's prisons was advocated and the idea of similar centres in the community, which would provide a focus for women who did not know how to obtain help, was also raised.

Resource centres in the community featured again in the report of the Wedderburn Committee (Prison Reform Trust 2000). No specific reference to release procedures was made but an expanded use of community penalties was recommended and, following the Scottish Office (1998), a number of key areas for specific provision within programmes of supervision identified. Given that such provision would require the services of a diverse range of agencies, a national network of Women's Supervision, Rehabilitation and Support Centres, run by the Probation Service, was recommended. These resource centres would provide supervision of court orders and access to a wide range of services, but could also give extended support to women after completion of sentence, support to non-offending women and support to protect family ties. These recommendations were taken up by NACRO (2001). Similar proposals for a 'time-out centre' have been made in Scotland by the Inter Agency Forum on Women's Offending (2001) and by the Ministerial Group on Women's Offending (Scottish Executive 2002), with proposals to introduce such a facility in Glasgow in 2003.

Overall, the focus of the penal critique has been on the need to help women. It is about rehabilitation and reintegration. It is also about preventing reoffending. Proposals are based on recognition of the fact that women's offending is inextricably linked with their life experiences and their social exclusion. Recent reports from within government take a very different approach.

The Halliday Report (2001) was principally about sentencing but its proposals in that respect involved a complete change to release procedures. Two main recommendations were made: that discretionary release should be abolished; and that sentences should be served in full – the first part in prison and the second part in the community. Release arrangements were then linked to three types of sentence: less than 12 months, 12 months or more, and a 'special sentence' for 'dangerous' offenders. Both recommendations are incorporated into the White Paper (Home Office 2002).

Halliday proposed that sentences of less than 12 months become 'custody plus'. Offenders would serve a minimum of two weeks in custody and a maximum of three months.[12] The second part of the sentence would be served in the community with a minimum of 6 months and a maximum of whatever would keep the total sentence to less than 12 months.[13] Release plans would be agreed by the court at the time of sentence and any modification would need a review hearing. The prison part of the sentence would be used to work on the content and implementation of the release plan and to begin programmes designed to tackle offending behaviour. The community part of the sentence would require the offender to take part in various programmes to tackle offending behaviour, and such programmes would involve partnerships between probation and the voluntary and statutory sectors. Breach of conditions would lead to recall and re-release of offenders recalled would only be possible for those with at least four months left to serve.

Sentences of 12 months and over would operate in a similar way to the present system but with a number of key changes. All prisoners, including those sentenced to four years and over, would be released at the halfway point. But all sentences would be served in full. The second half would be served in the community and would involve a 'package' of measures designed to tackle offending behaviour. These measures would include the same range of options available for community sentences. Again, the courts would play a major role in determining the content of both parts of the sentence. They would be required, at the time of sentence, to indicate to the Prison Service the type of work needing to be done in prison. Also, the Prison and Probation Services working together would be required to design the 'package' of measures to be applied post-release, based on their assessment of risk of reoffending. This 'package' would be put before a review hearing of the court where it would be endorsed or further advice commissioned. Low levels of compliance would result in applications for tougher sanctions and serious failure would result in immediate recall to prison. Recalled offenders would not be entitled to a review hearing until 12 months had elapsed.

Despite their arguments for abolishing discretionary release, the Halliday Committee recognised that it needed to be retained for certain types of offender who presented a risk of serious harm to the public. Thus, it recommended a 'special sentence' for certain violent or sexual offenders where release in the second part of their sentence would be subject to a decision of the parole board and where courts would have the power to extend the supervisory part of the sentence.

Halliday's proposals raise a number of potential problems. The White Paper, however, is far less precise on the way in which the new system will operate. The potential problems are discussed here under three general but related topics: the possible impact on women and the size of the women's prison population; proposed changes to the administration of justice; and the content of the sentences and programmes which women would undergo. Differences between Halliday and the White Paper are highlighted.

On the basis of discharge figures for 2000 (Home Office 2001a), the initial impact of the Halliday proposals would be that an additional 4427 women would be subject to conditions on release. Although not endorsed in the White Paper, the minimum length of such conditions is proposed at 6 months but could be considerably longer given the 12-month overall maximum. In addition, some 2179 women already subject to conditions on release would be subject to these conditions for longer periods; that is until the end of their sentence rather than to the three-quarters point as currently operates. According to the White Paper these conditions are likely to include drug testing and, for those on 'custody plus', 'going straight contracts' which will involve sanctions and rewards for non-participation and participation.[14] Since breach could lead to recall to prison, one concern is that many women will find themselves in prison for longer periods. Also, breach is to be an administrative decision and, although there is a right of appeal, there is no provision for legal aid except in the most serious disputes.

A related issue concerns the re-release of those recalled. The absence of the option of re-release for offenders with less than 4 months to serve for those on 'custody plus' and no further review for 12 months for those serving sentences of 12 months and over is an extremely punitive response and would appear to leave the shorter sentence prisoners in each group to be re-released without any further release plan. Thus, the potentially most difficult cases will face release without any post-release supervision. The White Paper contains little on enforcement of licences except to say that monitoring compliance is a matter for the local probation board, recall a decision of the Prison Service, and that recalls will be considered by the parole board.

One of the biggest concerns in relation to 'custody plus' is that sentencers, faced with a maximum period of imprisonment of 3 months, will resort to using sentences of 12 months and over. Indeed, Hudson (2002) has demonstrated the way in which the imprisonment of women has escalated as a result of sentencing policies that have emphasised risk of reoffending and persistent offending. Both concepts are central to the Halliday proposals.

Halliday is aware of the dangers and attempts to limit the likelihood that this will occur by emphasising how much more onerous the new 'custody plus' sentence will be. Focusing on women received into prison in 2000 (Home Office 2001a), one cannot but agree. Less than 10 per cent (n = 616) of the 7006 women received into prison under an immediate custodial sentence in 2000 were serving sentences of 6 months but less than 12 months and so might find themselves spending a shorter period in custody and more time under sentence in the community. But women serving sentences of less than six months, that is two-thirds (n = 4241) of sentenced receptions, will face much longer sentences if the proposed six-month minimum community element is implemented.

Although the Halliday Report is about sentencing and release procedures, it is also about the administration of justice. Many changes are proposed in this respect, some of which are related to release procedures. The overall aim is to stimulate better pre-release planning and to make decisions much more transparent. This is partly in recognition of the fact that resettlement work had become something of a 'poor relation'. In this respect the proposals are to be welcomed. Agencies are to be forced to discharge their responsibilities. It is clear, however, that considerable change in practice will need to be made in the courts, the Probation Service and the Prison Service and such changes will require a significant input of resources. According to Halliday, the courts are expected to assume responsibility for deciding on the content of the supervisory period and to operate review hearings, whilst the Prison Service is expected to work in partnership with Probation in preparing plans for review hearings. But such an approach is not endorsed in the White Paper. Here the emphasis is on the Probation Service whose role is considerably extended: at the time of sentence in terms of setting out needs in pre-sentence reports; at the time of release in terms of preparing release plans; and post-release in terms of offering more programmes and over a longer period of time. The role of the Prison Service is also extended in that more programmes will have to be provided during sentence. The main concerns here are the extent to which resources will be provided to finance this amount of planning and provision of services and programmes that will be required and the extent to which staff will be trained in new working procedures. Without such an input, offenders will merely be set up to fail, but there are other related concerns.

The proposed programmes in the community require the Probation Service to work in partnership with voluntary agencies. Such programmes will also require additional funding. NACRO (2001) stressed the lack of stable and systematic funding for the voluntary sector and the lack of state funding to sustain innovative pilot projects funded initially by charitable organisations. NACRO's Women Prisoners Resource Centre closed in 2000 after 15 years because of lack of funding and the Black Female Prisoners Scheme has also closed for the same reason. Even if funding were available, few voluntary agencies currently offer services across the whole of the female estate (NACRO 2001). Thus, there will need to be some assessment of the equity of programmes. Just as the Probation Service is subject to national standards, then so too will the quality of provision from the voluntary sector need to be monitored.

Finally, there are a number of interrelated problems concerning the content of the new sentences. In terms of 'custody plus', the content of supervision is to be decided on the basis of risk of reoffending. Lothian (2002) has documented the way in which the social, economic and welfare needs of women have been translated into criminogenic factors and currently into risk factors. Shaw and Hannah-Moffat (2000) have warned of the way in which the *What Works* agenda renders women individually responsible for their offending. Thus, to the extent that needs might lead to fairly onerous conditions on release then there is an incentive not to disclose. This is particularly relevant to women and their histories of victimisation, their drug use and difficulties with care of children.

The relevance of the sometimes very short custodial part of 'custody plus' also is not immediately obvious although Halliday suggests that it is an opportunity to work on the content and implementation of the post-release plan, to begin work to tackle offending behaviour, and to begin treatment for drug and alcohol use. A number of possible problems present themselves here. First, some women sentenced to short periods of imprisonment will have served their sentences on remand and, currently, would be freed at court following sentence. The danger is that because these women would now be subject to the community element, they might be given a longer custodial element in order to facilitate development and implementation of the release plan. Second, it assumes that such plans can be developed in quite short periods. This may not be the case, especially where joint working between a range of agencies is required. Sentence planning, which involves similar requirements, has been the subject of much criticism in this respect (Home Office 1997; Morris *et al.* 1995). Third, prisons are currently ill-equipped to provide programmes to very short sentence prisoners. Given the proportion of women currently serving such sentences, this will require a considerable input of funding and resources.

Fourth, the content of such short programmes in prison is far from clear, although Halliday suggests that sentence programmes would involve treatment for drug, alcohol and mental health problems, cognitive programmes, skills training, resettlement and relationships. There are two interrelated problems here. First, there is a danger that in demonstrating the relevance of the prison part of the sentence the emphasis at this stage will be on cognitive skills programmes and social circumstances may be ignored.[15] As demonstrated above, women's offending is interwoven with their social exclusion. Tackling their offending behaviour needs to be about integration and this in turn means prison and probation officers connecting up with a whole range of agencies outside prison and, if programmes are to begin in prison, bringing their work into a prison setting. Again, this will require a significant input of resources. There is also an added danger of refocusing work with short-term prisoners in this way. Concentrating on provision of courses to tackle offending behaviour may leave little time for and commitment to pre-release courses which deal with resettlement needs and for more general work in the area of resettlement. The second problem concerns the applicability of any programmes to women, whether these are delivered in a custodial setting or in the community. Currently, it is not clear that programmes which have been shown to work with men actually also work with women (Home Office 2001c; Kendall 2002; Rex 2001). There is also the added problem of ensuring that programmes are appropriate for some very different groups of women whilst recognising that numbers in any one establishment at any one time will be small.

Finally, whatever the content of programmes/courses, it is difficult to see to what extent these could run 'seamlessly' from prison to the community in the way envisaged, particularly where offenders serve their sentences long distances from home, as is the case for many women. To some extent Halliday recognises the problem. A dedicated part of the prison estate for short-term prisoners is considered 'useful' in that it may reduce the possible risks of disruption to programmes from overcrowding and subsequent transfer. It is suggested also that this part of the estate could be used for the resettlement of longer term prisoners. An immediate review of the 'intermediate' estate[16] is recommended, as is long-term planning of the estate to establish what sort of local prisons would best meet the needs of short-term prisoners. Thus, it appears that a separate type of prison system for short-term prisoners is being proposed.[17] This has huge implications for the imprisonment of women. As shown above, around three-quarters of women sentenced to immediate imprisonment in 2000 were serving sentences of less than 12 months and so presumably would be housed in this dedicated part of the estate. This would have two effects. First, it would leave a very small number of women sentenced to immediate imprisonment to be housed in the existing estate with the possible effect that these women would be housed in fewer establishments and, hence, some women would serve their sentences even further from home. It also raises the problem of where to place women on remand.

One alternative is that these women could be housed in a network of small, local secure units as recommended by the Prison Reform Trust (2000). Second, dispersal more locally of the larger group of women serving short sentences would still leave small groups of women in many areas. This raises questions about where such women might be housed and the recurring issue of units attached to male establishments (NACRO 1991). It also raises questions about the types of programmes that could be offered in a custodial setting to such small numbers, particularly since women, as stressed above, are not a homogeneous group, have diverse needs and will require therefore a range of programmes. One way out of this difficulty, which might help achieve cost effectiveness, would be to offer joint programmes locally to women in different parts of the criminal justice system: for example, women serving community sentences; women serving the community part of custodial sentences; women serving the short part of custodial sentences; and women preparing for resettlement from longer custodial sentences.

Taken to this conclusion, then again, the proposal of the Prison Reform Trust (2000) for a national network of Women's Supervision, Rehabilitation and Support centres becomes very relevant. The White Paper, however, favours 'campus' style prisons that would hold in separate sections adults, remands, young offenders and women.

Conclusion

After two decades of research on women's imprisonment, there is now considerable consensus about the problems and difficulties faced by women at the time of release and for the need for a change to release procedures. Two main points of debate remain.

First, the emphasis in the penal critique has been on the need to provide help to women by concentrating on the practical problems and difficulties which they face. Whilst the Halliday Report clearly recognises the problems and difficulties, the primary emphasis is very different: it is about risk of reoffending and the need for programmes aimed at reducing criminal behaviour. There is a danger here of repeating the mistakes of the past: the optimism of the 1960s around rehabilitation was associated with incursive, coercive and over-zealous programmes. Although Halliday recommends retaining proportionality in sentencing, it is not clear to what extent the content of sentences rather than their length may impact on this. Perhaps the biggest difference between the proposals is that the penal critique recognises that prevention of offending requires social intervention. The Halliday Report, on the other hand, is underpinned by a model of criminal justice that emphasises responsibility, free will and choice (Hannah-Moffat 2002).

Second, the biggest debates about changes to release procedures are likely to be around the structure within which release procedures might operate. There is considerable consensus about the need to involve a whole range of agencies working within the community; the question is one of how to organise this. Halliday was of the opinion that 'custody plus' needed to operate within a more localised structure. The provision of services through some form of centre designed specifically for women has also been envisaged in the penal critique. One potential difficulty is that these centres may face problems in trying to provide services to very different client groups, some of whom, as suggested above, could be non-offenders. But this problem has to balanced against the need to provide services which are cost effective in order to ensure that services are provided at all. The reorganisation of the prison estate, however, is perhaps the most far reaching of Halliday's proposals. No doubt it will be debated fiercely, particularly within prison establishments.

The Halliday Report provides a unique opportunity. We know a considerable amount about women's resettlement needs, new initiatives aimed at ensuring that women's needs are reflected in policy and practice are in place, and there is some indication that women's specific needs are becoming recognised by government. The challenge now is to ensure that these factors are brought to bear and that any new release procedures actually meet the needs of imprisoned women. The biggest parts of this challenge may be in ensuring that, at last, the organisation of the custodial estate is appropriate for the women held within it and that the government match their 'tough on crime' approach with an equally 'tough on the causes of crime' approach which gives due recognition to the fact that women's offending is underpinned by their social exclusion.

Notes

1   In order to ensure that the needs of women offenders are reflected in policy and practice, a Women's Policy Group was set up in 1998; women's prisons have been managed by a single operational manager since April 2000; a Programmes for Women Steering Group meets quarterly; and the government has published its strategy for women offenders (Home Office 2000) on which it has consulted widely (Home Office 2001c).

2   Under S.35 prisoners aged less than 22 years are subject to compulsory supervision by either the Probation Service or social services.

3   In 2000, some 6606 women were discharged after serving a custodial sentence: four-fifths (n = 5301) were serving sentences of 12 months or less; two-thirds (n = 4331) were serving six months and less; two-fifths (n = 2610) were serving three months and less; 15 per cent (n = 1018) were serving sentences of 12 months but less than 4 years and only 4 per cent (n = 287) were serving sentences of 4 years and over and so were released at the discretion of the parole board (Home Office 2001a).

4   Figures vary from around a quarter (Morris *et al.* 1995) to around a third (Dodd and Hunter 1992; Hamlyn and Lewis 2000; Home Office 1997).

5   The Wedderburn Committee (Prison Reform Trust 2000) welcomed a reassurance from the Women's Policy Group that education, training and employment opportunities now better reflected the resettlement needs of women. On the other hand, at a later date, the Chief Inspector of Prisons in a follow-up to his thematic review (Home Office 1997, 2001b) indicated that such opportunities were still insufficient.

6   Half of all women working full time and 80 per cent of those working part time earn below the Council of Europe's decency threshold of £6.31 an hour. Over 6.5 million women are low paid. Of those women, 4.5 million (43% of all women employees) earn less than £5 an hour (Low Pay Unit, 29 Armwell Street, London EC1R 1TL).

7   There are no actual statistics to reflect the number of women identifying in this way and there is no reason to suggest that lesbian women should be expected to 'out' themselves in order to provide these. But it is clear to researchers and practitioners that some imprisoned women do identify as lesbian and so their different needs should be recognised.

8   Obtaining help with such concerns in a prison setting may pose difficulties given that lesbian activity is an offence against prison discipline.

9   The Home Office has announced plans to increase provision for women in mixed hostels whilst not expanding provision of places in women only hostels (Home Office 2000). These proposals have been met with concern (for a discussion see Home Office 2001c).

10 Counselling, Assessment, Referral, Advice and Throughcare Service.

11 Home Office (2000) *Prison Service Draft Resettlement Standard*; Prison Service (2001) *Resettlement*, Prison Service Order No. 2300, Issue 134, 23 October 2001. The Prison Service is to introduce a resettlement key performance indicator (KPI) from April 2002 for employment but an accommodation target is only under consideration (Home Office 2001c).

12 Since these proposals would effectively abolish periods of custody of between three months and six months, there was some debate about whether the maximum should be six months.

13 A period of custody (maximum three months) without post-release supervision would be retained for a small group where no specific needs were identified.

14 These contracts were recommended by the Social Exclusion Unit (2002).

15   In designing effective programmes there is evidence to suggest that account must be taken of the social environment in which offenders are taking and acting upon decisions (Rex 2001).

16   This should encompass all types of accommodation including that owned by the prison and probation services and the independent or voluntary sector, whether used for temporary release, conditional release, offenders serving community sentences or ex-offenders receiving support voluntarily.

17   This links in also with Halliday's proposals for intermittent custody.

References

Auld Report (2001) *Report of a Review of the Criminal Courts of England and Wales.* London: Home Office.

Caddle, D. and Crisp, D. (1997) *Imprisoned Women and Mothers.* Home Office Research Study no. 162. London: Home Office.

Criminal Justice Act (1991) London: HMSO.

Crime and Disorder Act (1998) London: HMSO.

Dodd, T. and Hunter, P. (1992) *The National Prison Survey 1991.* London: HMSO.

Dodgson, K., Goodwin, P., Howard, P., Llewellyn-Thomas, S., Mortimer, E., Russell, N. and Weiner, M. (2001) *Electronic Monitoring of Released Prisoners: An Evaluation of the Home Detention Curfew Scheme.* Home Office Research Study no. 222. London: Home Office.

Halliday Report (2001) *Making Punishments Work: Report of a Review of the Sentencing Framework for England and Wales.* London: Home Office.

Hamlyn, B. and Lewis, D. (2000) *Women Prisoners: A Survey of their Work and Training Experiences in Custody and on Release.* Home Office Research Study no. 208. London: Home Office.

Hannah-Moffat, K. (2002) 'Creating choices: Reflecting on choices.' In P. Carlen (ed) *Women and Punishment: The Struggle for Justice.* Cullompton: Willan.

Home Office (1997) *Women in Prison: A Thematic Review by HM Chief Inspector of Prisons for England and Wales.* London: Home Office.

Home Office (2000) *The Government's Strategy for Women Offenders.* London: Home Office.

Home Office (2001a) *Prison Statistics, England and Wales 2000.* London: The Stationery Office.

Home Office (2001b) *Follow-up to Women in Prison: A Thematic Review by HM Chief Inspector of Prisons for England and Wales.* London: Home Office.

Home Office (2001c) *The Government's Strategy for Women Offenders.* Consultation report. London: Home Office.

Home Office (2001d) *Through the Prison Gate: A Joint Thematic Review by HM Inspectorates of Prisons and Probation.* London: Home Office.

Home Office (2002) *Justice for All.* Cm 5563. London: The Stationery Office.

Hudson, B. (2002) 'Gender issues in penal policy and penal theory.' In P. Carlen (ed) *Women and Punishment: The Struggle for Justice.* Cullompton: Willan.

Inter Agency Forum on Women's Offending (2001) *Second Year Report.* Glasgow: IAF.

Kendall, K. (2002) 'Time to think again about cognitive behavioural programmes.' In P. Carlen (ed) *Women and Punishment: The Struggle for Justice.* Cullompton: Willan.

Lothian, J. (2002) 'Women's prisons in England: Barriers to reform.' In P. Carlen (ed) *Women and Punishment: The Struggle for Justice.* Cullompton: Willan.

Morris, A. and Wilkinson, C. (2000) 'Breaking out of offending women after prison – lessons from the past, looking to the future.' *Prison Service Journal 132*, 44–47.

Morris, A., Wilkinson, C., Tisi, A., Woodrow, J. and Rockley, A. (1994) 'Managing the needs of female prisoners.' Report to the Home Office. Unpublished.

Morris, A., Wilkinson, C., Tisi, A., Woodrow, J. and Rockley, A. (1995) *Managing the Needs of Female Prisoners.* London: Home Office.

NACRO (1991) *A Really Fresh Start for Women Prisoners: The Implications of the Woolf Report for Women.* London: NACRO.

NACRO (1996) *Women Prisoners: Towards a New Millenium.* London: NACRO.

NACRO (2000a) *The Forgotten Majority: The Resettlement of Short-term Prisoners.* Resettlement Policy Committee. London: NACRO.

NACRO (2000b) *Race and Prisons, A Snapshot Survey.* London: NACRO.

NACRO (2001) *Women Beyond Bars: A Positive Agenda for Women Prisoner's Resettlement.* London: NACRO.

Player, E. (2000) 'Justice for women.' *Prison Service Journal 132*, 17–22.

Prison Reform Trust (2000) *Justice for Women, the Need for Reform: Report of the Committee on Women's Imprisonment, Chaired by Professor Dorothy Wedderburn.* London: Prison Reform Trust.

Rex, S. (2001) 'Beyond cognitive-behaviouralism? Reflections on the effectiveness literature.' In A. Bottoms, L. Gelsthorpe and S. Rex *Community Penalties: Change and Challenges.* Cullompton: Willan.

Rich, A. (1993) 'Compulsory heterosexuality and lesbian experience.' In H. Abelove, M.A. Barale and D.M. Halperin (eds) *The Lesbian and Gay Studies Reader.* London: Routledge.

Richards, M. and McWilliams, B. (1996) *Imprisonment and Family Ties.* Research Bulletin no. 38. London: Home Office.

Scottish Executive (2002) *A Better Way: The Report of the Ministerial Group on Women's Offending.* Edinburgh: The Scottish Executive.

Scottish Office (1998) *Women Offenders – A Safer Way: A Review of Community Disposals and the Use of Custody for Women Offenders.* Edinburgh: The Stationery Office.

Shaw, M. and Hannah-Moffat, K. (2000) 'Gender, diversity and risk-assessment in Canadian corrections.' *Probation Journal 47*, 3, 163–172.

Social Exclusion Unit (2002) *Reducing Re-offending by Ex-prisoners.* London: Office of the Deputy Prime Minister.

Wedderburn, D. (2000) 'Justice for women: The need for reform.' *Prison Service Journal 132*, 2–4.

Wilkinson, C. and Morris, A. (2000) 'Victims or villains: Challenging the use of custody for girls who offend.' *Prison Service Journal 132*, 48–52.

Wilkinson, C., Morris, A. and Woodrow, J. (2001) 'Issues of security and safety for women released from prison.' *Security Journal 14*, 2.

CHAPTER 9

Black Women and the Criminal Justice System

Ruth Chigwada-Bailey

Introduction

So far there has been very little information available on black women's experience of the criminal justice system. It remains subsumed in the experience of black men and homogenised with the experience of white women. Feminist criminology has largely overlooked the social, cultural and economic experiences of black women which make them uniquely vulnerable to unequal treatment in the criminal justice process (see Chigwada-Bailey 1997; Rice 1990). In this chapter I look at key issues around race, gender and class and argue that these compound to create a potential for inequality before the law that is particularly detrimental to black women in Britain.

The term 'black' is used in this chapter to refer to people of African descent. Except where the context clearly implies otherwise, the term 'ethnic minority' is reserved for other non-white groups such as people of Asian descent.

Background

Since the early 1990s the female prison population of all ethnic origins has increased sharply, and this has been most pronounced for black and 'Chinese/others'. Although Africans and Caribbeans make up only 2 per cent of the total population of England and Wales, they account for 19 per cent of the female prison population.[1] This disproportionate number is striking, fuelling the myth that the black community are more dangerous than their white counterparts, yet there is no substantiating evidence that black people are more prone to commit serious crimes than white people. The statistics give weight, therefore, to the widely held perception that those from the black community and other ethnic minorities are not treated fairly within the penal system and that this is caused by direct and indirect or institutional racism (Bowling and Phillips 2002; Chigwada-Bailey 1997).

The rise in prison figures is partly due to the 1990s introduction of more punitive sentencing policies and an increased tendency to use custodial sentences, and to use them for longer periods. Under the 1991 Criminal Justice Act aggravating and mitigating circumstances were restricted and linked to the offence itself and not to the offender. In consequence not only an increasing number of women with children were imprisoned, but so also were those with addictions, mental illness and histories of physical and sexual abuse. This meant that women committing crimes out of need were as readily imprisoned as those committing them out of greed. The insensitivity of this sentencing system which valued formal justice – dealing with all offenders alike – above substantive justice – doing what is appropriate for the individual case – impacted on men as well as women. However, because of the circumstances typically surrounding women's criminality, women were disproportionately affected, and women's imprisonment grew at a faster rate than men's (Hudson 2002). Black women, above all, suffered a triple disadvantage – they were poor, they were black and they were female.

Mainstream criminology

Within critical criminology literature, race, class and gender have each been given exclusive attention. What has been conspicuously absent has been the investigation of their various intersections – the set of configurations that are more than the sum of the individual parts. Each of these factors, on their own and in combination, shapes or structures the life course of an individual (Groves and Frank 1993). In other words, race, class and gender function to enhance or limit access to economic and political power, which in turn shapes the choices people have at their disposal. As a generality, men have more choices than women, whites have more choices than minorities and the wealthy have more choices than the poor. If you combine these factors it is obvious that wealthy white males have access to the greatest number of choices in their life course, while the poor, black and other minority women would appear to have the fewest. There is a compelling argument that those with the greater number of choices should be held more accountable for their behaviour (Groves and Frank 1993). In reality, criminal justice and legal practices tend to hold the powerless more accountable because, as we shall discuss, the impact of custodial sentencing on them is frequently more devastating.

Critical criminologists have also argued that those with economic power also have access to political power, and thus to the ability to influence the scope and shape of the law (Quinney 1980; Reiman 1979). This means that values found in law will generally be most consistent with the interests of the upper class. Since race, class and gender have a strong impact on economic power, the dominant race, class and gender will be more likely than other groups to control the political and legal process. Crime, which is a political phenomenon, will reflect this in that the less powerful a person is in terms of race, class and gender, the more likely that person is to be subjected to the controlling power of the law and the more likely it is that behaviours common to those disempowered groups will be treated as criminal. This becomes clear when we look at the issue of stereotyping.

It is important to remember that race, class and gender effects are not simply 'additive forces' (Anderson and Collins 1995). If, for example, someone is a lower class, black woman, she does not experience the simple negative additive effects of being 'female', 'black' and 'lower class'. Rather, her experiences are an outcome of how these forces intersect with each other through the social and economic structures. In other words the effect is contextual, not mathematical (Anderson and Collins 1995).

Economic pressure

Black women are a marginalised group. They are poorly represented in education, the professions, commerce, industry and politics. They suffer higher levels of unemployment than most groups. A study in London of income distributions shows the stark difference between minority ethnic groups with, for example, 76 per cent of the Bangladeshi population being among the lowest one-fifth of earners in London (Runnymede Bulletin 2001). Add to that the fact that 30 years after the Equal Pay Act women in the UK still earn substantially less than men (cited in Runnymede Bulletin 2002), and where does that leave black women?

Economic resources are often the key to a person's ability to control other aspects of their lives. Unemployment particularly affects the young (16- to 24-year-olds), which is significant because of the relatively young structure of minority groups within Britain. A contributing factor is related to schooling. Black children are more likely to be permanently excluded from schooling and the reasons given differ from those given for white children. Black students are excluded for 'challenging behaviour' while white pupils are excluded for 'swearing at the member of staff'. The reality is that black girls develop, early on, a particular set of subcultural values which stress strength, independence, resilience and perseverance – all necessary attributes when trying to compete in the racist and sex-segregated labour market.

Professor Osler, at the launch of the Rowntree report, asking why black girls were four times more likely to be expelled from school than their white contemporaries, despite the fact that they were achieving quite successfully, felt the answer lay partly in this acquired assertiveness. 'Teachers,' she said, 'do have a particular set of thoughts or expectations of behaviour...conscious or unconscious... Many black children would say they get into trouble because they stick up for themselves' (*Morning Star*, 10 January 2002).

There is a well-established link between school exclusion and crime. The Social Exclusion Unit's report on *Truancy and Social Exclusion* found that of the young people offending after exclusion, over 44 per cent had no previous recorded offences (Social Exclusion Unit 1998, cited in NACRO 2001). The report went on:

> Permanent exclusion from school exposes [young people] to new criminal opportunities, while rendering them more visible, and hence more vulnerable, to the attention of the police...the visibility-vulnerability factor emerged as a particular problem for some African-Caribbean young people. (NACRO 2001)

Kwame McKenzie (2001) notes that suicide rates are increasing among black people, particularly among black youths: 'If you have your aspirations thwarted either through not getting the job you wanted, being excluded from school, or not getting the promotion you want, then this doubles or triples the chances of getting depression.'[2]

Stereotyping womanhood

Changing views of womanhood and women's role in society have informed the ways in which criminal women have been perceived and treated throughout the criminal justice process. Lucia Zedner, in her studies of women's prisons in Victorian England, used the example of 'feeble-mindedness' to illustrate how, at the end of the nineteenth century, women were judged as much for moral behaviour as criminal activity (Zedner 1991). Under the Mental Deficiency Act 1913 those in receipt of poor relief when pregnant or at the time of giving birth could be, and often were, classified as feeble-minded and placed in asylums.

Deviant and criminal behaviour of women and girls was explained more often by biological factors than social or economic forces. Representations of their motives for committing offences, or the circumstances leading to their crimes, were often not understood or were distorted. Such critiques stemmed from sexist assumptions of predominantly, but not exclusively, male criminologists who tried to explain the phenomenon of women's crime without any understanding or insight into a woman's perspective.

In recent decades theories have emerged which try to explain the increase in the number of women arrested by claims that female offenders are becoming increasingly more aggressive and violent (Adler 1975; Simon 1975). Both Adler and Simon believed that female criminality had been kept under control in the past by limited aspirations and opportunities in the public sphere. They argued that social circumstances, not biology, explained gender differences in crime. For Adler, the lifting of restrictions on women's behaviour gave them the opportunity to act like men – that is, to be as violent, greedy and crime prone as their male counterparts. Simon took a more qualified stance based on her interpretation of the statistical evidence. Having found no increase in the number of women arrested for violent crimes, she reasoned that their increasing arrest for property crimes – especially larceny, fraud and embezzlement – might be explained by their increasing participation in the public sphere which presented more opportunities to commit such crime. Adler (1975) has been criticised for claiming a link between the goal of female emancipation and an increase in female crime, and Simon (1975) for assuming that such increases were due to new workplace opportunities, rather than increasing economic pressures. On a broader front, both have been challenged about whether the trends they described were actually occurring at all (see also Chapter 4 this volume).

Leonard (1982) believes that theoretical criminology is sexist because it unwittingly focuses on the activities, interests and values of men, ignoring a comparable analysis of women. Furthermore, the traditional approach does not take into account the situation of black women who, for example, have always had to work and function outside conventional roles. In order to understand the forces affecting women as a whole, it is important to acknowledge and incorporate into the debate the complex interconnections between racial, sexual and economic disadvantage and the oppression in the lives of black women.

One of the real problems with feminist theory which we see reflected in feminist criminology, as Spelman (1988) points out, is that it has confused the condition of one group of women with the condition of all. 'A measure of the depth of white middle-class privilege is that apparently straightforward and logical points and actions at the heart of much feminist theory guarantee the direction of its attention to the concerns of white middle-class women' (Chigwada-Bailey 1997, p.35).

The family is, for example, a main cause of contradictory experiences for black women in ways unknown to most white women. The number of one-parent families overall has trebled in Britain in the last 30 years. Nearly every other black family – 49 per cent – is headed by a lone parent, the highest by far of any other ethnic or mixed race family. Even though research shows that ethnic minority groups experience high levels of unemployment, black Caribbean lone parents are significantly more likely to be at work, and working full time, than any other group, and less likely to be getting benefits. This is because they are poorly paid and often their partners are unemployed. Therefore they have to take up full employment if they can find it. Black women, and in particular African women, continue to be employed in jobs below the level to which they are qualified. Poor pay necessitates working longer hours to make ends meet.

Although both black and white women may experience the family as an institution of violence and oppression, for black women it often functions as a source of support against harassment and racism. It provides a cultural and political retreat from white supremacy. Many black women consider their race a more primary factor than gender in their dealings with the criminal justice agencies. It is significant that white women tend not to think of themselves as white, but merely as women (Spelman 1988), whereas blacks think of themselves primarily as black. It is essential to recognise that the interests and concerns shared by black and white women are cut across in a variety of ways by the interests of class, sexuality, race and ethnicity.

Lewis (1981), for example, accounted for the different crime rates for black and white women by focusing on racism and sexism within the criminal justice process (see Fry 1983, cited in Chigwada-Bailey 1997). Sexism, he suggested, had previously been thought to explain the 'chivalry' or leniency shown to women, but Lewis noted that this only included women who adhere to dominant societal gender-role expectations. As black women are less often married than white women, more often charged with violent offences, and less 'feminine' in demeanour, they were less likely to match up to such expectations.

Lewis also suggests that different circumstances and cultural backgrounds led to the development of personal traits that may contribute to differences in the nature and extent of crime between black and white women (Lewis 1981). For example, black women live in greater relative poverty and are socialised to be independent and assertive. Arguments such as these, however, should be viewed with caution because of the risk of stereotyping and ignoring variations in black communities, though they are useful in as much as they help to develop a greater understanding of the different roles and expectations of women in different cultures. As Kennedy has argued:

> Until there is a clear appreciation of racism and the social factors which bring black people before the courts, and an understanding of the subtle

dynamics which work in the courts to discriminate against them, they will continue to be amongst the sections of community least well served by the law. (Kennedy 1992, p.34)

Stereotyping motherhood

It must be acknowledged that how society as a whole views different groups of women may come into play during sentencing. Since race affects dominant perceptions of women's 'goodness' or 'badness', it would help to have some information about how black women are viewed – for example, by judges and police officers – to determine whether there might be discrimination on the basis of societal perception. It also has to be recognised that behaviour that may be attributed to a 'good' woman in one culture may have the reverse meaning in another. An African woman who arranges for members of her extended family to care for her children while she spends many hours at the market or finding ways of supporting their children may not be seen in English courts as a 'good' and caring mother. It may be that black mothers are considered inadequate by the courts more often than white mothers because they fail to measure up to the dominant pattern of mothering that constitutes the white ideology of motherhood.

While white ideology of motherhood has dictated that white women stay at home, it recognises no contradiction in encouraging black women to be domestic workers in other people's homes; their own role as mothers thus going unrecognised and even being discouraged (Chigwada-Bailey 1997). Black women may be affected in complex and contradictory ways by the prevailing ideological expectations of combining motherhood and work. On the one hand, if they are to conform, they need to stay at home with the children while they are still young; on the other they have economic responsibilities to make ends meet. They may be seen as failed mothers if they work, even if they are single parents or living with a partner who is either unemployed or poorly paid.

As Kennedy (1992) points out, black mothers often feel that their bond with their children is perceived as less significant, and that their views on the children's welfare are less valuable than those of their white counterparts. She cites one mother who was sentenced to two months in prison for refusing access to her daughter's father, which incidentally is a civil matter. She felt that she was seen as bloody-minded and obstructive, when in fact she was trying to protect her child whose father was a drug user. The little girl returned from visits describing in detail his use of drugs and drug-related involvement with other people. The mother feared that the influence of drugs would affect his ability to care for the child and wanted any access to be supervised. In court her concerns were ignored:

> 'I think had I not had two children by different fathers, they would have viewed me as a different type of person,' she said. 'I think the judge was trying to say, "You can't have your children and do what you like with them". I think the colour factor comes into it, but it's something that can never be proved.' (Kennedy 1992, p.65)

Claudia Bernard (1995) describes how stereotyping of black mothers as bad parents has strongly influenced these women not to involve the child protection agencies in cases of childhood sexual abuse. Mothers in the study felt vulnerable to implied criticism of their parenting and their capacity to protect their children from abuse.

Media portrayal reinforces the public perception of black women, and in particular black mothers, as deviant because they do not conform to white societal norms of maternal behaviour. The following report appeared in the London *Evening Standard* (12 December 1987):

> Young black men commit a disproportionately high number of violent crimes in London because most black mothers, when they are young girls, have children out of wedlock and are not supported by the fathers. There appears to be fewer stigmas attached to single parenthood in the black community. The only hope is that somehow the West Indian marriage can be encouraged and supported.

Such reports only serve to criminalise black women. An article in the *Daily Mail* (17 December 2001) put it this way: 'Many Jamaican women see having children by more than one father as the equivalent of spreading investments. If one man deserts you, perhaps the other will stay. If one loses his job, or refused to support his child, well, maybe one of the others will help.'

This type of reporting reinforces public perception of black mothers as irresponsible and promiscuous, deserving of the punishment meted out to them. These attitudes permeate the criminal justice system, affecting the way black women are regarded by both the police and the courts. Research by Visher (1983) concluded that because black women are seen as capable of committing crime they are not seen as victims, and so don't benefit from the mitigating factors such as maternal responsibility that are afforded to 'normal' or middle-class white women.

Black women as suspects

The prevalent assumption that black people are more likely to commit crimes than white people is misplaced. African-Caribbean women are stereotyped as strong, over-excitable and dominant. Asian women, by contrast, are seen as 'passive' and 'hysterical', subject to oppressive practices within the family (see Chigwada 1991). Such stereotyping has permeated the legal system, affecting the ways in which both police and courts respond to black women. Kennedy (1992), for example, mentions the trial of a Ugandan woman for grievous bodily harm to her husband – she poured hot cooking fat over him. It came to light that although she had called the police repeatedly, her violent husband was never arrested. It was suggested in court that she was not telling the truth about making previous complaints. There was no record of the complaints and it was put to her in cross-examination that she was exaggerating her husband's brutality. It was a prosecution witness, a neighbour, who inadvertently came to her aid. He complained in the witness box about the number of times he had been awakened, first by her screams and then by police mistakenly ringing his doorbell when they came in to answer her calls.

The highly publicised case of Joy Gardner, a black woman of Jamaican origin who died in 1993 in London, lends support to the view that authorities can see black women as potentially violent. Joy Gardner had overstayed her visa and was visited by the Alien Deportation Group (Chigwada-Bailey 1997). Her wrists were handcuffed to a leather strap around her waist, another belt was strapped around her thighs and a third around her ankles. As she lay on the floor, 13 feet of adhesive tape were wound around her head and face. Mrs Gardner collapsed and died in hospital a few hours later. Until her tragic death the use of body belts, surgical tape and the existence of a special deportation squad were unknown to the general public. It subsequently came to light that two other African women had been deported in this way.

The alarming conclusion that underlies these events is that the treatment she received was considered to meet the legal requirements of being 'reasonable in all circumstances' (Chigwada-Bailey 1997). Some politicians used the events to hammer home their anti-black, anti-refugee message. Teresa Gorman, Conservative MP for Billericay, said of Mrs Gardner: 'She had been bumming on the Social Services for five years...she cost the taxpayer an enormous amount... If she had gone quietly none of this would have happened' (see Chigwada-Bailey 1997).

Penal outcomes depend on constructions of culpability – on how much offenders are held to blame for their crimes. There are no hard-and-fast distinctions between being a victim and being an offender, but rather there is a continuum of blameworthiness which has important criminal justice implications. Black men and women are at one end of the continuum and considered as wholly to blame for their crimes. They fit the stereotype of 'suitable enemy' rather than 'ideal victim' (see Daly 1994). White women are at the end other end of the continuum with white men in between. This means for white women the line between being a victim and being an offender is somewhat blurred and can be crossed (Hudson 1988).

Black women, who are perceived as independent and unconventional, as defiant rather than fearful, with a succession of partners and with children in care, are held more blameworthy than white women who have committed similar offences. What count as mitigating circumstances differs markedly for white and black mothers. For example, a study of probation reports found that when officers asked white mothers about the fathers of their children, the point of the question was to ascertain whether the fathers were supportive economically and in other ways (Hudson 1988). When black mothers were asked the same questions, the point was to find out if the children were from different fathers, or whether the women had a record of promiscuity and unstable relationships. In other words with white women the point at issue was the adequacy of the father's performance of his role.

With black women the point at issue was the mother's sexual lifestyle (Green 1991). These stereotype-led differences meant that for the white woman being a mother was likely to be a mitigating factor, whereas for a black woman it was used as proof of her fecklessness, and thus became an aggravating factor.

This distortion of perception is also reflected in attitudes to foreign nationals who account for an increasing proportion of the female prison population. The fact that their crimes are committed out of extreme poverty and as a way of supporting their children is unlikely to be seen as reducing their culpability. They are likely to be judged not as women who are going to extreme lengths to support their families, but as women who have left their families and who have neglected their responsibilities to their dependants.

It is significant that drug barons are targeting mothers who have no criminal records and women in Caribbean hospitals who need money for medical treatment. These women are nearly all single parents and sole providers for their children and elderly relatives. The majority have never travelled out of their countries before. A number of studies have looked at the extent to which women participate in the illicit drug economy and Green (1991) notes that although 80 per cent of couriers are men, virtually all journalistic and pressure group interest in couriers has been on women. The couriers, she says, who are 'poor, foreign, visible and vulnerable', have thus been reconstructed as traffickers who are 'wealthy, powerful, manipulative and dangerous'.

In June 1999 more than three-quarters (77%) of sentenced female prisoners who were foreign nationals were held for drug offences. Of this number a staggering 10 per cent were Jamaican passport holders, almost all proven or suspected mules. Women caught trying to smuggle drugs inside their bodies can expect a sentence of between 4 and 6 years, but sentences of up to 15 years are not unusual (Green 1991).

What makes these women take such huge risks – risks not only of long prison sentences, but of death through cocaine leakage into their bodies? What makes them risk leaving their children destitute? In the main it seems to be poverty and naivety. They are paid between £150 and £1500 per trip, but if they change their minds before departure they are threatened with death and locked up before being taken directly to the airport (Gordon

1985). Most women are unaware not only of the length of sentence they face in Britain if they are caught, but of the physical dangers they face. In 2001, 8 so-called 'mules' died after cocaine packets burst in their stomachs and 31 others were rushed to hospital after their packages began to leak.

Black women and the police

The experience that black women have of policing is quite often bound up with Britain's immigration and nationality laws. These laws have undergone considerable refinement and expansion in the post-war period but, as Paul Gordon (1985) argued, they have not been concerned simply with controlling who has right of entry to Britain: 'Immigration control has increasingly entailed the growth of controls and surveillance of those [black people] already here.' To this end the police and immigration services have been given ever-increasing resources, both in terms of personnel and technology, and these have resulted in the police stopping and questioning black people about their nationality, as well as conducting controversial passport raids on black communities.

Gordon argues that all black people are seen as immigrants. A typical authoritative view, he says, is summed up in the comment 'the only way to tell an illegal black from a legal one is to suspect the lot'. As a result many black people do not report crimes to the police for fear of their complaint being turned into an immigration enquiry. A case reported in *The Guardian* supports this view (17 March 1995). A 29-year-old black man of Nigerian parentage born in the UK went to a police station in South London in July 1993 to report the theft of his fiancée's car radio. He was arrested and detained for more than three hours while police questioned him about his immigration status. Police then took him in handcuffs to his home where he showed them his passport and birth certificate. He was taken back to the police station, fingerprinted and detained for another one and a half hours. He was not believed when he told police officers that he was born in this country. He later sued for false imprisonment, assault and discrimination under the Race Relations Act. He won an undisclosed but 'substantial' out-of-court settlement.

The problem of the use and abuse of immigration powers in relation to black women was also highlighted by a case reported in 'Campaign Against Racism and Fascism' in which an East African woman who stopped to ask a policewoman for directions was held at the police station until her passport could be produced (cited in Chigwada 1986). In another case a black woman was taken to the police station by police officers who had come to her flat to look for her partner. After the police had searched the house and found nothing, they took the woman with them to the police station 'to answer questions about a forged passport'. When she pointed out that the picture on the forgery bore no resemblance to her, the officers said: 'We know you black people, you disguise yourselves.' The police used family responsibilities to force a 'confession' out of her. She was further victimised in that she was not told of her rights and was not seen by a solicitor. On the second day of the hearing the passport charge was dropped (Chigwada-Bailey 1989).

Police and abuse of mental health powers

Section 136 of the Mental Health Act 1983 covers situations where a person's behaviour is causing a nuisance or offence. Incidents leading to the use of the section are usually reported to the police by members of the public and routinely involve minor offences. The provision reads:

> If a constable finds in a public place to which the public have access a person who appears to him to be suffering from mental disorder and to be in immediate need of care or control, the constable may, if he thinks it necessary to do so in the interests of that person or for the protection of other persons, remove that person to a place of safety. Somebody removed under section 136 can be detained at a 'place of safety' for up to 72 hours.

The intention behind the provisions is to ensure that 'mentally disordered' people are examined by a registered medical practitioner and interviewed by an approved social worker so as to make arrangements for their care. The appropriateness of police involvement in medical issues and the use of police vans instead of ambulances has been questioned by organisations such as MIND. The statutory definition of 'place of safety' includes a police station.

However the procedure followed in London – where the section is most frequently used – give the police greater power with which to detain and refer people, as a result of which both men and women tend to be admitted to hospital for three days following police detention, and are rarely assessed by social workers. Studies have shown that young African-Caribbean people born in Britain were admitted at four times the rate for whites (Littlewood and Lipsedge 1979; see also Dunn and Fahy (1990) on differences in admissions between black and white women). Dr S.P. Sashidhartam commented: 'The crisis in British psychiatry is not about large numbers of black people breaking down with any given psychiatric diagnosis, but how such individuals are being inducted into the mental health services and being labelled as having serious mental illness' (*The Guardian*, 4 November 1989).

The possibility that high rates of police admissions may be partly affected by conscious or unconscious racist attitudes has been a cause of concern among psychiatrists. Writing about their clinical experiences in the East End of London, Littlewood and Lipsedge (1979) suggest the police behaved 'in an overtly racist manner as an alternative to arrest, selectively picking out mentally healthy black people and taking them to psychiatric hospitals under Section 136'.

It could be that because cultural difference means that black women tend to speak loudly and gesticulate more frequently, their behaviour can be mis-interpreted as 'crazy' or in need of psychiatric attention. Certainly more women are detained under Section 136 than for criminal charges – this may be instead of being charged, of course – and the loss of rights and ramifications of this are serious. Under Section 136 there is no right to see a solicitor and any children may be taken into the care of the local authority. If employed, an individual's job may also be in jeopardy. Not only that, but if a woman is not diagnosed as in need of hospital treatment but released after the 72 hours allowed by the Act, she has no redress in law unless she can prove that the police acted 'in bad faith or without reasonable care'.

During a series of interviews with black women I found they had extremely negative views about their treatment at the hands of the police. They felt they were viewed as suffering from some kind of paranoia, just because they were black. Lorraine, who was pregnant at the time of her arrest, said:

> The police pushed me about and took me to the police station with my brother's girlfriend, who was also pregnant. While in the police cell, the police went back to my flat, broke the door and searched the flat. There was no need for that…they could have asked me for the keys. They found nothing but took my filofax, babyclothes and photographs. It was wrong for them to do that. I should have been present. I did not know about all this until the next day. They would not treat a pregnant white woman like that. (Chigwada-Bailey 1989, pp.100–101)

Police officers have been known to take no action if the person responds well to them and behaves respectfully. The way a woman is dressed also seems to matter. Police officers in Elaine Player's (1989, p.47) research stated: 'They would be more likely to arrest a woman who behaved aggressively or who was verbally abusive or obstructive than a woman who was trying to be helpful or appeared to regret what she had done.'

The way the police treat and speak to black women may contribute to the way black women respond to them.

Black women and the courts

Historically British law has been made or determined mainly by socially dominant white males, and the great majority of people in senior positions within the judicial institutions are still white men. Apart from setting out criminal offences the law in effect defines acceptable behaviour in areas such as marriage, sexual relations, domestic relationships, care of children, and so on. It sets the parameters of what is 'normal' and 'proper'. This 'man-made' law sets the context within which courts respond to women, and to particular groups of women such as black women, mothers, victims of domestic violence, prostitutes and lesbians. The largely middle- or upper-class judges and magistrates then administer the law. Kennedy (1992) maintains that the law mirrors society and continues to reflect the subordination of women while the construction of defendants as white and British, or perhaps nowadays European, reinforces and perpetuates racism.

There has been no direct focus as yet on black women's experience of sentencing practices. There are certain clues, however, which suggest there is a need for concern. Women in general who, because of their behaviour or lifestyle, or even their dress or hairstyle, do not appear to conform to the stereotypical norm, may receive different sentences from those who do. This also applies to women whose sexuality or racial origins appear to challenge the courts' definition of 'normal' or 'acceptable'. This is supported by Hedderman and Hough's (1994) research which suggests that in general women may receive more lenient sentences than men unless they transgress the boundaries of stereotypical acceptability, when the converse may be true. Black women would be particularly vulnerable to this aspect of discrimination.

Certainly black women are more frequently refused bail than white, and this may partly be because of not having what is perceived to be a stable family background. There appears to be a general assumption that ethnic minority women will 'disappear into their own subculture' which it will then be difficult for the police to penetrate (Chigwada-Bailey 1997). In addition, poverty within the black community often means that it is difficult to obtain financial sureties or a security. Such considerations mean that black women who should be on bail may find it being refused.[3]

Another problem area for black defendants in general is the difficulty in deciding whether to have a white lawyer whom they believe is less likely to lose the sympathy of the court, or a black lawyer who understands their own culture. Black women wanting to change their lawyers may also experience difficulties. In the interviews I conducted with a range of black women it is, of course, difficult to know how much of the dissatisfaction stemmed from the solicitor being unhelpful, and how much was due to disappointment with the outcome of a case, or indeed how much was due to the inherent mistrust between black women and criminal justice agencies.

All the women I spoke to were convinced that judges and magistrates were racist. For example, Edith said: 'I feel you are found guilty the minute they see your colour. I don't think they should go through the procedure of hearing the case when they have made up their minds the minute they saw you.'

Many women talked about judges that were known by the black community to be anti-black. 'I have been in trouble with the law a few times,' said Anthea. 'Where I live every black person knows about this judge in the Crown Court. He is definitely anti-black and dishes out long sentences to blacks.'

During an interview Judge Pickles tried to put the other perspective: 'A Rastafarian standing in front of you with dreadlocks can look rather intimidating,' he said. 'If we could understand their minds better, we might be able to better understand what they are doing and why they are doing it. There is no deliberate racism but there may be unconscious bias because we don't know enough about the people' (*The Voice*, 11 September 1990).

All the women interviewed felt aggrieved and were dissatisfied with the sentences they were given. After discussing them with other women in prison they realised that white women get shorter sentences compared to black. This remark from Dawn summarises the feelings of many of them:

> Courts are not fair. I had one and a half kilo of cocaine and was given ten years and have done four years so far. Since I have been in prison I have found that some white women, although they had more cocaine on them, got lesser sentences. One white woman here had six kilos and was given five years. I feel it's unfair as it's my first offence.

It is difficult to say how much of this apparent disparity in sentencing was due to legitimate considerations – such as the seriousness of the offence, the offender's past criminal record and the exact circumstances of the offence – and how much was due to extra legal variables like being black, being a woman and being working class.

Black women in prison

Up to a third of women in prison in England and Wales are drug couriers or 'mules' from other countries who will be deported after serving their prison sentence. In addition to the problems usually associated with imprisonment, such women have to face the difficulties of coping with a different culture, with a language they may not speak, or speak very inadequately, with isolation and lack of family contact as well as acute anxiety about the welfare of children who are either in care or in poverty-stricken conditions in their home country.

Some of these women prisoners lack adequate clothing, having been arrested at ports of entry with only one set of clothes and unsuitable shoes. Penny Green notes:

> The vast majority of foreign national couriers arrive in Britain with an expectation of staying only five or so days – they bring enough clothes only for these few days, and if they arrive in summer they have no clothing adequate for the British winters ahead. Those they have with them are then all they have when they find themselves in prison for six to ten years. One Nigerian woman interviewed burst into tears as she lifted her blouse to show she had no underwear at all, her plastic sandals were totally inadequate for the British climate. (Green 1991, p.54)

Discrimination in custody also includes a paucity of basic information in their own language and a lack of even the most basic interpreting services, poor catering for special diets and a failure to access education classes because of the cultural problems they present. Many black women are in prison for sentences of less than 12 months. Had they been men, certainly white men, this group of offenders would have been targeted for community service or probation.

All women in prison experience difficulties, but for black women there are additional burdens which they encounter on remand as well as during their sentence and on their release. Many feel acutely the bias with which they are viewed by prison officers. 'We [black women] are…mad and we commit crime and we sponge off the system... Black women are not even allowed the patronising treatment of being seen as "fragile little creatures" that must be protected. We are supposed to be able to cope in whatever situations arise' (Black Women in Prison 1985). In prison black women are often viewed as so violent they have to be dealt with by male officers (Chigwada-Bailey 1997).

The *Race Relations Manual* for prison officers states that racist behaviour or abuse is a serious, disciplinary matter. Launching the manual in 1991, Angela Rumbold, Home Office minister with responsibility for prisons, said:

> We all know that discrimination does still occur in our prisons, against
> both prisoners and staff. Some is overt, perhaps racial abuse of prisoners or
> harassment of ethnic minority officers. While some is unintentional, like
> stereotyping which leads to false assumptions about a person's behav-
> iour...I...firmly believe that prisoners...regardless of colour, race or
> religion, should be treated with equality, humanity and respect. (NACRO
> 1991)

The minister emphasised race and colour without mentioning gender, as if
racial discrimination is not sometimes, as argued throughout this chapter,
likened to gender or class discrimination. To this list of discrimination, must
be added yet another – religious discrimination – since the Home Office has
consistently refused to recognise Rastafarianism as a religion; thus adding to
the institutionalised discrimination already experienced by black women
Rastafarians.

Genders and Player (1989) found that the prevailing perception among
most prison officers was that Asians are 'clean' and 'hardworking' and 'no
trouble' while blacks are 'arrogant', 'hostile to authority' and have 'chips on
their shoulders'. Race relations officers could also experience difficulties
with their colleagues. One was referred to as the 'Sambo Samaritan'.

This experience of multi-faceted discrimination expressed by black
prisoners was confirmed by a report put out by the Oxford University Centre
for Criminological Research which found a wide gap between the actual
number of racial incidents recorded by the prison service, which was low,
and the high number of complaints reported to them. The researchers
concluded that black prisoners were indeed subjected to victimisation by
prisoners and staff, unfairly treated over access to facilities and education,
and subjected to racial abuse, harassment, unfair discipline, bullying and
assault (Genders and Player 1989).

One south east London probation officer noted that although black
women who served long sentences for drug offences were 'almost all
dignified, respectful and unworldly...[they] tend to get all the shit jobs in the
prison, like working in the kitchens from 6.0 am to 5.0 pm, but they don't
complain because it keeps them occupied. They prefer it because they don't
have time to think about their families' (cited in Chigwada-Bailey 1997).

Conclusion

Feminist penologists have rightly been critical of the construction of equality that is inscribed in law and criminal justice, but this does not mean they are opposed to an ideal of equality. The thrust of feminist critique in and beyond criminal justice is that to treat people equally has in the past been taken to mean to treat them the same (see Carlen 1990; Eaton 1986; Hudson 1998). In law, as in other institutions within liberal societies, this means treating women the same as men, and treating black women the same as white women.

According to Hudson (2002), Equality versus Difference has been the big debate among feminist theorists in so-called 'second wave' feminism, and takes as its point of departure the realisation that rights and other bedrock concepts of law are constructed from a male view of the world. The political–legal structure of modern societies is based on a masculine imagery. The cultural complex of which law is part is based on constructions of subjectivity based on masculine philosophies. It is based on masculine desires, masculine imaginings of the life they would lead, and masculine fears about the structures and other subjectivities that are likely to obstruct the fulfilment of their desires and ambitions (see Hudson 2002). Any further gains for women can only be achieved through interposing a feminine imagery, which can develop its own ideas about the rights, freedoms, rules and protections women need to fulfil their hopes and to permit their development as free, authentic females (Cornell 1995; Irigaray 1994). The feminine imagery would need to include race and class to represent all women.

The reasonable behaviour, the reasonable person of the law, is not just a male person but a white, middle-class male person, constantly reproduced through legal thinking and legal practice (Lloyd 1994; Naffine 1990). The yardstick for a reasonable woman's behaviour for the court is a white, middle-class female. The reasonable woman yardstick has to be cultural and class sensitive if 'justice' is to prevail. This is about acknowledging other cultures as different, not inferior.

In this chapter I have tried to demonstrate how race, gender and class interlink in a way specific and unique to black women, contributing to their over-representation in prison. Apart from obvious and blatant racism, there is a more insidious and subtle racism that reaches right into the heart of the British criminal justice system. Not only is there a need for black people to be properly represented within the legal profession itself, but the institutional racism that pervades British criminology also needs to be clearly identified and recognised. At the moment nearly all research into the workings of the legal system is done by the Home Office. We need more independent criminologists who can conduct independent research, and we need ethnic criminologists to be included into the mainstream. Unless the criminal justice system is class, race and gender blind, and seen to be so, it will continue to be a tool not for justice but of oppression.

Notes

1   On 30 June 1999, ethnic minority groups made up 25 per cent of the female prison population compared to 18 per cent of the male prison population. Black prisoners (Africans and Caribbeans) comprised 19 per cent of the female prison population (12% males). Africans and Caribbeans make up 2 per cent of the total population of England and Wales. Of those whose nationality was recorded, 15 per cent of female prisoners were foreign nationals compared with 8 per cent men. Using British nationality as a proxy for this, and limiting the comparison to the general population aged between 15 and 64, in 1999 there were proportionately more black and 'Chinese and other' women and proportionately fewer South Asian women in prison than in the general population (Home Office 2000).

2   Dr Kwame McKenzie, speech at Race, Gender Criminal Justice, held at St. Alban's Centre, London, organised by Criminology in the New Millenium on 25 October 2001.

3   Dr McKenzie (2001) states that 85 per cent of the Caribbean population in the UK has less than £1000 saved.

References

Adler, F. (1975) *Sisters in Crime*. New York: McGraw-Hill.
Anderson, M.L. and Collins, P.H. (1995) *Race, Class & Gender*, 2nd edn. Belmont, CA: Wandsworth.
Bernard, C. (1995) 'Childhood sexual abuse: The implications for black mothers.' *Rights of Women Bulletin*, winter.

Black Women in Prison (1985) *Black Female Prisoners and Political Awareness.* London: Black Women in Prison.

Bowling, B. and Phillips, C. (2002) *Racism, Crime and Justice.* London: Longman.

Carlen, P. (1990) *Alternative to Women's Imprisonment.* Milton Keynes: Open University Press.

Chigwada, R. (1986) 'Policing of black women.' In E. Cashmore and E. McLaughlin (eds) *Policing of Black People.* London: Routledge and Kegan Paul.

Chigwada-Bailey, R. (1989) 'Criminalisation and imprisonment of black women.' *Probation Journal 36,* 100.

Chigwada-Bailey, R. (1997) *Black Women's Experiences of Criminal Justice: Discourse on Disadvantage.* Winchester: Waterside Press.

Cornell, D. (1995) *The Imaginary Domain.* London: Routledge.

Daly, K. (1994) *Gender, Crime and Punishment.* New Haven: Yale University Press.

Dunn, J. and Fahy, T.A. (1990) 'Police admissions to psychiatric hospital: Demographic and clinical differences between ethnic groups.' *British Journal of Psychiatry 156,* 373–378.

Eaton, M. (1986) *Justice for Women? Family, Court and Social Control.* Milton Keynes: Open University Press.

Genders, E. and Player, E. (1989) *Race Relations in Prison.* Oxford: Clarendon Press.

Gordon, P. (1985) *Policing Immigration: Britain's Internal Controls.* London: Pluto Press.

Green, P. (ed) (1991) *Drug Couriers.* London: The Howard League for Penal Reform.

Groves, W.B. and Frank, N. (1993) 'The sociology of structured choice.' In G. Newman, M.J. Lynch and D. Galaty (eds) *Discovering Criminology.* New York: Harrow and Heston.

Hedderman, C. and Hough, M. (1994) 'Does the criminal justice system treat men and women differently?' *Research Findings 10.* London: Home Office, Research and Statistics Department.

Home Office (2000) *Statistics on Race and the Criminal Justice System. A Home Office Publication under Section 95 of the Criminal Justice Act 1991.* London: Home Office.

Hudson, B. (1988) 'Content analysis of social enquiry reports written in the borough of Haringey.' Unpublished report, Middlesex Area Probation Service.

Hudson, B. (1998) 'Doing justice to difference.' In A. Ashworth and M. Wasik (eds) *Fundamentals of Sentencing Theory.* Oxford: Clarendon Press.

Hudson, B. (2002) 'Gender issues in penal policy and penal theory.' In P. Carlen (ed) *Women and Punishment: The Struggle for Justice.* Cullompton: Willan.

Irigaray, L. (1994) *Thinking the Difference.* Trans. K. Montin. London: Athlone.

Kennedy, H. (1992) *Eve was Framed.* London: Chatto and Windus.

Leonard, E. (1982) *Women, Crime and Society.* London: Longman.

Lewis, D. (1981) 'Black women offenders and criminal justice: Some theoretical considerations.' In M. Warren (ed) *Comparing Female and Male Offenders.* CA: Sage.

Littlewood, R. and Lipsedge, M. (1979) *Transcultural Psychiatry.* London: Churchill-Livingstone.

Lloyd, G. (1994) *The Man of Reason: 'Male and Female' in Western Philosophy.* London: Methuen.

NACRO (1991) *A Fresh Start for Women Prisoners.* London: NACRO.

NACRO (2001) *Safer Society Magazine,* summer, 13.

Naffine, N. (1990) *Law and the Sexes.* London: Allen and Unwin.

Penal Affairs Consortium (1996) *Race and Criminal Justice.* London: Penal Affairs Consortium.

Player, E. (1989) *Women and Crime in the City.* London: Macmillan.

Quinney, R. (1980) *The Social Reality of Crime.* Boston: Little, Brown.

Reiman, J. (1979) *The Rich Get Richer and the Poor Get Prison.* New York: Wiley.

Rice, M. (1990) 'Challenging orthodoxies in feminist theory: A black feminist critique.' In L. Gelsthorpe and A. Morris (eds) *Feminist Perspectives in Criminology.* Milton Keynes: Open University Press.

Runnymede's Quarterly Bulletin (2001), December.

Runnymede's Quarterly Bulletin (2002), March.

Simon, R. J. (1975) *Women and Crime.* Boston, MA: Lexington

Social Exclusion Unit (1998) *Reducing Re-offending by Ex-prisoners.* London: HMSO.

Spelman, E. (1988) *Inessential Women.* Boston, MA: Beacon Press.

Visher, C. (1983) 'Gender, police arrest decisions and notions of chivalry.' *Criminology 21,* 5–27.

Zedner, L. (1991) *Women, Crime and Custody in Victorian England.* Oxford: Clarendon Press.

PART III

Contemporary Issues

CHAPTER 10

Risk, Dangerousness and Female Offenders

Hazel Kemshall

Introduction

Risk has become the core business of criminal justice agencies (Kemshall 1995, 1998). This is exemplified by policy and legal developments across the UK in which public protection, victim and community safety and the identification of high-risk offenders are central features. In England and Wales the 1990s saw the rapid development of penal policies to identify and regulate those offenders deemed to present 'a significant risk of harm to the public' (Wasik and Taylor 1991, p.21), defined by legislation as sexual and violent offenders (Criminal Justice Act 1991, Criminal Justice and Court Services Act 2000). In Scotland similar concerns were raised about serious sexual and violent offenders (Scottish Office 1997), with the MacLean report recommending that 'high risk' should mean those offenders whose 'offence(s) or antecedents or personal characteristics indicate that they are likely to present particularly high risks to the safety of the public' (MacLean 2000, p.4). MacLean accepted the 'underlying supposition...that something special may need to be done for this group' (p.4) above what is already available in the criminal justice system. The report subsequently recommended 'An Order for Lifelong Restriction' (OLR) be introduced for such offenders, including mentally disordered offenders and those with a personality disorder, and supervision and management plans should be in place for each OLR.

Such policies were steeped in a climate of public and governmental concern about risk, particularly sex offender and paedophile risks (Nash 1999), and various instances where violent offenders released into the community had committed grave crimes (for example, the case of Michael Stone). The reliable identification of the 'critical few' 'dangerous and potentially dangerous offenders' became a central feature of much criminal justice policy in the decade (Home Office 1996, 1997, 2001) paralleled by attention to the risk of recidivism and the appropriate targeting of effective programmes of intervention (Holt 2000). These trends were reflected in agency policies and practice development, most particularly in the research and development of risk assessment tools. The early part of the decade saw attention almost exclusively focused on the risk of recidivism through various tools to assess 'criminogenic needs' (Andrews 1995; Andrews and Bonta 1995), with rather less attention to the more unpredictable dangerous offender (Kemshall 1998). This resulted in a twin-track approach to offender risk, and on occasion an unhelpful conflation of recidivism and danger (Kemshall 1998).

Risk assessment tools have reflected this twin concern with recidivism and the identification of those offenders most likely to commit acts of serious harm to the public. Tools have predominantly been of two types: statistically based actuarial tools such as the Offender Group Reconviction Score (OGRS) and Offender Assessment System (OASys) that generate probability scores of reoffending; and structured clinically based tools that provide an assessment of individual criminogenic needs, in essence a risk profile of the individual based upon an inventory of those factors most associated with reconviction. Whilst reasonably successful in the area of recidivism (Lloyd, Mair and Hough 1994), the transfer of such tools to those offenders who pose a significant risk of harm has been less successful (Kemshall 2001), not least because actuarial risk prediction is less accurate where base rate behaviours are low (Monahan 1981). The more infrequent a behaviour in the population at large, the more difficult it is to predict accurately (Monahan 1981). This problem is exacerbated where such acts are committed by particular sections of the population such as ethnic minorities or women. The central principle of the actuarial method is a comparison of the similarities of an individual's profile to the aggregated knowledge of past events. This can however result in a 'statistical fallacy' (Dingwall 1970) where the aggregated properties of a general category are incorrectly attributed to the individual. In a review of various prediction studies Grubin and Wingate (1996) identified that factors from one specific population do not necessarily transfer to another. Whilst risk tools have traditionally been presented as value neutral (for example, OGRS), actuarial predictors have been derived from retrospective studies of the recidivist risks of male prisoners or parolees (Copas, Ditchfield and Marshall 1994), and meta-analyses of largely male reconviction studies (McGuire 1997). As such their roots in male patterns and profiles of offending have been seen as a key problem in their application to the distinctive nature of female offending (Shaw and Hannah-Moffat 2001), and particularly in the assessment of female violence (Rumgay 1999) and sexual offending (Grubin 1998). Their transferability and predictive utility in work with female offenders have been increasingly challenged (Shaw and Hannah-Moffat 2001; Worrall 2001).

The discovery of female 'criminogenic needs'

The significant differences between male and female offending have been extensively reviewed (Gelsthorpe 1999; Hedderman, Chapter 4 this volume; Worrall 1990, 1997) and will only be briefly revisited here. The key differences have been presented as length and type of criminal career (women's are shorter and less serious); female offending is less extensive than male offending; and women's offending is largely acquisitive and rooted in their financial difficulties (Carlen 1988). The overall differences have been attributed to structural inequalities in the labour market and income; differing attitudes to criminal activity; differing opportunities to offend between men and women (particularly young men and women); and different societal expectations of men and women (Gelsthorpe 1999; Heidensohn 1996; Kemshall and Wright 1995). Female offending has been less extensively studied than male offending, and as a consequence there is less research on female risk taking, risk factors and risk profiles.

The increased attention to female offending from the late 1980s onwards by both academics and practitioners (Hedderman and Hough 1994; Kennedy 1992; Rumgay 1996; Worrall 1990) led to a focus upon the most relevant provision for female offenders (Kemshall and Wright 1995), particularly alternatives to custody (Worrall 1989), and examination of the context and reasons for female offending (Worrall 1990). This work included the application of feminist theory to work with female offenders (for example, in group work, Donnelly 1986); work by practitioners to make community sentences more relevant to female offending patterns and needs (Hay and Stirling 1998; Kemshall and Wright 1995); and more recently attention to the distinctive nature of women's criminogenic needs (Clarke and Howden-Windell 2001; see also Chapter 11 this volume), in order to produce risk of recidivism tools valid for female offenders (Bonta, Pang and Wallace-Capretta 1995). Such needs are not seen as exhaustive, but rather are limited to those deemed to have a direct connection to offending behaviour (Aubrey and Hough 1997), and other 'social' and 'welfare needs' are delegitimated (Kemshall 1998).

However, the trend to develop risk tools and inventories of criminogenic needs for women has attracted criticism (Rumgay 1996; Shaw and Hannah-Moffat 2001; Worrall 2001). Rumgay, for example, bases her reservations upon extensive 'research findings for which there is agreement across a range of studies' (p.105) completed in the Anglophone countries. From this extensive database she identifies key reasons for rejecting the male-oriented approach to risk and criminogenic needs in favour of a needs-led approach to women offenders. In brief these are as follows:

1   Women have less involvement in the criminal justice system; hence the use of previous convictions as a major predictor of recidivism is partially hindered.

2   Women are less involved in serious and violent crime. For example, women are responsible for very few homicides, and even where percentage increases in female violent crime are recorded these 'big percentage changes are produced from very small numerical increases' (p.106).

3   Women are not necessarily treated more leniently than men, and sentencers are able to respond to the different criminal histories and offence severity between men and women (p.107).

4   Risk prediction instruments applied to women show poor predictive accuracy and merely adapting male-based tools has not been successful.

5   Women have different pathways into crime from men. Whilst this area has been difficult to investigate and direct correlations difficult to establish, abusive relationships and 'impoverished backgrounds' have been shown to be significant in women's choices and experiences of crime.

6   The contexts of male and female offending are often different, reflecting differential positions in society and structural inequalities of gender.

7   Women's offences frequently have a relational quality; for example, women who commit homicide are more likely to kill a partner or other family member. In accounting for their acquisitive crime women are more likely to cite family responsibilities and financial hardship (summarised from Rumgay 1996, pp.105–110).

Rumgay concludes by arguing for a needs-based approach that acknowledges the links between women's personal histories, problems and offending experience. Worrall (2001) has expressed similar concerns in respect of interventions and sentencing of young girls and has argued that the increasing use of a risk-based approach has resulted in a greater criminalisation of their behaviour. In effect, this has resulted in a recasting of 'troublesome young women' as 'nasty little madams' (p.86), despite the fact that 'the number of female juveniles found guilty or formally cautioned in England and Wales has not risen overall since 1994 (Home Office 2000)' (p.87). She also importantly points out that being young, a member of an ethnic minority and of the so-called 'underclass' are increasingly deployed in the risk demonisation of young women. The co-option of race as a risk marker rather than as an indictor for anti-discriminatory practice has been particularly disappointing (Gottfredson and Jarjoura 2000; Walker-Barnes and Mason 2001).

The 'new penality' of actuarially based justice (Feeley and Simon 1992, 1994) has resulted in a criminal justice preoccupation with classifications and audits of risk (Kemshall *et al.* 1997; Muncie 2000) in which the identification, assessment and categorisation of risk levels are central (Kemshall 1998). Shaw and Hannah-Moffat (2001) have argued that in the rush to implement risk-based classification systems male-based tools have been adopted in an uncritical and gender-neutral way. Based upon an extensive study of the implementation of a universal actuarial tool in Canadian female prisons, they outline key issues in transferring male-based tools to women and ethnic minority offenders. In particular, they take issue with the underpinning assumptions of contemporary risk-based classification systems. For example:

1   The failure of such systems and the risk tools they rely upon to recognise the significance of gender, race and social disadvantage in offending behaviour.

2   The inability of such tools to view problems holistically. Risk inventories tend to direct attention away from the broader societal contexts of offending and pathways into crime. The restriction of such inventories to 'criminogenic needs' and objective facts diminishes the importance of context and situational factors in offending choices and crime causation.

3   Actuarially based risk tools are rooted in particular explanations of crime. Predominantly rooted in psychological and individualising discourses of offending, this results in what Shaw and Hannah-Moffat term a *'disciplinary perspective'* that 'places greater emphasis on individual pathology than on contextual and institutional factors in explaining events or behaviour' (p.169).

4   Risk tools provide a veneer of objectivity that hides the 'multiple judgements made by classification officers' (p.168), thus eroding reflective anti-discriminatory practice and significant attention to diversity and difference (summarised from Shaw and Hannah-Moffat 2001, pp.168–170).

The attention to 'criminogenic needs' and risk factors for both men and women has transformed the subject into an actor in need of 'moral re-socialisation' (Cruickshank 1996; Rose 1996). Rose (1996, 2000) has labelled this 'responsibilisation', a technique of managing society not through overt state control and regulation but through the self-management of individuals. The individual must govern his or herself, assess and manage his or her own risks, and in the case of offenders learn and deploy techniques of self-risk management (Bush 1995; Kemshall 2002). Whilst problematic for all offenders for whom the choice, resources and opportunity to self-govern may be limited (Kemshall 2002), the implications for women offenders may be particularly severe. As Shaw and Hannah-Moffat (2001) express it, women have long been subject to social over-regulation, and techniques that increase this whilst also increasing a blaming attitude to 'self-induced' risk factors are unwelcome. As Hannah-Moffat puts it: 'risk technologies are part of a wider programme of neo-liberal governance that seeks to discipline and responsibilize the female offender' (1999, p.88).

'Dangerous' women

Within a criminal justice system framed largely in actuarial terms, 'needs' have been increasingly transformed into 'risk markers' (Hannah-Moffat 1999). Paralleling concerns with criminogenic needs and the prediction of recidivism has been attention to 'dangerousness' and the accurate identification of those offenders most likely to commit acts of serious harm to the public (Kemshall 1998). The usefulness of the term 'dangerousness' has been doubted (Brooks 1984), and most recent tools have tended to focus on those behaviours and circumstances most likely to contribute to a 'risk of harm' (OASys tool). The desire accurately to identify 'dangerous offenders', particularly for more intrusive community measures and preventative sentencing, has preoccupied numerous researchers and the varying tools in use in Anglophone countries are reviewed in Kemshall (2001). Almost exclusively the tools have been derived from research with male (usually white) offenders and transference to use with women, young offenders and ethnic minorities has been prone to similar problems as those encountered by risk of recidivism tools (Kemshall 2001). As Rumgay puts it, despite the curiosity value of one-off cases of female violence and the percentage increases in female violent offending, serious violent offending by women is rare (1999). Scarcity of a phenomenon within the population as a whole makes its accurate prediction by actuarial methods extremely difficult (Monahan 1981), and this is particularly acute for female sexual and violent offending.

Risk factors can however be identified and the knowledge base upon which assessments can be based is growing (Rumgay 1999). Three key areas can be discerned in the research literature:

- risk factors for female violent offending
- risk factors for female sexual offending
- risk factors for women who kill.

Risk factors for female violent offending

> There are more girls in gangs, more girls in the drugs trade, more girls carrying guns and knives, more girls in trouble...They are more violent, they get angry quicker, they are trying to prove they are just as tough as the boys... I'm noting more girls on the corner with the drugs trade than a year ago. They are more physical than girls used to be. (*New York Times*, 25 November 1995, cited in Maher and Curtis 1995, p.148)

This quote illustrates both the 'discovery' of female violence and the accompanying media and moral panic that tends to follow. 'Girl gangs' and the spectre of the 'girl gangsta' are cases in point with amplification of both risk perceptions and responses (Worrall 2001). As Rumgay puts it: 'the periodic "discovery" of a new generation of violent women is greeted with a curious excitement' (1999, p.106), although the extent to which female violent offending has actually increased continues to be a matter of extensive academic debate (Fitzroy 2001; Maher and Curtis 1995; Shaw 1999; see also Chapters 2 and 4 this volume). Within both the research literature and subsequent policy and practice two responses to female violence can be discerned: either a trend towards their 'masculinisation' and demonisation or attempts to render women pathetic, helpless and thereby harmless (Maher and Curtis 1995). Such explanations are largely the product of overly individualised analyses of female violence and risk tools uncritically transferred from male offenders. Simplistically violent women are portrayed as 'aping men' (Adler 1975), for example, girl gangs, or as the victimised and unwilling accomplices of male perpetrators (Felson 1997a, 1997b). Whilst there may be some merit in such explanations, Maher and Curtis importantly remind us that female violence also needs to be located in the 'violent, social, economic and cultural contexts within which women live and work' (1995, p.147). This would require risk assessment to pay attention to a 'contextual examination of women's violence', to locale and immediate environment, and to social forces as well as individual pathology. In such analyses restricted economic opportunities and race would play a more significant role (Acker 1988; Carlen 1988; Goldberg and Kremen 1987; Sommers and Baskin 1991).

The importance of immediate locale, networks and relational factors is also supported by research evidence on female homicide and serious assaults. Sexual partners and children under one year of age are most likely to be the victims of female homicide (Kruttschnitt 1993), and women are unlikely to harm people with whom they do not have an interpersonal relationship (Felson 1997a). Attacks on non-familial members are most often associated with impoverished urban areas in which women are overly exposed to violent situations (Baskin and Sommers 1998) or where women resolve threats to themselves violently (Maher and Curtis 1995). Baskin and Sommers (1998) have seen these factors as particularly relevant to the high homicide rates amongst black women in America. Stressful and impoverished environments (although not exclusively so) are also indicated in female homicides of their children, along with early motherhood, social isolation and 'poor' parenting skills (Mann 1996).

Violent women are perhaps more easily characterised by their social and economic location in situations of disadvantage, stress and exposure to routine violence (Baskin and Sommers 1998), rather than by any increased masculinisation of their offending or by being cast as pathetic victims of violent men. Based upon an extensive literature review Rumgay concludes:

> The conditions in which women engage in serious violence thus appear to be extreme. Female violence emerges within a context of familiarity with violence as witness and/or victim. It is often a response to strong, fre-

quently repeated provocation that threatens personal safety. Attacks on weaker victims, particularly children, reflect profound and multiple psychological, social and economic difficulties. Where female violence reflects a lifestyle choice, that choice is made in the context of deep and chronic social and personal disadvantage. (Rumgay 1999, p.119)

This strongly suggests that risk assessment needs to incorporate knowledge of such extreme social, cultural and economic conditions for women as well as attention to individual pathologies.

Risk factors for female sexual offending

Women who abuse children are rare (Adshead, Howett and Mason 1994) although between 50 and 100 women each year are convicted of sexual offences against children in England and Wales. This rarity has resulted in lack of knowledge about female sexual offending (especially against children) and the inappropriate imposition of male models of sex offending. Lack of aggression and the absence of fantasy have been seen as key factors in female sexual offending (Adshead *et al.* 1994). Female sexual murderers such as Rosemary West are extremely rare (only a handful have ever come to notice), a factor attributed by most feminist theorists of sexual crime to the location of female sexual offending within a system of patriarchy (Cameron 1999). At its crudest this results in analyses of female sexual offending as an 'appendage' of male offending (e.g. 'The Wests'), and the assertion that more men than women abuse simply 'because they can' (Cameron 1999, p.79). As Cameron puts it, there is no 'equal opportunity in sex murder' (p.79), nor does sexual liberation and feminism necessarily mean that there will be more Rosemary Wests. Rather, for Cameron, it merely indicates that male sexual violence and the relative lack of female sexual violence are rooted within an established gender hierarchy of patriarchy. Patriarchy can however be transcended not just by re-enacting abuse or adopting violence as a coping mechanism, but by becoming a 'survivor' and a 'resister'.

In a comparative study of male and female sexual abusers of children Allen (1991) found that although similar in some respects there are important distinguishing factors between male and female offenders. Women abusers were more likely to have been the victims of familial abuse themselves (including sexual victimisation); to come from 'unstable' homes; to be more sexually active than their partners; and to have a higher need for sexual and emotional fulfilment. The study also noted that female sex offenders may experience harsher spousal relationships and that the female respondents had committed spousal violence at almost every level of severity. The study also notes that female offenders tend to abuse or be abused by men, and male offenders tend to abuse or be abused by women.

Female abusers also have higher levels of denial for their actions and higher levels of resistance to investigative procedures, although the impact of this on accurately determining prevalence rates is not clear. Issues of prevalence, incidence and hence risk levels are also obscured by societal factors such as gender stereotyping and the 'myth of motherhood', with the result that we are 'reluctant to face any challenges to our socially constructed notions of the maternal and the feminine' (Crawford and Conn 1997, p.280). Abuse is then simplistically reconstructed as a 'perversion of the maternal instinct' (Welldon and Seamark 1996, p.40), rather than more adequately located in an understanding of female abuse as an expression of female 'domestic power' (p.47).

Peluso and Putnam (1996) argue that traditional interviewing techniques and a reluctance to believe children, especially boys, helps to hide the relative commonality of unwanted adult female sexual contact directed at young boys. The 'idealization of women' and attendant cultural myths also inhibit recognition of the female sexual abuse of children (Hetherton 1999). Workers are not immune from these processes and risk assessments are therefore skewed, with victims paying the price. Hetherton urges workers to suspend their inappropriate belief that women do not harm children.

Grubin (1992) argues that there is a need for reliable statistics on the incidence of sexual offending, both within and across countries, so that comparisons can be made both transnationally and also across time. He argues that this would enable key questions about the impact of changes in the role of women in society, media portrayals of sexual and violent behaviour and cultural changes towards violence to be explored. Certainly the 'ultimate taboo' of women who sexually abuse children (including their own) has been broken (Wolfers 1993), and increased research knowledge has debunked the myth of the female child sexual abuser as a 'psychotic, drunken, drugged, or intensely promiscuous woman' (Hanks and Saradjian 1992, p.vii). Whilst Faller (1987) found from a very small sample (40 respondents) that women abusers were characterised by marked difficulties in psychological and social functioning, and mental ill health, Hanks and Saradjian suggest that other typologies are more useful. They argue that there are two main groups of female abusers: those who abuse children alone, and those who abuse children in conjunction with others. These can be subdivided further into women who abuse their own children, women abusing in conjunction with men, women abusing as part of a married couple, women abusing as part of a lesbian couple, women abusing children with learning difficulties, and women who abuse male and female adolescents (Hanks and Saradjian 1992, p.vii). Hanks and Saradjian contend that three common strands link all these groups:

- almost all were sexually abused as children

- other forms of maltreatment, particularly emotional abuse are present

- mothers who abuse their own children commonly see the child as an extension of themselves (Hanks and Saradjian 1992, p.viii).

Saradjian (1996) argues that assessments of female abusers must be rooted in a sound body of knowledge and focus on risk, especially the risk of reoffending, and establish an effective therapeutic working relationship in order to deliver work that will reduce that risk. The lack of an extensive knowledge base on the aetiology of female sexual offending inhibits reliable actuarial risk prediction, but Saradjian argues that sufficient information can be collected to identify those behaviours and attitudes which are likely to result in significant harm for a child, and indicate specific factors that can increase or decrease the risks in that individual case. In essence, the production is recommended of an in-depth and practically useful clinical assessment for individual case management, rather than an actuarial risk prediction for a generic offence type.

Women who kill

Female homicide is rare. Hence it has been difficult to establish an aetiology of female homicide and lethal violence. However, some key characteristics have been established: women are more likely to kill people they know and within this more often to kill sexual partners and their own children under one year of age; such homicides are 'expressive' rather than 'instrumental' in nature; and the context of 'love triangles' is important with 'females murdering their partners and males murdering their rivals' (Felson 1997a, p.148). Female serial killing is even rarer, although the recent cases of Beverly Allitt and Rosemary West in the UK have raised uncomfortable issues for societal recognition and acceptance that such 'female monsters' may be in our midst (Cameron 1999). Relatively little is known about this small group, although key features revealed by a cross-national study are that they are 'place-specific killers' operating mainly at home or in healthcare settings (Wilson and Hilton 1998), using low profile modus operandi such as drug overdoses and poisoning.

Whilst comparisons by gender have increased, there has been less attention to comparisons by race. Jones and McJetters (1999) found that 'the causes of homicidal behaviour for White and Black women may differ significantly' (p.125) and point to class as well as race as significant in producing differential causes and motivations. Black women are more likely to be poor and to murder for money. For Jones and McJetters this means paying attention to race as well as gender-specific at-risk populations, both in terms of assessment and intervention programmes.

Women who commit filicide are largely characterised by experiences of sexual and emotional victimisation, substance abuse of varying degrees, and self-harm such as suicide attempts (Crimmins *et al.* 1997), demonstrating a strong link between self-damage and filicide. However, crude caricatures around 'mad or bad' are unhelpful as these divert attention away from the important processes, traumas and dilemmas that underpin these complex acts (Crimmins *et al.* 1997; Wilczynski 1991, 1997). In-depth qualitative studies and use of self-accounting from women (Crimmins *et al.* 1997; Wilczynski 1997) indicate that women are cumulatively exposed to stressful environments and cumulative social risk factors linked to their gender role, and high social expectations associated with motherhood often exacerbated by single parenthood. However, sentencing tends to medicalise these problems rather than locate them within gendered social and economic conditions, hence psychiatrically driven defences and disposals. As

Crimmins *et al.* put it: 'Low self-esteem, reliance upon a dysfunctional partner, and feelings of worthlessness characterised these women to the extent that their judgement about safety for themselves and their children was impaired' (p.55).

Risk, prediction and dangerousness

Some concluding remarks about female offenders

The recognition of risk and danger is always aided by the luxury of hindsight. Hence the risk factors for the serial killer Beverly Allitt seem extremely compelling with the benefit of hindsight knowledge (Welldon and Seamark 1996). However, risk prediction remains a risky business, with many tools operating at little better than chance (Moore 1996), applying inventories of statistically generated risk factors to individuals who are often more distinguished by their uniqueness than by their similarity (Dingwall 1970). Women offenders, particularly those committing the most dangerous and harmful crimes, remain relatively rare and as such the transference of male-based actuarial tools is inappropriate. Rather than continue to pursue the inappropriate amendment of such tools to risk prediction with women, perhaps the research and practice agenda should focus upon extending our understanding of the specific conditions, circumstances and characteristics of female violent and sexual offending so that we can better identify and respond to those risk circumstances that indicate likely dangerous behaviour.

Acknowledgement

My thanks to Joe Yates who carried out the literature search for this chapter. However, the views expressed are entirely my responsibility.

References

Acker, J. (1988) 'Class, gender and the relations of distribution.' *Signs: Journal of Women in Culture and Society 13*, 473–497.

Adler, F. (1975) *Sisters in Crime: The Rise of the New Female Criminal.* New York: McGraw-Hill.

Adshead, G., Howett, M. and Mason, F. (1994) 'Women who sexually abuse children: The undiscovered country.' *Journal of Sexual Aggression 1*, 1, 45–56.

Allen, C.M. (1991) *Women and Men Who Sexually Abuse Children: A Comparative Analysis.* Brandon, VT: Safer Society Press.

Andrews, D. (1995) 'The psychology of criminal conduct and effective treatment.' In J. McGuire (ed) *What Works: Reducing Reoffending, Guidelines from Research and Practice.* Chichester: Wiley.

Andrews, D. and Bonta, J. (1995) *The Level of Supervision Inventory Revised.* Toronto: Multi-Health Systems.

Aubrey, R. and Hough, M. (1997) *Assessing Offenders' Needs: Assessment Scales for the Probation Service. A Report for the Home Office Research and Statistics Directorate.* London: Home Office.

Baskin, D.R. and Sommers, I.B. (1998) *Casualties of Community Disorder: Women's Careers in Violent Crime.* Boulder, CO: Westview Press.

Bonta, J., Pang, B. and Wallace-Capretta, S. (1995) 'Predictors of recidivism among incarcerated female offenders.' *The Prison Journal 75*, 277–294.

Brooks, A.D. (1984) 'Defining dangerousness of the mentally ill: involuntary commitment.' In M. Craft and A. Craft (eds) *Mentally Abnormal Offenders.* London: Ballière Tindall.

Bush, J. (1995) 'Teaching self-risk management to violent offenders.' In J. McGuire (ed) *What Works: Reducing Reoffending, Guidelines from Research and Practice.* Chichester: Wiley.

Cameron, D. (1999) 'Rosemary West: Motives and meanings.' *Journal of Sexual Aggression 4*, 2, 68–80.

Carlen, P. (1988) *Women, Crime and Poverty.* Milton Keynes: Open University Press.

Clarke, D. and Howden-Windell, J. (2001) 'A retrospective study of criminogenic factors in the female prison population.' Internal Home Office report, March 2000.

Copas, J., Ditchfield, J. and Marshall, P. (1994) 'Development of a new reconviction score.' *Research Bulletin 36*, London: HMSO.

Crawford, C. and Conn, L. (1997) 'Female sexual abuse: Unrecognised abuse and ignored victims.' *Journal of the British Association for Counselling 1*, 278–280.

Crimmins, S., Langley, S., Brownstein, H. and Spunt, B.J. (1997) 'Convicted women who have killed children: A self-psychology perspective.' *Journal of Interpersonal Violence 12*, 41–59.

Cruickshank, B. (1996) 'Revolutions within: Self-government and self-esteem.' In A. Barry, T. Osborne and N. Rose (eds) *Foucault and Political Reason.* London: UCL Press, pp.231–252.

Dingwall, R. (1970) 'Some problems about predicting child abuse and neglect.' In O. Stevenson (ed) *Child Abuse: Public Policy and Professional Practice.* Hemel Hempstead: Harvester Wheatsheaf.

Donnelly, A. (1986) *Feminist Social Work with a Women's Group.* Norwich: University of East Anglia monograph.

Faller, K.C. (1987) 'Women who sexually abuse children.' *Violence and Victims 2*, 4, 263–276.

Feeley, M. and Simon, J. (1992) 'The new penology: Notes on the emerging strategy of corrections.' *Criminology 30*, 4, 449–475.

Feeley, M. and Simon, J. (1994) 'Actuarial justice: The emerging new criminal law.' In D. Nelken (ed) *The Futures of Criminology.* London: Sage.

Felson, R.B. (1997a) 'Anger, aggression and violence in love triangle.' *Violence and Victims 12*, 4, 345–362.

Felson, R.B. (1997b) 'Routine activities and involvement in violence as actor, witness or target.' *Violence and Victims 12*, 3, 209–221.

Fitzroy, L. (2001) 'Violent women: Questions for feminist theory, practice and policy.' *Critical Social Policy 21*, 1, 7–34.

Gelsthorpe, L. (1999) *Review of Theory in Hereford and Worcester Probation Service. Programme for Women Offenders: Theory Manual.* Version 7, unpublished.

Goldberg, G.S. and Kremen, E. (1987) 'The feminization of poverty: Only in America?' *Social Policy 17*, 3–14.

Gottfredson, S.D. and Jarjoura, G.R. (2000) 'Race, gender, and guidelines based decision making.' *Journal of Research in Crime and Delinquency 33*, 1, 49–69.

Grubin, D. (1992) 'Sexual offending: a cross-cultural comparison.' *Annual Review of Sex Research 3*, 202–217.

Grubin, D. (1998) *Sex Offending Against Children: Understanding the Risk.* Home Office Police Research Paper no. 99. London: Home Office.

Grubin, D. and Wingate, S. (1996) 'Sexual offence recidivism: Prediction versus understanding.' *Criminal Behaviour and Mental Health 6*, 349–359.

Hanks, H. and Saradjian, J. (1992) 'The female abuser.' *Community Care*, 25 June.

Hannah-Moffat, K. (1999) 'Moral agent or actuarial subject.' *Theoretical Criminology 3*, 1, 71–94.

Hay, A. and Stirling, A. (1998) 'Women need women.' *Probation Journal 45*, 1, 36–38.

Hedderman, C. and Hough, M. (1994) *Does the Criminal Justice System Treat Men and Women Differently?* Home Office Research Findings no. 10. London: HMSO.

Heidensohn, F. (1996) *Women and Crime.* Basingstoke: Macmillan.

Hetherton, J. (1999) 'The idealization of women: Its role in the minimization of child sexual abuse by females.' *Child Abuse and Neglect 23*, 2, 161–174.

Holt, P. (2000) 'Take-up and roll-out: Contexts and issues in the implementation of effective practice in the Probation Service.' Community and Criminal Justice Monograph no. 1. Leicester: DeMontfort University.

Home Office (1996) *Protecting the Public: The Government's Strategy on Crime in England and Wales.* London: HMSO.

Home Office (1997) *The Management and Assessment of Risk in the Probation Service (Training Manual).* London: ACOP/Home Office.

Home Office (2000) *Criminal Statistics for England and Wales 1999.* Cm 50. London: The Stationery Office.

Home Office (2001) *Initial Guidance to the Police and Probation Services on Sections 67 and 68 of the Criminal Justice and Court Services Act 2000.* London: Home Office.

Jones, C.B. and McJetters, Y. (1999) 'Gender, race and homicide: A preliminary analysis.' *Western Journal of Black Studies 23,* 2, 119–128.

Kemshall, H. (1995) 'Risk in probation practice: The hazards and dangers of supervision.' *Probation Journal 42,* 2, 67–72.

Kemshall, H. (1998) *Risk in Probation Practice.* Aldershot: Ashgate.

Kemshall, H. (2001) *Risk Assessment and Management of Known Sexual and Violent Offenders: A Review of Current Issues.* Police Research Series Paper no. 140. London: Home Office.

Kemshall, H. (2002) 'Effective practice in probation: An example of "advanced liberal" responsibilisation.' *Howard Journal of Criminal Justice 41,* 1, 41–58.

Kemshall, H. and Wright, L. (1995) 'Service delivery to women offenders: How can we get it right?' *VISTA 1,* 2, 21–30.

Kemshall, H., Parton, N., Walsh, M. and Waterson, J. (1997) 'Concepts of risk in relation to organisational structure and functioning within the personal social services and probation.' *Social Policy and Administration 31,* 3, 213–232.

Kennedy, H. (1992) *Eve was Framed.* London: Chatto and Windus.

Kruttschnitt, C. (1993) 'Violence by and against women: A comparative and cross-national analysis.' *Violence and Victims 8,* 3, 253–270.

Lloyd, C., Mair, G. and Hough, M. (1994) 'Explaining reconviction rates: A critical analysis.' Home Office Research Study no. 136. London: HMSO.

MacLean, (2000) *A Report on the Committee on Serious and Violent Sexual Offenders.* Edinburgh: The Scottish Executive.

McGuire, J. (1997) 'A short introduction to meta-analysis.' *VISTA 2,* 3, 163–176.

Maher, L. and Curtis, R. (1995) 'In search of the female urban "Gangsta": Change, culture, and crack cocaine.' In B.R. Price and N.J. Sokoloff (eds) *The Criminal Justice System and Women: Offenders, Victims, and Workers,* 2nd edn. New York: McGraw-Hill.

Mann, C.R. (1996) *When Women Kill.* Albany: State University of New York Press.

Monahan, J. (1981) *The Clinical Prediction of Violence.* Beverley Hills, CA: Sage.

Moore, B. (1996) *Risk Assessment: A Practitioner's Guide to Predicting Harmful Behaviour.* London: Whiting and Birch.

Muncie, J. (2000) 'Pragmatic realism? Searching for criminology in the new youth justice.' In B. Goldson (ed) *The New Youth Justice.* Lyme Regis: Russell House.

Nash, T. (1999) *Police, Probation and Protecting the Public.* London: Blackstone Press.

OASys (undated) *Offender Assessment System.* London: Home Office.

Peluso, E. and Putnam, N. (1996) 'Case study: Sexual abuse of boys by females.' *Journal of the American Academy of Child and Adolescent Psychiatry 35,* 1, 51–54.

Rose, N. (1996) 'Governing "advanced" liberal democracies.' In A. Barry, T. Osborne and N. Rose (eds) *Foucault and Political Reason.* London: UCL Press, pp.37–64.

Rose, N. (2000) 'Government and control.' *British Journal of Criminology 40*, 321–339.

Rumgay, J. (1996) 'Women offenders: Towards a need-based policy.' *VISTA 2*, 2, 104–115.

Rumgay, J. (1999) 'Violent women: Building knowledge-based intervention strategies.' In H. Kemshall and J. Pritchard (eds) *Good Practice in Working with Violence.* London: Jessica Kingsley Publishers, pp.106–127.

Saradjian, J. (1996) *Women Who Sexually Abuse Children: From Research to Clinical Practice.* Chichester: Wiley.

Scottish Office (1997) *A Commitment to Protect.* Edinburgh: The Scottish Office.

Shaw, M. (1999) '"Knowledge without acknowledgement": Violent women, the prison and the cottage.' *Howard Journal of Criminal Justice 38*, 3, 252–266.

Shaw, M. and Hannah-Moffat, K. (2001) 'Gender, diversity and risk assessment in Canadian corrections.' *Probation Journal 47*, 3, 163–172.

Sommers, I. and Baskin, D. (1991) 'The situational context of violent female offending.' Paper presented at the Annual Meetings, American Society of Criminology, San Francisco, November.

Walker-Barnes, C.J. and Mason, C.A. (2001) 'Perceptions of risk factors for female gang involvement among African American and Hispanic Women.' *Youth and Society 32*, 3, 303–336.

Wasik, M. and Taylor, R. (1991) *Blackstone's Guide to the Criminal Justice Act 1991.* Oxford: Blackwell.

Welldon, E.V. and Seamark, J. (1996) 'Female sex offenders.' *Prison Service Journal 107*, 39–47.

Wilczynski, A. (1991) 'Images of women who kill their infants: The mad and the bad.' *Women and Criminal Justice 2*, 2, 71–80.

Wilczynski, A. (1997) 'Mad or bad? Child-killers, gender and the courts.' *British Journal of Criminology 37*, 3, 419–437.

Wilson, W. and Hilton, T. (1998) 'Modus operandi of female serial killers.' *Psychological Reports 82*, 495–498.

Wolfers, O. (1993) 'The paradox of women who sexually abuse children.' In M. Elliot (ed) *Female Sexual Abuse of Children: The Ultimate Taboo.* Chichester: Wiley.

Worrall, A. (1989) 'Working with female offenders: Beyond "alternatives to custody".' *British Journal of Social Work 19*, 2, 77–94.

Worrall, A. (1990) *Offending Women: Female Lawbreakers and the Criminal Justice System.* London: Routledge.

Worrall, A. (1997) *Punishment in the Community.* Harlow: Longman.

Worrall, A. (2001) 'Girls at risk? Reflections on changing attitudes to young women's offending.' *Probation Journal 48*, 2, 86–92.

CHAPTER 11

The 'Criminogenic' Needs of Women Offenders

Carol Hedderman

Introduction

In the late 1990s, the government in England and Wales began to devise a national curriculum of offending behaviour programmes for those under supervision in the community and in prison. Programmes are usually expected to make use of cognitive behavioural techniques, which assume that working to change offenders' attitudes and understanding has a positive impact on behaviour (McGuire 2000; Vennard, Hedderman and Sugg 1997). They must also be delivered in accordance with 'what works' principles which are said to maximise impact (see Vennard and Hedderman 1998 for a review). They were also expected to focus on a range of 'dynamic criminogenic' factors. These are personal traits or conditions which a range of research studies have concluded are associated with reoffending and which may be subject to change. The usual list (e.g. Home Office 2000a) includes:

- holding antisocial attitudes
- strong ties to and identification with antisocial/criminal models
- weak (pro)social ties and strained family relationships
- displaying high levels of dependency on drugs and alcohol
- having financial difficulties
- unemployment

- low educational attainment

- having poor cognitive skills.

In fact, current evidence (e.g. May 1999) suggests that static factors (age, sex, number of previous convictions, etc.), which cannot be changed by external intervention, are statistically speaking stronger predictors of reconviction than are dynamic ones. Although, as Taylor (1999) points out, criminal history may be a strong predictor of reconviction partly because it acts as a proxy for dynamic factors.

The decision to encourage the use of cognitive behavioural techniques, to abide by 'what works' principles and to focus on dynamic criminogenic factors is said to be 'evidence-based' (Home Office 2000a). What this actually means is that these principles have been derived from meta-analyses (e.g. Andrews *et al.* 1990; Lipsey 1992) of the results of small-scale empirical studies conducted over the last 20 years about the onset, persistence and desistence of criminal offending. Most of these studies have looked exclusively at young male offenders. Few have been methodologically rigorous and nearly all of them have been carried out in the USA or Canada (Vennard and Hedderman 1998). This raises obvious questions about how safe it is to base male offending programmes in the UK on this evidence. Nevertheless, the Accreditation Panel has concluded that 'there is very good evidence about what is effective' (Home Office 2000a, p.4) in relation to men, although it has acknowledged that the evidence in relation to female offending is thin. This chapter first considers the state of research on women offenders. It then explores the question of whether they share men's criminogenic factors or have additional or different needs. It concludes with some initial thoughts about what the results imply about the focus of offending programmes for women.

Research on women offenders

After more than 100 years of disputes about the causes of crime, few would now argue against the idea that it is explained by a mixture of factors. These include: the likelihood of detection and punishment; opportunities to offend; individual disposition; levels of social integration; attitudes and beliefs favourable to offending; levels and efficacy of informal social controls; and extent of antisocial and criminal commitment among family members or associates.

We know from self-report studies that girls and women offend less frequently than boys and men; that the women start offending later and generally desist earlier (Flood-Page *et al.* 2000; Graham and Bowling 1995; Jamieson, McIvor and Murray 1999). We also know from self-report and official statistics that when women do offend they tend to commit acquisitive rather than violent crime (e.g. Jamieson *et al.* 1999). For example, about half of all women as opposed to around a quarter of men commencing probation supervision or received into prison under sentence have been convicted of theft and handling or fraud and forgery (Home Office 2000b, 2001). They also tend to specialise more than men. Whereas women initially convicted of theft who reoffend are also convicted of theft (Mair and May 1997), men tend to be generalists (Farrington 1996).

Gelsthorpe's recent review (1999) concludes, as do previous accounts (e.g. Heidensohn 1996), that the substantial sex differences in offending are related to gender differences in opportunity, upbringing and expectations across our society. However, there is still considerable disagreement about the precise contribution each factor makes and the mechanisms whereby they influence behaviour at the individual level. It is also unclear how far each factor is associated with persistence or desistence as opposed to initially becoming an offender.

Very few studies of women offenders have examined the link between static or dynamic factors and reconviction. For example, less than 2 per cent of the 1606 studies included in the CDATE meta-analysis database involved women offenders.[1] Most of the research that has been conducted about the characteristics of female offenders has tended to use qualitative techniques, so it is not usually possible to say what proportion of women offenders share a characteristic (regardless of whether it is related to reconviction). Part of the explanation for this is that such research tends to be exploratory, but it also reflects the difficulties involved in obtaining large enough samples to sustain quantitative analysis.

The advantage of techniques such as unstructured or semi-structured interviewing is that they capture women's own views about their problems (see, for example, Carlen *et al.* 1985). In other words, they are less likely to falsely restrict the ground an interview covers than a structured interview. To give an obvious example, if women are only asked the same questions as men, information on whether they have the same problems to the same extent may be answered but we will not be able to identify any additional problems they have outside this framework.

Aside from the fact that these studies tell us little about the number or proportion of women offenders who share such characteristics, they also tend to be of little *predictive* value because they do not examine the links between having particular problems and being reconvicted.

Do women share men's criminogenic needs?

In the absence of conclusive evidence about women's dynamic risk factors, it has been assumed that male ones play a large part in explaining female offending too, although the precise mixture might be different and there may be other factors – such as a history of sexual abuse or domestic violence – that are related to offending by women. Only recently have researchers begun to investigate whether this is actually the case, either through primary research or reviews of existing studies.

One of the most recent reviews (Howden-Windell and Clark 1999) examined a selection of the literature to discover whether women did display male dynamic risk factors. It concluded that such factors are relevant for women, although their importance and explanatory value might be different, particularly in the case of educational attainment, substance misuse and criminal associates. However, the authors also considered that there may be *additional* risk factors peculiar to women, but that the research base was not strong enough to be conclusive about precisely what these were. In line with Farrington (1996), they also suggest that different factors may be related to the onset of offending and maintenance and desistence. Moreover, Jamieson *et al.* (1999) suggest that the salience of factors related to onset and desistance is likely to vary with age.

Gelsthorpe's (1999) review took a more wide-ranging approach to the literature to include descriptive studies. Factors which commonly emerged as *characteristics* of women offenders were: having financial problems; high levels of sexual and physical victimisation in childhood and as an adult; relationship problems; mental health issues; childcare problems; and difficulties in being assertive. The difficulty with this type of material is that at least some problems, such as childcare problems experienced by imprisoned women, are as likely to be a consequence as a cause of their offending. Similarly, Howden-Windell and Clark (1999) suggest that the higher levels of mental illness generally observed among female prisoners may be caused by their reaction to incarceration rather than being evidence of a pre-existing condition. Another difficulty is that such studies tend to focus on women in prison, so there is limited understanding of whether the same factors are relevant for women on probation. Under these circumstances it is worth revisiting the literature to examine exactly what evidence does exist about the factors associated with offending by women.

Evidence about women's risk factors

A history of previous offending

A history of previous offending is a good predictor of future offending for women as well as men (Lloyd, Mair and Hough 1994). As for men, age, age at first conviction, number of previous offences, number of custodial sentences served and type of current offence are all significantly related to reconviction (i.e. they are static risk factors). This has recently been confirmed by May's (1999) study of 7000 offenders on community sentences, 10 per cent of whom were women; and Clark and Howden-Windell's (2000) recent records-based study of 215 women released from prison in 1995.

Antisocial attitudes

Women offenders are reconvicted less frequently for less serious offences and their criminal careers are shorter than men's. This might suggest that they generally have less antisocial attitudes. Evidence to support this comes from Barnfield and Tonglet's (2000) recent British self-report study of 304 apprehended shoplifters and 417 shoppers (including current and former thieves). The results indicate that while male and female shoplifters were relatively uncritical of rule breaking in general compared to non-shoplifters, male shoplifters were more likely to indicate that they would shoplift in the future and had to express fewer moral concerns about doing so.

In Mair and May's (1997) study of nearly 2000 offenders on probation, 9 per cent of women compared with 16 per cent of men said they would not reoffend, while 21 per cent said they found probation helpful compared with 15 per cent of men. These somewhat contradictory findings may be a sign that women are not keen to pursue a criminal lifestyle, but believe that they will reoffend given their material circumstances. It also suggests that they may not take full moral responsibility for their offending as they perceive themselves as having little control over their offending or other aspects of their lives (Cook 1997). Support for this idea comes from two recent studies. Barriga *et al.* (1999) found that antisocial behaviour was more common among 192 male and female student subjects who had 'self-serving cognitive distortions' (i.e. rationalising attitudes and beliefs which neutralise empathy such as blaming others or portraying behaviour as a momentary aberration). In the second US-based study, Walters and Elliott (1999) found that efforts to deny the reality of one's negative behaviour and its consequences were strongly associated with recidivism during the first 12 months after release from a state correctional facility for a sample of 118 women. Jamieson *et al.*'s (1999) finding that women who offended were keen to portray themselves as desisting even if they were not – which they attributed to the stigma associated with being a woman who offends – might also be interpreted as supporting this position.

An alternative explanation put forward by Gilligan (1982) is that women in general operate according to a moral code which is contextual and focused around meeting the needs of their families and dependants. In contrast, male standards of morality are more abstract and rule based and, Gilligan argues, these are the ones espoused by wider society and embodied in the criminal law.

In Clark and Howden-Windell's (2000) study of the records of over 200 women released from prison, evidence that they regretted their offences was noted in 54 per cent of cases.[2] There was a difference in reconviction according to whether or not women were recorded as having experienced remorse. Of those who were not reconvicted in two years 68 per cent had the fact that they were remorseful recorded on their file as opposed to only 35 per cent of those who were reconvicted.

Strong ties to and identification with antisocial/criminal models and weak (pro)social ties/strained family relationships

The men and women in Mair and May's probation sample were equally likely (42%) to have family members who had been convicted. Fourteen per cent of both men and women had criminal parents, but women were more likely to have a spouse/partner or child who had also been convicted, whereas men were more likely to have criminal siblings (see also Jamieson *et al.* 1999). Women were less likely to have friends who had been in trouble with the law and those who did know other offenders tended to know fewer of them. Women were also more likely to report that they concealed their offending from their families and when their families did know they were on probation to describe their reaction as 'shocked and disgusted'.

Women and men differed very little in the extent to which they discussed problems with their family or personal problems with a probation supervisor, although women were more likely to describe such conversations as helpful. Given this, it is noteworthy that Clark and Howden-Windell (2000) found that women prisoners who had established good relationships with staff and other inmates were less likely to be reconvicted.

Mair and May found that around 10 per cent of men and women offenders had lived with a foster family and about a fifth had spent time in a residential children's home. Only 4 per cent of the women compared with 14 per cent of men had spent time in a borstal or young offender's unit. Another noteworthy difference was that 28 per cent of the women compared with 20 per cent of the men had been brought up in a one-parent family. Once again, Clark and Howden-Windell's (2000) study is one of the few to have examined the relationship between such factors and reconviction for women. They found that women who came from a 'broken home' were more likely to be reconvicted than other women, but other factors, such as problems with current relationships, were not associated with differences in reconviction.

Dependency on drugs and alcohol

Recent research (Bennett 2000) suggests that drug use among male and female arrestees is comparable but that women had a significantly higher rate of positive tests for opiates. They also reported higher average weekly spending on drugs (£171 vs £123 for males); and 60 per cent of the female users were arrested for acquisitive offending compared to 48 per cent of men. In their research on 205 offenders referred to drug services by criminal justice agencies, Edmunds *et al.* (1999) found that 55 per cent of women said that they funded their habits by shoplifting and 29 per cent committed fraud. Men were just as likely to admit to shoplifting but only mentioned fraud in 11 per cent of cases. They were much more likely to sell drugs (35%) or commit burglary (25%). In a 1997 survey of psychiatric morbidity among prisoners, just over 40 per cent of male and female sentenced prisoners reported a measure of drug dependence in the year before being incarcerated, but a higher proportion of the women were dependent on opiates (Home Office 2001). In Mair and May's (1997) study of offenders on probation, women were less likely overall to take drugs than men, but their use of amphetamines, methadone, heroin and crack cocaine was more comparable. Also, although women probationers were less likely to take drugs than male probationers, they were more likely to take them than men in the general population. Alcohol abuse was lower for women in this study in that they drank less and drank less frequently than men. They were also less likely to report getting drunk or being unable to stop drinking.

May's (1999) research also found that problems with alcohol were less frequent for women than men (see also McIvor and Barry 1998). However, in this study of more than 7000 probation records, drug problems were more common among women. For both sexes, drug abuse was associated significantly with being reconvicted within two years, after factors such as criminal history had been taken into account. Similarly, Clark and Howden-Windell (2000) found that drug abuse was strongly related to two-year reconviction rates for women released from prison but alcohol abuse was not.[3]

Financial difficulties

As noted above, most female offending is acquisitive. It may therefore seem rather obvious to note that their offending is associated with experiencing financial difficulties. In fact, as McGuire (2001) points out, such unidimensional explanations are unlikely to tell the whole story. Even a single offender's motives may change over time. Cook (1997) has suggested that women's offending may occur for a complex set of reasons. These include being an act of desperation, as the product of a woman perceiving herself to be socially excluded or having narrowing options for employment, in response to opportunity, perceiving legitimate avenues to money to be blocked and as a means of asserting economic independence. Nevertheless there is strong evidence that acquisitive offending is fuelled by perceived or actual economic hardship. For example, Moore's (1984) study of 300 US shoplifters found that financial benefit was the main motive for offending in 68 per cent of cases. Two-thirds of the sample (N = 203) were regular shoplifters. Economic disadvantage was a contributing factor in 72 per cent of these cases. Three of the most common reasons given for offending in a study of 1057 mothers in prison were financial (Caddle and Crisp 1997): having no money (54%); needing to support children (38%); having no job (33%). At least two of the other three reasons – drink or drugs (35%), family problems (33%) and mixing with the wrong crowd (46%) – may also have financial aspects. Similarly, in May's (1999) reconviction study, drug misuse was related to unemployment which, he suggests, is consistent with the idea that drug users commit crime to finance their habits. In Morris *et al.*'s (1995) follow-up of 200 women on release from prison, almost half of the 47 who were known to have reoffended said that they were not managing financially compared with a quarter of the others. More than a third said that drug use was a drain on their income compared to 3 per cent of those who were thought not to have reoffended.

Mair and May's (1997) study of offenders serving community sentences also indicated that women were more likely than men to report having financial problems to their supervisors. Financial problems were also associated with being convicted of acquisitive crime or a motoring offence as opposed to personal crimes (sex, violence) or drug offences. Mair and May also suggest that financial hardship is a factor in women's offending in that

41 per cent of women compared to 25 per cent of men said that needing things or money was a key factor in their current offence. The proportion of women who gave this as a reason for their first offence was also higher than the proportion of men. May, Edmunds and Hough (1999, p.4) suggest that other offending by women may have a financial element:

> Viewing sex workers as rational decision-makers in the face of poverty or other forms of social inequality is supported by various studies... Women have been known to enter sex working to earn money for mortgages, or to supplement low incomes, social security benefits or student grants. Women may thus choose to enter sex work as a response to limited conventional opportunities.

Unemployment

While unemployment may be linked to offending because both are associated with having financial difficulties, there is remarkably little robust evidence of a direct relationship between unemployment and offending. Exceptions are Farrington's research (1996) which shows that periods of being unemployed are linked to periods of offending; and May's (1999) work which identified a link between reconviction rates and unemployment. However, the former results were derived from a study of male offenders and in the latter women were less likely to have problems with employment recorded. May suggests that this may because many of the women in his sample were looking after children so that unemployment was not viewed or recorded as a problem.

It is also noteworthy that only 34 per cent of women compared to 59 per cent of men in Mair and May's research described themselves as 'unemployed'. Forty-two per cent of women described their employment status as 'looking after children'. As 32 per cent of the women were also living alone with dependent children compared to only 1 per cent of men, it may be that financial hardship was regarded as a more immediate problem than unemployment for this group. Support for the idea that a lack of money is more important than unemployment for women also comes from Clark and Howden-Windell's (2000) prison-based study, where having previously been in receipt of welfare benefits and being in unskilled employment were both significantly related to reconviction.

In a recent meta-analysis of educational and vocational programmes, Pearson and Lipton (1999) found that job-seeking and job-placement programmes yielded some improvement in employment chances. They suggest that programmes can be made more effective in reducing offending if they are offered as modules in the context of other treatment forms such as a therapeutic community or a cognitive behavioural programme. However, separate results for women offenders were not available and it seems unlikely, given Mair and May's findings, that standard employment programmes designed to encourage offenders into full-time work will be attractive to women offenders or be so effective with them.

Low educational attainment

In Mair and May's (1997) study, 51 per cent of women on probation and 48 per cent of men had left school without qualifications compared to 42 per cent of women in the general population and 34 per cent of men. Howden-Windell and Clark (1999) report that prison service tests conducted in 1997 indicate that women in prison are somewhat more literate than are imprisoned men. They were able to find only one (North American) study which had examined the link between educational qualifications and reconviction for women and this showed no effect. Clark and Howden-Windell's own subsequent study (2000) did find such an association, but the relationship did not reach statistical significance.

It is also worth noting that a CDATE meta-analysis of educational and vocational programmes has concluded that there is as yet no evidence that correctionally based literacy training and GED (high school equivalency degree), vocational training or college course work has any impact on recidivism (rearrest and reconviction). However, of the 1606 studies on the database only 72 covered education and employment and none of them were coded as having a completely satisfactory methodological approach (Pearson and Lipton 1999).

Mental health problems

Mental health and emotional well-being were said to be linked to offending in nearly 70 per cent of pre-sentence reports prepared by Hereford and Worcester Probation Service on a sample of 198 women (reported by Gelsthorpe 1999). However, it should be noted that this includes problems (e.g. unhappiness) which would fall outside clinical definitions of mental illness. Mair and May (1997) found that 17 per cent of men compared to 33 per cent of women in their probation sample reported suffering from a mental disorder or depression for longer than six months.

A number of the studies reviewed by Howden-Windell and Clark (1999) show that women in custody tend to have more mental health problems than incarcerated men. More recent information (Home Office 2001) suggests that twice as many female prisoners (40%) reported receiving help for a mental or emotional problem in the 12 months before being imprisoned. However, it is not clear whether these results reflect sex differences in the incidence of mental illness in the general population, willingness to report such problems or responses to incarceration rather than being an indication of a link between mental illness and offending.

Physical and sexual abuse

While various studies (e.g. Morris *et al.* 1995; Walmsley, Howard and White 1992) have noted that many women in prison have experience of current and previous (physical and sexual) abuse, there is little evidence about the link between this and offending. One the few studies which has examined this (Bonta, Pang and Wallace-Carpetta 1995), indicated that childhood abuse was not predictive of offending, although physical abuse as an adult did seem to be related. Indeed, women with a history of abuse were actually less likely to reoffend. Clark and Howden-Windell's (2000) British study also found no significant relationship between abuse and reconviction. One possible explanation for these findings is simply that women's experience of abuse is generally greater than men's and its incidence among women offenders reflects this. Another could be that childhood abuse is related to onset of offending but not to persistence.

Poor cognitive skills

It has not been possible to trace any evidence on the extent to which women offenders suffer from cognitive skills deficits or how far this is linked to their reconviction. However, the review of other factors above suggests that while women offenders may suffer from cognitive distortions, most of their offending is in some senses a rational response to restricted opportunities, social inequality and poverty. However, their offending is a form of 'bounded rationality' in that while there may be a level at which their offending makes sense to them (e.g. stealing because a benefits cheque has not arrived), this is within a very restricted frame of reference (Carroll and Weaver 1986).

Implications for offending behaviour programmes for women

The small number of women commencing community rehabilitation orders or prison sentences each week (see Chapter 4 of this volume) makes it tempting, on the grounds of both costs and logistics, to suggest that offending programmes for women should be generic. However, running a generic programme for women would run counter to 'what works' principles which require that factors which have contributed to offending should be targeted and interventions tailored to specific levels of risk and need (Vennard *et al.* 1997).

Official statistics show that most offending by women is acquisitive. Financial considerations also play a part in other crimes such as drug dealing and prostitution. Sometimes these financial concerns are exacerbated by bearing sole responsibility for dependent children and/or funding drug dependency. Given this, it seems reasonable to propose that at least one of the first programmes for women should focus on those whose offending is financially motivated.

The limited evidence available suggests that other important 'criminogenic' factors include:

- a distorted or limited appreciation of the negative consequences of offending

- the existence of relationships supportive of antisocial behaviour (including having a partner who is an offender and/or who may coerce a woman to offend through physical violence)
- having no or few qualifications and leaving school early
- drug abuse.

The available evidence suggests that women who commit financially inspired offending have made a 'rational choice' to offend. In other words, they do weigh up the costs and benefits of offending. However, because their decision making reflects their distorted or limited perception of the risks and rewards (Clarke and Homel 1996), this is 'bounded rationality' (Carroll and Weaver 1986). This suggests that offending behaviour work with women should focus less on enhancing cognitive skills and more on challenging cognitive distortions and encouraging longer term planning.

Having sole responsibility for childcare, having a drug habit, being poorly qualified and having a criminal record will almost certainly impose some real limits on women's options for financial security. Any effective programme must therefore increase their options by:

- providing advice on benefits and money management
- increasing access to vocational training by providing childcare facilities and running courses at times which are compatible with school hours and holidays
- encouraging women to consider part-time and home-working opportunties rather than unrealistically pushing them towards full-time jobs.

Some women are concerned to keep their families from knowing about their offending. This suggests that the ways girls are socialised and societal expectations of women's behaviour may work against reconviction. However, the same socialisation process encourages women to feel that they have little control over their lives and actions. They may also have partners who coerce them into offending. In these cases, work with women offenders needs to tackle poor self-esteem and offer assertiveness training to ensure that once women appreciate or extend the range of non-offending options open to them, they feel able to take them.

Although many women offenders do appear to have suffered some form of abuse in childhood and this is sometimes assumed to be a risk factor, the (limited) existing evidence has not shown a relationship with recidivism.[4] This makes it difficult to justify treating abuse as a 'criminogenic' factor but does not mean that it should be ignored. Those running programmes for women should be aware that a history of abuse may be disclosed and should record its existence so that its relationship to reconviction can be tested. Arrangements for referral to an appropriate service should also be in place.

At least some of the women involved in acquisitive crime are supporting expensive drug habits. Clearly they are unlikely to desist unless they are also able to get their drug use under control. A decision about whether this happens as part of a programme or by referral to specialist services depends on better information on prevalence becoming available.

Overall, the available evidence suggests that programmes which focus on male criminogenic factors are unlikely to be as effective in reducing reconviction among women offenders as they are for men. This is not only because they focus on factors which are less relevant to or operate differently for women, but also because they fail to address factors which are unique to, or more relevant for, women who offend.

Notes

1   The Correctional Drug Abuse Treatment Effectiveness Project (CDATE) is funded by The National Institute on Drug Abuse (NIDA) at the National Institutes of Health in New York. The database contains data from evaluation studies conducted between 1968 and 1994. This is used to assess the effects of correctional interventions on various outcome measures (e.g. drug use, recidivism). (See www.preventingcrime.org for further information.)

2   As the authors note, some caution must be exercised in extrapolating from this research, as it was based on official records. Thus, some information, such as whether the offender expressed remorse, may not always have been recorded in every case. On the other hand, there is no obvious reason why there should have been systematic recording bias.

3   The fact that North American researchers (Bonta et al. 1995), who interviewed a sample of Canadian women in prison and examined their reoffending data at three years, found that substance abuse did not predict recidivism is difficult to explain. Possible explanations may include their conflating drug and alcohol

abuse; using a different period and measure of reoffending; and/or the fact that they interviewed inmates (thus obtaining a fuller picture of substance misuse than might be captured in official records).

4   The profile of women offenders suggests that onset, as opposed to persistence, could be related to the absence of significant adults (e.g. being brought up in care). Alternatively, the significant adults to whom the child is attached may not promote prosocial attitudes and behaviour (e.g. parents or older siblings who offend). This remains to be tested empirically.

References

Andrews, D.A., Zinger, I., Hoge, R.D., Bonta, J., Gendreau, P. and Cullen, F.T. (1990) 'Does correctional treatment work? A clinically relevant and psychologically informed meta-analysis.' *Criminology 28*, 369–404.

Barnfield, J. and Tonglet, M. (2000) 'Understanding criminogenic behaviour: How shoplifters shop the store.' Paper presented to the British Criminology Conference, Leicester, July.

Barriga, A.Q., Morrison, E.M., Liau, A.K. and Gibbs, J.C. (1999) 'Explaining the gender difference in externalising behaviour: a moral-cognitive study.' Unpublished 1999.

Bennett, T. (2000) *Drugs and Crime: The Results of the Second Developmental Stage of the NEW-ADAM Programme.* Home Office Research Study no. 205. London: Home Office.

Bonta, J., Pang, B. and Wallace-Capretta, S. (1995) 'Predictors of recidivism among incarcerated female offenders.' *The Prison Journal 75*, 277–294.

Caddle, D. and Crisp, D. (1997) *Imprisoned Women and Mothers.* Home Office Research Study no. 162. London: Home Office.

Carlen, P., Hicks, J., Christina, D. and Tchaikovsky, C. (1985) *Criminal Women: Autobiographical Accounts.* Oxford: Blackwell.

Carroll, J. and Weaver, F. (1986) 'Shoplifters' perceptions of crime opportunities: A process tracing study.' In D.B. Cornish and R.V. Clarke (eds) *The Reasoning Criminal: Rational Choice Perspectives on Offending.* New York: Springer-Verlag.

Clark, D. and Howden-Windell, J. (2000) *A Retrospective Study of Criminogenic Factors in the Female Prison Population.* Internal Home Office report, March.

Clarke, R.V. and Homel, R. (1996) 'A revised classification of situational crime prevention techniques.' In S.P. Lab (ed) *Crime Prevention at the Crossroads.* Cincinnati, OH: Anderson.

Cook, D. (1997) *Poverty, Crime and Punishment.* London: CPAG.

Cornish, D.B. and Clarke, R.V. (eds) (1986) *The Reasoning Criminal.* New York: Springer-Verlag.

Edmunds, M., Hough, M., Turnbull, P.J. and May, T. (1999) *Doing Justice to Treatment: Referring Offenders to Drug Services.* London: Home Office, Drugs Prevention Advisory Service Headquarters.

Farrington, D.P. (1996) 'The explanation and prevention of youthful offending.' In J.D. Hawkins (ed) *Delinquency and Crime: Current Theories.* Cambridge: Cambridge University Press.

Flood-Page, C., Campbell, S., Harrington, V. and Miller, J. (2000) *Youth Crime: Findings from the 1998/99 Youth Lifestyle Survey.* Home Office Research Study no. 209. London: Home Office.

Gelsthorpe, L. (1999) *Review of Theory in Hereford and Worcester Probation Service, Programme for Women Offenders: Theory Manual.* Version 7. Unpublished.

Gilligan, C. (1982) *In a Different Voice.* Cambridge, MA: Harvard University Press.

Graham, J. and Bowling, B. (1995) *Young People and Crime.* Home Office Research Study no. 145. London: Home Office.

Heidensohn, F. (1996) *Women and Crime.* Basingstoke: Macmillan.

Home Office (2000a) *What Works: First Report of the Joint Prison/Probation Accreditation Panel 1999-2000.* London: Home Office.

Home Office (2000b) *Probation Statistics, England and Wales, 1999.* London: Home Office.

Home Office (2001) *Statistics on Women and the Criminal Justice System: A Home Office Publication under Section 95 of the Criminal Justice Act 1991.* London: Home Office.

Howden-Windell, J. and Clark, D. (1999) *The Criminogenic Needs of Female Offenders: A Literature Review.* London: HM Prison Service. Unpublished.

Jamieson, J., McIvor, G. and Murray, C. (1999) *Understanding Offending Among Young People.* Edinburgh: The Stationery Office.

Lipsey, M.W. (1992) 'The effect of treatment on juvenile delinquents: Results from meta-analysis.' In E. Losel, T. Bliesener and D. Bender (eds) *Psychology and Law: International Perspectives.* Berlin: de Gruyter.

Lloyd, C., Mair, G. and Hough, M. (1994) *Explaining Reconviction Rates: A Critical Analysis.* Home Office Research Study no. 136. London: Home Office.

McGuire, J. (2000) *Cognitive-Behavioural Approaches.* London: HMI Probation.

McGuire, J. (2001) 'Property Offences.' In C.R. Hollin (ed) *Handbook of Offender Assessment and Treatment.* Chichester: Wiley.

McIvor, G. and Barry, M. (1998) *Social Work and Criminal Justice Vol.6: Probation.* Edinburgh: The Stationery Office.

Mair, G. and May, C. (1997) *Offenders on Probation.* Home Office Research Study no. 167. London: Home Office.

May, C. (1999) *Explaining Reconviction Following a Community Sentence: The Role of Social Factors.* Home Office Research Study no. 192. London: Home Office.

May, T., Edmunds, M. and Hough, M. (1999) *Street Business: The Links Between Sex and Drug Markets.* Police Research Series Paper no. 118. London: Home Office.

Moore, R.H. (1984) 'Shoplifting in Middle America: Patterns and motivational correlates.' *International Journal of Offenders Therapy and Comparative Criminology* *28*, 1, 53–64.

Morris, A., Wilkinson, C., Tisi, A., Woodrow, J. and Rockley, A. (1995) *Managing the Needs of Female Prisoners*. London: Home Office.

Pearson, F. and Lipton, D.S. (1999) 'The effectiveness of educational and vocational programs: CDATE meta-analyses.' Paper presented to ASC, Toronto, Canada, November.

Taylor, R. (1999) *Predicting Reconvictions for Sexual and Violent Offences Using the Revised Offender Group Reconviction Scale*. Research Findings no. 104. London: Home Office.

Vennard, J. and Hedderman, C. (1998) *Effective Interventions with Offenders, Reducing Reoffending: An Assessment of Research Evidence on Ways of Dealing with Offending Behaviour*. Home Office Research Study no. 187. London: HMSO.

Vennard, J., Hedderman, C. and Sugg, D. (1997) *Changing Offenders' Attitudes and Behaviour: What Works*. Research Findings no. 61. London: Home Office.

Walmsley, R., Howard, L. and White, S. (1992) *The National Prison Survey, 1990*. Home Office Research Study no. 128. London: Home Office.

Walters, G.D. and Elliott, W.N. (1999) 'Predicting release and disciplinary outcome with the Psychological Inventory of Criminal Thinking Styles: Female data.' *Legal and Criminal Psychology 4*, 15–21.

CHAPTER 12

Women, Drug Use and the Criminal Justice System

Margaret S. Malloch

There's no one specific thing among females that we could say started them off on drugs. But it's either drug offences or shoplifting and prostitution that brings them back in. So when they get lifted for shoplifting they're usually full of drugs. In fact, about 90% of them are full of drugs when they come in. (Prison officer quoted in Malloch 2000b, p.91)

To them we're just junkies. They don't care. We're nothing to them and they make it worse for us. (Woman prisoner quoted in Malloch 2000b, p.99)

Introduction

Sheila Henderson (1990, p.12) notes that: 'Women who use illicit drugs are beyond the moral pale. Their behaviour goes against people's expectations of the feminine and is typified as selfish, deviant, criminal.' The sentiments expressed indicate societies' moral distaste for women who use illegal drugs, views that are also applied to women who 'overindulge' in alcohol (Kennedy 1992; McDonald 1994). Being drunk or drugged is considered to be inappropriate behaviour for women, particularly for women with children. While there are similarities in the depiction and problematisation of women who use illegal drugs and alcohol, this chapter will focus on illegal drug use and the issues that can arise for women drug users in their contact with the criminal justice system. Legalised alcohol use and illegal drug use are both implicated in offending behaviour and both can have adverse social consequences for women who use them. However, the illegal status of drug use results in the criminalisation of the user.[1] This chapter will consider the consequences of drug use and the process of criminalisation for women who subsequently come into contact with the criminal justice system. It will highlight some of the key issues this raises for criminal justice social workers and probation officers in their provision of services for women.

Women and drug use

It is not possible to provide exact figures for the extent of drug use in the UK. However, estimates suggest that there are between 85,000 and 215,000 adult problem drug users in England and Wales (Drugs Prevention Advisory Service 1999), and approximately 55,800 users of opiates and benzodiazepines in Scotland (Hay, McKeganey and Hutchinson 2001). Women constitute around one-third of all drug users in contact with services (Drugscope 2000; Scottish Drug Misuse Database 2000) and a significantly lower proportion of criminal justice referrals to drug services, in some cases as low as 14 per cent of all referrals (Edmunds *et al.* 1999). Their contact with drug workers, probation officers and criminal justice social workers is therefore limited. This is disconcerting in the current political climate where the criminal justice system is increasingly being identified as a key mechanism for putting drug users in touch with appropriate services to reduce drug use and consequently drug-related crime. As HM Inspectorate of Probation (1996) have noted, the needs of women are not seen as a priority when local partnerships are being developed to deal with drugs and alcohol.

The impact of drug use on women's offending behaviour has been noted in various contexts. In particular, the high numbers of women who use drugs prior to and during periods of imprisonment has been highlighted by Inspectorate Reports into individual penal establishments and through examinations of the broader aspects of the imprisonment of women (HM Inspectorate of Prisons 1994, 1997, 2001; HM Inspectorate of Prisons for Scotland 2001; Scottish Office 1998; Scottish Prison Service 2001).

Academic texts and research have addressed this issue (Carlen 1998; Devlin 1998; Loucks 1998; Loucks, Chapter 7 this volume; Loucks and Knox 2001; Malloch 2000a, 2000b) while the media have regularly drawn attention to the extent and nature of drug use in prisons. Such concerns have led to the recognition, from both the criminal justice and welfare services, for the need to develop increased resources for drug users in the community (Carlen 1990; Dorn, James and Lee 1992; Henderson 1990). The provision of services for women is particularly problematic, with many resources being more suitable for and accessible to male drug users. This is reflected throughout the criminal justice system, in both voluntary and statutory settings. In 1998 the Scottish Office Health Department noted that women are often reluctant to contact statutory services due to childcare issues. Indeed, when services are specifically aimed at women they are regularly directed towards pregnant women or women with children, intended to protect and respond to the needs of children.[2]

Given the relatively small number of women drug users who come into contact with the criminal justice system, the potential that their needs will be overlooked and 'deviance' exaggerated is high (Lloyd 1995). Socially constructed norms of 'appropriate' masculinity and femininity often form the basis for judging an individual's reputation and character. Women's behaviour and self-presentation is often used to depict them as 'respectable', 'bad' or 'inadequate' (Skeggs 1997). While criminal activity is seen as a deviation from standards of 'appropriate womanhood', the problematic use of drugs by a woman is additionally seen to be an indication of questionable morality. This is considered even more problematic if the woman is pregnant and/or a mother. The perceived deviance of women drug users is exacerbated by the hedonistic associations of drug use (getting 'high' or 'out of it') generally considered inappropriate for women (Ettorre 1992; Malloch 1999; Perry 1991; Sargent 1992; Taylor 1993). Subsequently, for women lawbreakers and users of illegal drugs, a number of additional stereotypes and images are employed in defining them as 'triple' deviants.[3]

Drug use is regularly assumed to be an 'unfeminine preoccupation' (Ettorre 1992; McDonald 1994; Malloch 1999; Perry 1991; Taylor 1993) dominated by male users and 'macho' images. Traditionally, drug use has been viewed as a 'masculine' activity leading to the sustained dominance of stereotypical assumptions.[4] The use of 'hard' drugs (particularly heroin) has regularly been associated with young, working-class males (Parker, Bakx and Newcombe 1988). Women's role in drug use has been identified as peripheral or as secondary to the central position of men (Young 1994), with women presented as 'passive' spectres in the background of the drug 'scene'. Traditionally, men have been viewed as the more active participants, introducing their female partners or friends to initial experiences of drug use. Parker *et al.* (1988) identified that women in their study who came into treatment were more likely to have been introduced to heroin through a male user. However, the women in their study who had not sought treatment were more likely to have been introduced to heroin use by their women peers. The findings presented by Taylor (1993) indicate that both male and female friends were instrumental in introducing the women in her study to drug use.

Women have often been viewed as dependent on men for their continued supply of drugs and the finance required to support their drug use and subsistence. However, as Taylor (1993) illustrates, an examination of the daily lives of women drug users clearly challenges those traditional perceptions. Indeed women are frequently expected to maintain their male partners drug use as well as their own. This would appear to underpin many women's involvement in minor property offences and prostitution (Sargent 1992; Taylor 1993). Taylor (1993) illustrates the ways in which women drug users often have the main responsibility for 'scoring and grafting'. The gender dimensions which are prevalent in the depiction of 'hard' drug use are significantly different from those surrounding the use of medically prescribed drugs, notably tranquillisers and anti-depressants, which are often identified as more 'appropriate' forms of addiction for women.[5] The legally controlled, medical relationship between doctor and patient is portrayed as a more 'appropriate' relation of dependency for women than the chaotic, unpredictable and often dangerous practice which characterises the use of street drugs (Ettorre and Riska 1995).[6]

Women who use drugs are frequently presented as irresponsible, hedonistic, polluted[7] (McGrath 1993; Weeks 1989, 1995) and incompetent mothers. These images are additionally mediated by the structural relationships of class, 'race'/ethnicity and sexuality which have a profound impact on the experiences of women as both offenders and drug users. The impact of social structures can significantly affect the experiences of working-class, black/ethnic women and lesbians in their dealings with the criminal justice system (Lees 1997; McRobbie 2000; Skeggs 1997, 2001). The stereotypes and images that persist of women lawbreakers also influence how women offenders are presented in the court setting. This is evident in the ways in which women are responded to as 'victims', notably as victims of male violence (Lees 1997; Malloch forthcoming; Soothill and Soothill 1993; Temkin 1996) as well as 'lawbreakers', presenting a major challenge to conceptualisations of the 'justice' system as neutral and objective. The presented images of drug-using women are likely to have a significant impact on their negotiations with the criminal justice system. Dominant ideologies relating to appropriate constructions of femininity are institution-alised and come to affect policies and practices (Howe 1994; Malloch 1999). Subsequently ideological constructs profoundly affect the ways in which punishment and social control are regulated (Heidensohn 2000). For women, reputations and stereotyped images are constructed and transmitted through patriarchal ideologies. Thus criminalisation itself constitutes a power relation which forms part of a structural, political process.

Men constitute the vast majority of all known offenders and official statistics indicate that women who come before the courts are more likely than men to receive non-custodial sentences (Home Office 2000, 2001; Scottish Executive 2001b, 2001c). This has often been taken to mean that women receive preferential treatment. However, an examination of the statistical data reveals that apparent 'leniency' in sentencing can be attributed not to chivalry on behalf of the judiciary, but in terms of the offences which women typically commit. Women's offending behaviour differs from that of men, with women committing far fewer and less serious offences. Many women who come before the courts have no previous convictions and will not go on to commit further crimes. In practice however, law enforcement agencies tend to intervene earlier in the criminal careers of women. The differential treatment of women offenders has been highlighted by a number of theorists and researchers (Carlen 1983, 1985, 1998; Eaton 1993; Edwards 1996; McIvor 1998; Worrall 1990). Their work illustrates how women who come into contact with the criminal justice system (as both victims and law breakers) are frequently judged on their ability to conform to conventional gender roles. Such roles include normative concepts of the 'good' wife and/or mother, highlighting the importance attached to gender roles within the family. Women who are viewed as 'non-conformist' to 'appropriate' gender roles subsequently receive harsher treatment than men, and than women who conform in some measure to socially ascribed roles (Carlen 1983; Kennedy 1992; Worrall 1990). Women are more likely to be sentenced in relation to their social circumstances rather than in direct response to the offence committed. While this may appear to constitute a welfarist/treatment response, the underlying basis of punishment cannot be ignored (Carlen 1998; Howe 1994; Hudson 1993; Malloch 2000b). Illegal drug use is generally seen as contrary to acceptable behaviour and may result in the punishment of the woman drug user. Hedderman and Dowds (1997) note that sentencers may attempt to avoid custodial sentences for some women offenders. However recidivist drug offenders are treated similarly to their male counterparts, while women drug users are more likely than men to be placed on some form of supervision for a first offence.

Women, drug use and the criminal justice system

Drug use is one of the key issues facing the criminal justice system today and is particularly significant when examining concerns relating to women offenders. Academic research and institutional inspectorate reports have consistently highlighted the need to identify and respond to the distinctive issues women offenders bring to the criminal justice system. Women make up a very small proportion of known offenders[8] and subsequently of the prison population.[9] Despite an increase in the use of probation and community service these disposals have had a negligible effect on the numbers of women being sent to prison. Increasing levels of illegal drug use in the community have had a clear impact on the rising rates of imprisonment throughout the UK but have had a significant effect on the imprisonment of women. Between 1993 and 2000 the average population of women in prison in England and Wales rose by 115 per cent compared to an increase of 42 per cent for men (Home Office 2001) and is currently at its highest level since 1901. In Scotland, between 1991 and 2000, the female prison population increased by 42 per cent, twice the growth of the male prison population (Scottish Executive 2001c). This increase is affected by the lengthy sentences which can be given for drug offences, particularly for the supply of drugs, and by the use of custodial disposals for frequent minor drug-related offences. It is not unusual for sentencers to use custody in an attempt to force the offender to 'come off' drugs (Mallon 2001). However, there is now some recognition that imprisonment is unlikely to achieve this objective. Alternative ways of dealing with women offenders need to be considered, particularly for women who commit frequent but minor offences which are often associated with illegal drug use (Carlen 1990).

Individual sentencing preferences and regional policies can impact on the variable nature of 'justice'. Such variations illustrate the diverse nature and practices of the administration of justice, indicating that it is far removed from a neutral, scientific process. Indeed, research conducted by Hutton and Tata (1995) indicated significant statistical variation in the sentences imposed by courts in Scotland. Their findings 'suggested that there were variations in sentencing by individual judges which could not be explained by the seriousness of the offence and might be more directly attributable to differences between the judges themselves in their approach to sentencing' (Scottish Office 1996, p.35: 8.10). These differences are influenced by individual and social attitudes to women as offenders and drug users, affected by constructs of 'reputation' and 'respectability'. Furthermore, the structural inequalities of society are reflected throughout the criminal justice system and the majority of individuals processed through the system are economically marginalised. In England and Wales, a disproportionate number of prisoners are from black/ethnic communities. This is particularly evident in the female prison population where women from ethnic minority groups made up 25 per cent of the prison population in 2000, compared to 19 per cent of the male prison population (Home Office 2001). Many women who come to the attention of the courts have experienced a range of social, economic and emotional difficulties. These include drug and/or alcohol misuse, inadequate housing and employment opportunities and a general lack of relevant support services in the community (HM Inspectorate of Prisons 1997; Loucks 1998; Malloch 2000a, 2000b; Scottish Office 1998; Scottish Prison Service 2001). As official reports have illustrated, a significant number of women prisoners have been the victims/survivors of violence (HM Inspectorate of Prisons 1997; Loucks 1998; Prison Reform Trust 2000; Scottish Prison Service 2001). Historically, women's offending has often been viewed as pathological, explained in terms of depression or relationship problems leading to medical or psychiatric disposals (Allen 1987; Worrall 1990). However there has been a growing recognition that women's offending is inextricably linked to experiences of poverty and/or drug use.[10]

> If I didn't take drugs there's no danger, no way I would be in here. I wouldn't be stealing, I wouldn't be soliciting, I wouldn't be doing anything to keep the habit, because I wouldn't need it.

> I don't think I would have offended at all if I wasn't taking drugs. Because our savings were finished from using I needed to get money from somewhere. I wouldn't turn to prostitution so the best thing was fraud…Most of the time I have to take something (drugs) to do it…If you've got something in you it gives you the confidence to go out and steal. (Women prisoners quoted in Malloch 2000b, p.84)

A substantial number of women who come into contact with the criminal justice system do so for the commission of offences such as theft (shoplifting) and fraud, offences which are often related to poverty and/or drug use. Indeed HM Inspectorate of Prisons (2001) and the Scottish Office (1998) have identified drug use as a risk factor that increases the likelihood of reoffending.[11] In 2000 the main offence groups among the population of sentenced women offenders were drug offences (37%) and theft and handling (20%) (Home Office 2001). Black women are over-represented among the former group, with 69 per cent of black sentenced women prisoners incarcerated for drug offences (Home Office 2000). In June 2000 more than 75 per cent of sentenced female foreign nationals were held for drug offences (see Green 1991). Similarly, many women accumulate fines for offences which may ultimately result in a custodial sentence. The relatively high incidence of fines imposed as a disposal for women offenders is problematic, although Hedderman and Dowds (1997) note that sentencers appear to be reluctant to use fines for women in certain circumstances. This reluctance could lead to greater leniency, for example, discharge, or greater severity, generally due to the imposition of a higher tariff community penalty. Despite these findings, the use of fines as a disposal for women is particularly significant. Up to 52 per cent of female prison sentenced admissions in Scotland in 1998 were for fine default, despite the recommendations of the 1996 White Paper *Crime and Punishment* (Scottish Office 1996, p.40: 9.1) which stated that 'custody should not be used for want of a suitable community-based disposal and is particularly inappropriate for fine default'.

Attempts to alleviate the use of custody for fine defaulters have led to the introduction in Scotland of Supervised Attendance Orders (SAO) as an additional disposal available to the courts. In research conducted on the use of SAOs, McIvor and Levy (2001) argued that these orders might be particularly appropriate for women fine defaulters. However, the majority of SAOs in the six areas studied were made for males (85%), despite the high proportion of women in custody in Scotland who are imprisoned for fine default (Scottish Executive 2001b, 2001c). For women with a drug problem and limited financial resources, the imposition of a fine is very likely to result in fine default and potentially custody, often for an offence that does not merit imprisonment initially. The imposition of fines in circumstances where the recipient is unable to pay often increases the likelihood of repeat offending. This is particularly evident when fines are imposed for offences relating to prostitution and minor property offences such as theft/ shoplifting.

The failure to provide adequate non-custodial facilities for women held on remand is particularly problematic, despite attempts to develop Bail Support Schemes throughout the UK. Where these services operate, agencies often report a significant under-representation of women being referred from courts and local remand centres. The Prison Reform Trust (2000) has noted sentencers' reluctance to place drug users on bail, a situation that is exacerbated by the lack of appropriate bail facilities. The high number of drug users held on remand is particularly problematic and the conditions of custody are often significantly poorer than for sentenced prisoners (Malloch 2000b). Many women held on remand for reports or trial do not go on to receive a custodial sentence (Home Office 2001; Scottish Executive 2001b).

The increase in the female prison population and the conditions which women experience in custody have been a focus of recent attention for policy-makers and practitioners in both Scotland (Scottish Office 1998; Scottish Prison Service 2001) and England and Wales (HM Inspectorate of Prisons 1997, 2001; HM Inspectorate of Probation 1996; HM Prison Service 2000; Prison Reform Trust 2000). Despite prison service policies aimed at reducing levels of drug use in custody (education, support services, drug-free units, increased security measures and mandatory drug testing) the extent of drug use in prison is high. This is particularly problematic in women's prisons where high numbers of prisoners have previously used drugs (Malloch 2000a, 2000b). Inspectorate reports have consistently highlighted this issue with estimates that more than 90 per cent of women in prison have used drugs (HM Inspectorate for Prisons in Scotland 2001). Indeed a report by Dr Malcolm Faulk, HM Inspectorate of Prisons specialist in healthcare, made headline news when he stated that the use of illegal drugs in HM Prison and Young Offender Institution Styal was so severe that it was possible for a woman to 'enter a shoplifter and leave an addict' (HM Inspectorate of Prisons 1994).

Problems of drug withdrawal and the continued demand and supply of drugs in the prison environment have caused considerable and ongoing problems for both prisoners and prison staff (Carlen 1998; Devlin 1998; Malloch 2000a, 2000b). The disproportionately high incidence of suicides in Cornton Vale, Scotland's main prison for women, as in other women's prisons throughout the UK, has been tentatively linked to the problems of drug use and withdrawal in custody.[12] Despite the introduction of improved conditions and services in prisons throughout the country, the deeper problems presented by the imprisonment of women continue to be unresolved. Following the publication of the latest Inspectorate Report on Cornton Vale in September 2001, the improved conditions which were acknowledged in the report were outlined in glowing terms by the media. *The Herald* (6 September 2001) printed the headline 'Suicide Jail is Now Looked on as a Haven' adding that 'conditions at Cornton Vale, dubbed the suicide jail after a spate of deaths five years ago, have improved so much that some courts are now sending women there in an effort to save their lives'. Within weeks following the report's publication, two more women took their own lives (*The Herald*, 27 October 2001; *The Guardian*, 1 November 2001).

The recognition that prison is often inappropriate, and frequently dangerous for women drug users, has resulted in calls to expand and develop services in the community, increasing support options and expanding services that could operate as alternatives to custody. This is not a new problem. In 1968 a Home Office policy document noted:

> Imprisonment as at present conceived is unlikely to serve any useful purpose in cases of drug addiction, prostitution and drunkenness. It is necessary therefore to consider what alternative punishments or treatments are available and how we can most effectively deal with the problems posed by drugs, prostitution and drunkenness. (Home Office 1968, p.10)

More recently, a range of official reports has recommended that alternatives to custody are developed and their use expanded for drug users (Advisory Council on the Misuse of Drugs 1988, 1989, 1991, 1993, 1996; Home Affairs Committee 1998; Ministerial Drugs Task Force 1994; Scottish Affairs Committee 1994; Scottish Office 1996; Scottish Office Health Department 1998). Such reports have also recognised the need to provide specific services for women drug users which are 'sensitive' to their needs. While these recommendations have never been fully implemented, their significance has been upheld in subsequent reports (HM Inspectorate of Prisons 1997; Home Office 1995, 1998; Prison Reform Trust 2000; Scottish Executive 1999, 2000; Scottish Office 1998).

Following government strategies to tackle drug use (Home Office 1995, 1998; Anti-Drugs Co-ordinator 2001; Scottish Executive 1999, 2000),[13] a vast array of resources has been developed resulting from policy commitments to tackle offending in order to protect communities. Aimed at rehabilitative and support services as well as education programmes, this funding has also been diverted to the criminal justice system. It has been used to develop arrest referral schemes and court diversion programmes aimed at an early intervention in drug-related offending (Drugs Prevention Advisory Service 1999). In Scotland, pre-prosecution diversion to social work has led to the development of a number of schemes which focus on drug and/or alcohol use as the basis for diversionary provision (Barry and

McIvor 2000). Similarly attempts to identify and engage with women drug users prior to sentence have led to the introduction of innovative schemes intended to link women drug-using offenders with criminal justice social work or probation services (Turnaround 2000). Drug Treatment and Testing Orders are also in use in Scotland, England and Wales while the operation of a Drug Court in Glasgow is one of the most recent initiatives to be introduced. HM Inspectorate of Prisons (2001, p.13: 2.149) welcomed the introduction of Drug Treatment and Testing Orders, commenting that 'this is of particular value to women whose offending is often exclusively drug-related and who are particularly disadvantaged by custody. However its success for women depends on there being sufficient treatment resources suitable for them in the community.' This is of some concern. As the Prison Reform Trust (2000) has noted, services for women are often limited, particularly residential services which are prepared to accept women with their children.

Issues for social work and probation

The increased focus on criminal justice interventions with drug users and the development of community-based provision are likely to have a significant impact on the work of probation officers and criminal justice social workers. As the majority of individuals who commit offences are male, it inevitably means that probation officers and criminal justice social workers have a largely male client group. In 2000, male offenders accounted for 83 per cent of probation orders in Scotland (Scottish Executive 2001b) and 88 per cent of clients supervised by the Probation Service in England and Wales (Home Office 2001). This can often have consequences for the smaller number of women who receive criminal justice social work or the services of probation officers. Due to the relatively low number of women offenders who come to the attention of local authority social work departments and probation services, it is often assumed that women do not need a specific service, and they are often subsumed into services with/for men. This criticism has frequently been made in relation to services for women drug users (Dorn, James and Lee 1992; Drugscope 2000; Henderson 1990).

As previously argued, the criminal justice system reflects social and political structural formations. Accordingly the services provided by probation officers and criminal justice social workers are themselves affected by broader institutional practices. Normative constructions of gender roles and identities are evident in the practices of both criminal justice and welfare services and may also vary in respect of ethnic groups (HM Inspectorate of Probation 1996). The differential sentencing of women is influenced by the way men and women are portrayed in Pre-Sentence Reports (England and Wales) and Social Enquiry Reports (Scotland).[14] This is also likely to reduce the consideration of women for particular disposals such as community service (McIvor 1998). Practitioners often focus on the individual character-istics of women (ability to 'cope', childcare issues) rather than on broader contexts such as economic provisions (Brophy and Smart 1985; Buchanan, Collett and McMullen 1991; Worrall 1990). Worrall (1990) examined the ways in which women were presented in court reports, concluding that women were depicted within the context of wholly inappropriate categories, related to gender and family roles. Inappropriate emphasis was often placed on the domestic role of the woman or on her perceived needs, rather than focusing on her offending behaviour (see also Dickie 1995). This could then culminate in equally inappropriate solutions being recommended. HM In-spectorate of Probation (1996) noted that the preparation of Pre-Sentence Reports on women offenders did not always give full consideration to relevant issues, particularly drug use and financial circumstances.[15] Reports on women tend to focus on individual characteristics and lifestyle, while women themselves highlight structural factors such as poverty or drug use, as underpinning their offending behaviour (Prison Reform Trust 2000; Scottish Office 1998).

A woman's use of drugs may affect the recommendations made by social workers and probation officers. Problem drug use is frequently individual-ised and decontextualised from the structural factors of the user's life and experiences. As a result, the individual drug-using woman is often presented as 'inadequate' and in need of intervention. A study carried out in Merseyside (quoted in Scottish Office 1998, p.29) indicated that women with drug problems were more likely to have their cases adjourned for court reports. This process often resulted in women being 'up-tariffed', sentenced on the basis of a perceived need for intervention in the woman's life, rather than in direct response to the offence committed. While this may have the potential to provide support and services for women on an individual basis (and this is not always the case), it will also mean that should she reoffend or fail to comply then she may be returned to court and sentenced for the original offence and a breach of the order. It would also appear that orders imposed on drug users are likely to impose additional conditions (such as attending for drug treatment). Additional conditions were placed on 10 per cent of all probation orders made for women, compared to only 6.9 per cent of orders made on men (Scottish Executive 2001b). This is a reflection of the presentation of the circumstances of individual offenders, rather than an indication of the severity of offences committed. The presentations of women in Pre-Sentence and Social Inquiry Reports are often prime factors in the over-representation of women on probation orders and their under-representation on community service (McIvor 1998; Worrall 1990). Figures suggest that sentencers are overcoming their reluctance to place women on community service orders (Home Office 2001). However women drug users may be less likely to receive community service while drug users who have not controlled their use of drugs are more likely to be allocated to teams rather than individual placements (Prison Reform Trust 2000). The nature and organisation of work-teams may not always be appropriate for women.

Probation officers and criminal justice social workers are frequently limited in their ability to provide drug-focused intervention for clients. This often means that service users are directed to drug agencies, while the focus of the probation order, its management and objectives can be unclear. The availability of appropriate services can be crucial when sentencing decisions are taken. The allocation of funding clearly impacts significantly on women who are often restricted in their use of resources for quite general reasons. Few residential rehabilitation services exist specifically for women; few will take women with dependent children; local authorities are sometimes reluctant to provide the financial resources for such services. The inadequacy of services for women is regularly excused due to the relatively limited numbers of women in need of such provision, hence the restricted resource allocation. However the consequences this has for women themselves, particularly women who come into contact with the criminal justice system, are significant. The operation of Drug Strategies throughout the UK has resulted in a focus on 'high-risk' groups in the attainment of 'community safety'. This has meant that services have been diverted to deal specifically with offenders and particularly those designated 'high risk'. This has had some impact on services in the community and is likely to have profound consequences for women drug users who may be defined as 'risky' in terms of their lifestyle but not necessarily in terms of their offending behaviour. This appears to have a significant impact on women's access to particular services. The emphasis given to the development of short-term service provision and the resulting reduction in emphasis, in practice, on after-care has also affected the form and availability of services for women (Eaton 1993).

The Prison Reform Trust (2000) has emphasised the need to offer specific drug services for women as both offenders and non-offenders. The report states (2000 p.64: 5.41): 'there are other good reasons to argue for women's drug treatment facilities to be community resources used by all women and not just those who have been identified as offenders'. Without the availability of credible community-based treatments for drug-using offenders (as options available to the courts and as accessible support services for individuals on release from prison), the courts will continue the trend toward custodial sentencing. This is increasingly likely, given current fears and concerns relating to increasing levels of drug use and crime in local communities.

Conclusion

The need to develop increased services for women generally and women drug users in particular has been an ongoing concern for many involved both in the criminal justice and welfare/social services. It is a crucial factor in the development of services aimed at providing sentencers with appropriate alternatives to, or diversions from, custody, a responsibility which criminal justice social workers and probation officers clearly have. However, with the changing political climate and continued moves to strengthen and maintain 'law and order', greater emphasis is given to the need to 'tighten up' non-custodial disposals and their requirements (Hudson 2001).

The problematic association of drug use and crime, where the two are presented as inevitably correlated, and calls for more punitive approaches to offenders, will undoubtedly impact on attempts to utilise community provisions aimed at the reduction of the prison population. Assessments of 'dangerousness' and 'risk' (Castel 1991) are significantly influenced by perceptions of drug users when community disposals are being considered. Such perceptions appear particularly problematic in terms of women drug users and the deployment of stereotypical images that frequently result in the allocation of a 'high-risk' categorisation, which bears little relationship to the actual offence committed (Shaw and Hannah-Moffat 2000). However this does not necessarily result in 'high-risk' women being directed towards intensive community provisions. Given the nature of women's offending, they may be sentenced in lower courts thus being excluded from innovative initiatives, but in practice receiving custodial sentences.

The representation of drug-using women impacts on the responses of the courts and probation and criminal justice social work services. The focus of intervention for social workers and probation officers often depends on their understanding of the specific problems that drug use can result in, and is frequently underpinned by a very limited awareness of the gender dimensions that are associated with this. Individual attitudes and definitions affect institutional practices and can themselves propagate stereotypes and misrepresentations. This can have very real consequences for individual drug-using women who come into contact with the criminal justice system.

Notes

1   Most drug users do not participate in other forms of crime.

2   For example the Scottish Executive Report (2001a) *Getting Our Priorities Right: Policy and Practice Guidelines for Working with Children and Families Affected by Problem Drug Use* is couched in gender-neutral language but in practice is likely to apply more specifically to women who will have greater childcare responsibilities.

3   Feminists have argued that women lawbreakers are seen as 'doubly deviant'. Their lawbreaking goes against social norms, but in addition they are viewed as

transgressing ascribed gender roles. It is suggested here that illicit drug use constitutes an additional level of deviance in the depiction of women offenders.

4   The depiction of 'dance drugs' as part of youth culture suggests a greater gender balance in their use.

5   This applies particularly to well-known brands such as prozac and valium.

6   A chemically induced assistant to 'coping' is considered an appropriate function of medical intervention (Ettorre 1992).

7   The often over-estimated relationship between drug use and sex work results in women drug users being perceived in a similar way to the symbolic representation of prostitutes, associated with the transmission of infection and disease (notably HIV and hepatitis).

8   In 2000, only 19 per cent of known offenders were women (Home Office 2001).

9   In 2000 women made up 5.2 per cent of the overall prison population in England and Wales (Home Office 2001), and 3.8 per cent of the total Scottish prison population.

10   This is not a new phenomenon. Joe Sim (1990) cites the Prison System Enquiry Committee of 1922, which noted that drunkenness with aggravation was the most common crime for which women were imprisoned, followed by prostitution.

11   In both Scotland, England and Wales, national drugs strategies have been linked with governmental attempts to promote social inclusion (Hay *et al.* 2001; Home Office 1995, 1998; Scottish Executive 1999, 2000; Scottish Social Inclusion Network 1999).

12   The Scottish Office (1998) notes: 'No one reason for suicide emerges from recent Fatal Accident Inquiries... but a history of drug abuse and withdrawal problems shortly after being locked up is, with few exceptions, a common factor for remand and convicted prisoners.'

13   In Scotland a £100 million package of expenditure was provided to support the Scottish Executive's Drugs Action Plan. See the *UK Anti-Drugs Co-ordinator's Annual Report* (2001) for a breakdown of spending throughout the UK.

14   Between 2000 and 2001 in Scotland, 86 per cent of Social Inquiry Reports were made on men (Scottish Executive 2001b).

15   This point has also been made by the Prison Reform Trust (2000) who argued that Pre-Sentence Reports on women offenders should be examined for quality and consistency and that research should be conducted to ascertain the use of these reports by courts.

References

Advisory Council on the Misuse of Drugs (1988) *Aids and Drug Misuse: Part One.* London: HMSO.

Advisory Council on the Misuse of Drugs (1989) *Aids and Drug Misuse: Part Two.* London: HMSO.

Advisory Council on the Misuse of Drugs (1991) *Drug Users and the Criminal Justice System.* London: HMSO.

Advisory Council on the Misuse of Drugs (1993) *Aids and Drug Misuse Update.* London: HMSO.

Advisory Council on the Misuse of Drugs (1996) *Drug Misusers and the Prison System – An Integrated Approach.* London: HMSO.

Allen, H. (1987) *Justice Unbalanced: Gender, Psychiatry and Judicial Decisions.* Milton Keynes: Open University Press.

Anti-Drugs Co-ordinator (2001) *United Kingdom Anti-Drugs Co-Ordinator's Annual Report 1999/2000.* London: HMSO.

Barry, M. and McIvor, G. (2000) *Diversion From Prosecution to Social Work and Other Service Agencies.* Edinburgh: Scottish Executive Central Research Unit.

Brophy, J. and Smart, C. (eds) (1985) *Women In Law.* London: Routledge and Kegan Paul.

Buchanan, J., Collett, S. and McMullen, P. (1991) 'Challenging practice of challenging women?' *Probation Journal 38,* 2, 56–62.

Carlen, P. (1983) *Women's Imprisonment: A Study in Social Control.* London: Routledge and Kegan Paul.

Carlen, P. (1985) *Criminal Women.* Cambridge: Polity Press.

Carlen, P. (1990) *Alternatives to Women's Imprisonment.* Milton Keynes: Open University Press.

Carlen, P. (1998) *Sledgehammer.* London: Macmillan.

Castel, R. (1991) 'From danger to risk.' In G. Burchell, C. Gordon and P. Miller (eds) *The Foucault Effect.* London: Harvester Wheatsheaf.

Devlin, A. (1998) *Invisible Women.* Winchester: Waterside Press.

Dickie, D. (1995) 'Women offenders and social enquiry reports.' Unpublished thesis for MSc in Social Work Management, University of Stirling.

Dorn, N., James, B. and Lee, M. (eds) (1992) *Women, HIV, Drugs: Criminal Justice Issues.* London: ISDD.

Drugscope (2000) *Summary of UK Drug Situation.* London: Drugscope.

Drugs Prevention Advisory Service (1999) *Drugs Intervention in the Criminal Justice System: Guidance Manual.* London: Home Office.

Eaton, M. (1993) *Women After Prison.* Buckingham: Open University Press.

Edmunds, M., Hough, M., Turnbull, P. and May, T. (1999) *Doing Justice to Treatment: Referring Offenders to Drug Services.* DPAS Paper no. 2. London: Home Office.

Edwards, S. (1996) *Sex and Gender in the Legal Process.* London: Blackstone Press.

Ettorre, E. (1992) *Women and Substance Use.* London: Macmillan.

Ettorre, E. and Riska, E. (1995) *Gendered Moods: Psychotropics and Society*. London: Routledge.

Green, P. (1991) *Drug Couriers*. London: The Howard League.

Hay, G., McKeganey, N. and Hutchinson, S. (2001) *Estimating the National and Local Prevalence of Problem Drug Misuse in Scotland*. Glasgow: University of Glasgow and NHS Scotland.

Hedderman, C. and Dowds, L. (1997) *The Sentencing of Women*. Research Findings no. 58. London: Home Office Research and Statistics Directorate.

Heidensohn, F. (2000) *Sexual Politics and Social Control*. Buckingham: Open University Press.

Henderson, S. (ed) (1990) *Women, HIV, Drugs: Practical Issues*. London: ISDD.

HM Inspectorate of Prisons (1994) *HM Prison and YOI Styal*. London: Home Office.

HM Inspectorate of Prisons (1997) *Women In Prison: A Thematic Review*. London: Home Office.

HM Inspectorate of Prisons (2001) *Follow-up to Women in Prison: A Thematic Review by HM Chief Inspector of Prisons for England and Wales*. London: Home Office.

HM Inspectorate of Prisons for Scotland (2001) *Report on HMP and YOI Cornton Vale*. Edinburgh: The Scottish Executive.

HM Inspectorate of Probation (1996) *A Review of Probation Service Provision for Women Offenders*. London: Home Office.

HM Prison Service (2000) *The Government's Strategy for Women Offenders: A Consultation Document*. London: Home Office.

Holme, C. (2001) 'Second prisoner within three days found hanging at Cornton Vale.' *The Herald*, 27 October.

Home Affairs Committee (1998) *Alternatives to Prison Sentences: Third Report Volume One*. London: HMSO.

Home Office (1968) *Prison Policy: Women and Girls. PD4 Study*. London: HMSO.

Home Office (1995) *Tackling Drugs Together: A Strategy for England 1995–1998*. Cm 2846. London: Home Office.

Home Office (1998) *Tackling Drugs To Build a Better Britain: The Government's Ten-Year Strategy for Tackling Drugs Misuse*. Cm 3945. London: HMSO.

Home Office (2000) *Statistics on Women and the Criminal Justice System*. London: Home Office.

Home Office (2001) *Statistics on Women and the Criminal Justice System*. London: Home Office.

Howe, A. (1994) *Punish and Critique: Towards a Feminist Analysis of Penality*. London: Routledge.

Hudson, B. (1993) *Penal Policy and Social Justice*. London: Macmillan.

Hudson, B. (2001) 'Human rights, public safety and the Probation Service: Defending justice in the risk society.' *The Howard Journal 40*, 2, 103–113.

Hutton, N. and Tata, C. (1995) *Patterns of Custodial Sentencing in the Sheriff Court*. Edinburgh: Scottish Office Central Research Unit.

Kennedy, H. (1992) *Eve Was Framed*. London: Vintage.

Lees, S. (1997) *Ruling Passions: Sexual Violence, Reputation and the Law*. Buckingham: Open University Press.

Lloyd, A. (1995) *Doubly Deviant, Doubly Damned*. Harmondsworth: Penguin.

Loucks, N. (1998) *HMPI Cornton Vale: Research into Drugs and Alcohol, Violence and Bullying, Suicides and Self-Injury and Backgrounds of Abuse*. Scottish Prison Service Occasional Papers no. 1/98. Edinburgh: Scottish Prison Service.

Loucks, N. and Knox, J. (2001) *Custodial Remands in Scotland*. Scottish Prison Service Occasional Papers no. 1/2001. Edinburgh: Scottish Prison Service.

McDonald, M. (ed) (1994) *Gender, Drink and Drugs*. Oxford: Berg.

McGrath, R. (1993) 'Health education and authority.' In V. Harwood *et al. Pleasure Principles*. London: Lawrence and Wishart.

McIvor, G. (1998) 'Jobs for the boys? Gender differences in referral to community service.' *The Howard Journal 37*, 3, 280–290.

McIvor, G. and Levy, L. (2001) *National Evaluation of the Operation And Impact of Supervised Attendance Orders*. Crime and Criminal Justice Research Findings no. 54, Edinburgh: The Scottish Executive Central Research Unit.

McRobbie, A. (2000) *Feminism and Youth Culture*, 2nd edn. London: Macmillan.

Malloch, M. (1999) 'Women, drugs and the social construction of femininity.' *Women's International Research Forum 22*, 3, 349–358.

Malloch, M. (2000a) 'Caring for drug users? The experiences of women prisoners.' *The Howard Journal 39*, 4, 354–368.

Malloch, M. (2000b) *Women, Drugs and Custody: The Experiences of Women Drug Users in Custody*. Winchester: Waterside Press.

Malloch, M. (forthcoming) '"Risky" women, sexual consent and criminal "justice".' In M. Cowling and P. Reynolds (eds) *Making Sense of Sexual Consent*. London: Ashgate.

Mallon, M. (2001) 'Suicide jail is now looked on as a haven.' *The Herald*, 6 September, 9.

Ministerial Drugs Task Force (1994) *Drugs In Scotland: Meeting the Challenge*. Edinburgh: The Scottish Office.

Parker, H., Bakx, K. and Newcombe, R. (1988) *Living with Heroin*. Milton Keynes: Open University Press.

Perry, L. (1991) *Women and Drug Use: An Unfeminine Dependency*. London: ISDD.

Prison Reform Trust (2000) *Justice for Women: The Need for Reform*. London: Prison Reform Trust.

Sargent, M. (1992) *Women, Drugs and Policy in Sydney, London and Amsterdam*. Aldershot: Avebury.

Scott, K. (2001) 'Two deaths at suicide-prone women's jail.' *The Guardian*, 1 November.

Scottish Affairs Committee (1994) *Drug Abuse in Scotland: First Report Vol. 1*. London: HMSO.

Scottish Drug Misuse Database (2000) *Drug Misuse Statistics Scotland*. Edinburgh: The Scottish Executive.

Scottish Executive (1999) *Tackling Drugs in Scotland: Action in Partnership*. Edinburgh: The Stationery Office.

Scottish Executive (2000) *Drugs Action Plan: Protecting Our Future*. Edinburgh: The Scottish Executive.

Scottish Executive (2001a) *Getting Our Priorities Right: Policy and Practice Guidelines for Working with Children and Families Affected by Problem Drug Use*. Edinburgh: The Scottish Executive.

Scottish Executive (2001b) *Criminal Justice Social Work Statistics 2000–2001*. Edinburgh: Scottish Executive National Statistics Publication.

Scottish Executive (2001c) *Statistical Bulletin: Prison Statistics Scotland 2000*. Edinburgh: The Scottish Executive.

Scottish Office (1996) *Crime and Punishment*. Edinburgh: The Scottish Office.

Scottish Office (1998) *Women Offenders: A Safer Way*. Edinburgh: The Scottish Office.

Scottish Office Health Department (1998) *Planning and Provision of Drug Misuse Services*. Edinburgh: The Scottish Office.

Scottish Prison Service (2001) *Women Offenders: Effective Management and Intervention*. Occasional Paper Series no. 4/2001. Edinburgh: Scottish Prison Service.

Scottish Social Inclusion Network (1999) *Progress Report: Social Inclusion Strategy Evaluation*. Edinburgh: The Scottish Office.

Shaw, M. and Hannah-Moffat, K. (2000) 'Gender, diversity and risk assessment in Canadian corrections.' *Probation Journal 47*, 3, 163–172.

Sim, J. (1990) *Medical Power in Prisons*. Milton Keynes: Open University Press.

Skeggs, B. (1997) *Formations of Class and Gender: Becoming Respectable*. London: Sage.

Skeggs, B. (2001) 'The toilet paper: Femininity, class and misrecognition.' *Women's Studies International Forum 24*, 3/4, 295–307.

Soothill, K. and Soothill, D. (1993) 'Prosecuting the victim? A study of the reporting of barristers' comments on rape cases.' *The Howard Journal 32*, 1, 12–24.

Taylor, A. (1993) *Women Drug Users*. Oxford: Clarendon Press.

Temkin, J. (1996) 'Doctors, rape and criminal justice.' *The Howard Journal 35*, 1, 1–20.

Turnaround (2000) *Throughcare 2000 Project*. Glasgow: Turning Point, Scotland.

Weeks, J. (1989) 'Aids, Altruism and the New Right.' In E. Carter and S. Watney (eds) *Taking Liberties*. London: Serpent's Tail.

Weeks, J. (1995) *Invented Moralities*. Cambridge: Polity Press.

Worrall, A. (1990) *Offending Women*. London: Routledge.

Young, M. (1994) 'The police, gender and the culture of drug use and addiction.' In M. McDonald (ed) *Gender, Drink and Drugs*. Oxford: Berg.

CHAPTER 13

Working with Girls and Young Women

Susan Batchelor and Michele Burman

Introduction

Effective working with girls and young women who have been drawn into the criminal justice system is considerably hampered by a set of interrelated problems.[1] The first of these stems from their low numbers and relative invisibility in a system dominated by, and designed primarily for, men. A second set of problematic issues arises from the increasing recognition that offending girls and young women have particular and identifiable needs, stemming from what are frequently characterised as individualised troubles, which are difficult to meet effectively within a criminal justice framework. A third and related set of problems stems from their status as troublesome young females, and the persistence of perceptions characterising this particular group of offenders as intractable, malevolent and extremely difficult to work with (see, for example, Alder 1998; Chesney-Lind and Shelden 1998; Worrall 1999, 2000). Furthermore, in Britain, programmes and initiatives designed specifically with girls in mind are few and far between. There has been relatively little attention paid to the provision of services for girls, and there is a limited understanding of effective working with girls.[2] These issues, and their implications in terms of the availability and content of targeted interventions and programmes for girls and young women, are the subjects of this chapter.

Putting girls' and young women's offending in context

Compared to young men, girls and young women form a clear minority at all stages of the criminal justice process. While, in recent years, and in many jurisdictions, concern has been registered about the increasing number of girls and young women being drawn into both juvenile and adult justice systems (Alder 1996; Batchelor, Burman and Brown 2001; Chesney-Lind 1997, 2001a; Chesney-Lind and Shelden 1998; NACRO 2001), the fact that boys and young men are responsible for the large part of detected youth crime is well documented (see, for example, Chapter 2 this volume). A recent report by Audit Scotland (2001), for example, noted that in Scotland there are three times as many recorded male offenders as female offenders in the 8 to 21 age band. According to data from the Scottish Executive (2000), there are eight times as many convictions for males as for females in the 16- to 21-year age band. The figures for England and Wales show a similar picture. In the 10- to 17-year age group, approximately 152,600 young men were found guilty or cautioned in 2000 (all offences), compared to 36,400 girls and young women (representing a gender ratio of 4:1). The figures for 18- to 20-year-olds were 175,000 and 27,000 respectively (6.5:1) (Home Office 2001). In the USA the gender ratio for both total crime and index crime juvenile arrests runs at 3:1 (US Dept of Justice 1999) and young women account for less than 20 per cent of those dealt with by juvenile justice systems in Australia (Wundersitz 2000).

The relative invisibility of girls and young women can also be accounted for by the types of offending they commit. In Scotland, female young offenders are most likely to have been convicted of miscellaneous offences (such as simple assault and breach of the peace) and crimes involving dishonesty (mainly shoplifting) (see Table 13.1). In Canada, they are likely to be charged with minor property and minor assault offences, as well as failure to attend court and breach of probation (Reitsma-Street 1999). Young women in Australia tend to be charged with less serious forms of property offences (such as larceny and receiving) and for offences against 'good order' (Wundersitz 2000). In the USA, male and female young offenders can be taken into custody for both criminal acts and status offences that violate parental authority (such as running away and being 'beyond control'). Status offences and the more trivial property offences, such as shoplifting, play a major role in girls' delinquency (Chesney-Lind 1997).

Table 13.1 Females aged under 21 with a charge proved by ten most common charges proved, Scotland 2000		
Main charge proved	Number	Percent (N = 3059)
Shoplifting	518	17
Simple assault	443	15
Breach of the peace	376	12
'Other' miscellaneous offences (including non-payment of TV licence and breach of probation/community service)	278	9
'Other' theft (includes forgery, embezzlement and reset)	252	8
Crimes against public justice (includes perjury, contempt of court, bail offences and failing to appear at court)	199	7
Unlawful use of vehicle	184	6
Vandalism	117	4
Drugs	108	4
'Other' crimes of dishonesty	78	3

Source: *Criminal Proceedings in the Scottish Courts, 2000* (Scottish Executive 2001a).

Against this backdrop, the last 15 years have seen some changes in patterns of young female offending. In the USA, for example, female representation in the total juvenile index crime arrests has increased from 13 per cent in 1990 to 25 per cent in 1997, while male representation has decreased from

87 per cent to 75 per cent (cited in Schnelle 2000, pp.121–122). In Scotland, the number of girls referred to the Children's Hearing System[3] on offence grounds has risen from 8 referrals per 1000 population in 1985 to 13 referrals per 1000 population in 1995. Meanwhile referral rates for boys have remained stable (at around 40 to 45 offence referrals per 1000 population in the 8 to 15 age group) (cited in Hogg 1999). Of course, increases in the number of girls and young women apprehended do not necessarily imply that more are becoming involved in crime; nor do they mean an increase in the number of young females found guilty of a criminal offence. As Worrall (2001) has pointed out, drawing on recent Home Office figures, contrary to popular belief the number of juvenile females convicted in England and Wales has not risen overall since 1994.

The past 15 years have also witnessed increased concern about violent crime rates for girls and young women (Batchelor *et al.* 2001). In the USA, a special report on juvenile crime based on the 1997 US Uniform Crime Reports highlighted increases in juvenile crime, particularly in the proportion of violent crime committed by young females. The percentage of female juveniles arrested for violent crime increased by 101 per cent during the period 1988 to 1997, whereas male juvenile arrests increased by 42 per cent (cited in Zager 2000, p.90). In Canada, violence by adolescent girls is the only area consistently showing an increase in reported rates of violent offending (Statistics Canada 1999, cited in Leschied *et al.* 2000). In England and Wales, the biggest growth in violent offending by females has been in the 14- to 18-year age group (cited in Gelsthorpe 2000).

These figures, although much heralded by the media as a sign of the emergence of a new young female violent offender, belie a much more complex picture. In all jurisdictions, the figures reflect an increase in the number of young women charged with minor, non-sexual assault rather than serious acts of violence (which remain overwhelmingly the province of men) and it remains unclear whether such changes can be attributed to actual crime rates or changing responses to crime. It should also be remembered that serious crimes of violence form a very small proportion of overall offending by girls and young women, and that this group make up a very small proportion of the overall violent crime statistics. In Scotland, for example, females (of all age groups) accounted for 7.5 per cent of non-sexual crimes of violence in 2000. In terms of actual numbers, 315 women had a charge proven against them and of this group less than one-third (96 or 30%) were under the age of 21 years (Scottish Executive 2001a).[4] This low base rate means that a small number of cases can make a great deal of difference in terms of percentage rises (Batchelor 2001; see also Chapter 2 this volume).

Sentencing patterns and paradoxes

Debates about the significance of gender in relation to the ways in which male and female offenders are treated by the courts, and in particular whether women are treated more leniently than men, are well known. This is a very complex area, characterised by methodological dispute, theoretical inconsistency and local variation. That said, some themes in relation to girls and young women are discernible. Empirical studies of the processing of young men and young women through the criminal justice system have shown that at each key point in the system, girls and young women are less likely to receive the more serious of the options available (e.g. Chesney-Lind 1997; Wundersitz 2000). Compared to their male counterparts, they are more likely to receive a police warning, less likely to be prosecuted, and less likely to be referred to court (Samuel and Tisdall 1996; Wundersitz 2000). At court, sentencers are less likely to use the full range of disposals for young women, compared to young men. In Britain, for example, they are less likely to receive a custodial sentence or community service order (McIvor 1998) and more likely to be given an admonition or absolute discharge (Burman 1999; Samuel and Tisdall 1996). Probation is the most common type of sentence for female juvenile offenders in the USA, where they are less likely to be ordered to long-term correctional facility custody than male juveniles (Lippincott 2000).

That said, there is evidence to suggest that in England and Wales the rates of cautioning and absolute discharge for young women have fallen in recent years (Home Office 2000; Worrall 2001), while in both Britain and in the USA the rate of detention is increasing faster for girls than for boys. According to some commentators, this constitutes a strong sign that responses to troublesome girls and young women have undergone a fundamental shift, from the more traditional 'benevolent' welfare-oriented

approach to an increasingly punitive form of formal criminal justice intervention (Chesney-Lind 1997; Chesney-Lind, Artz and Nicholson 2001;
Howard League 1997; Reitsma-Street 1999; Worrall 2000, 2001). Recent
Howard League figures (2001) indicate that the number of girls received
into prison in England and Wales increased from 79 in 1992 to 302 in 1998.
Table 13.2 shows the steady increase in receptions into prison under an
immediate custodial sentence for both male and female young offenders,
over the ten-year period from 1988 to 1998. During 1999, a total of 1233
sentenced young females (aged 15 to 21 years) were received into prison,
more than double the number in 1995. There were 317 young females
under sentence at mid-1999, a slight rise on the previous year; the average
sentence length for young female offenders was 7.7 months (Home Office
2000). Fourteen per cent of all women in custody in mid-1999 were aged
under 21 years old (Home Office 2001). Girls and young women also make
up a growing proportion of the national prison population in Scotland,
where there was a 19 per cent increase (to 336) in the number of custodial
sentences for females aged under 21 between 1999 and 2000 (Scottish
Executive 2002). Custody dispositions for female juveniles have also
increased in Canada and the USA, despite legislative attempts to promote the
use of alternatives to imprisonment in Canada (Reitsma-Street 1999) and
moves to de-institutionalise US status offenders (Chesney-Lind 2001b;
Chesney-Lind *et al.* 2001).[5]

Table 13.2 Male and female young offenders sentenced
to immediate custody 1988-1998, England and Wales*

	No. of prisoners (thousands)					
	1988	1990	1992	1994	1996	1998
Males						
15–17 yrs	3.7	3.3	4.0	5.1	5.3	5.5
18–20 yrs	10.3	9.4	10.5	11.8	12.4	14.3
Females						
15–17 yrs	0.1	0.1	0.1	0.2	0.3	0.4
18–20 yrs	0.3	0.3	0.4	0.5	0.8	0.9

*Excludes fine defaulters.

Source: Home Office (2001, Table 7.2).

The drift towards confinement can also be seen, in Britain, in the over-representation of girls in local authority secure accommodation. Young people can enter such institutions as a result of welfare and/or criminal justice interventions. Although the majority of young people in secure accommodation are boys, the number of girls taking up places has increased substantially in recent years (Dept of Health 2001). Of the 87 children detained in secure accommodation in Scotland as at 31 March 2000, 16 were girls. This represents an increase from 31 March 1993, when only 10 of the 84 residents were female (Scottish Executive 2001b).

The welfare model which has been prominent in relation to responses to female criminality fosters a view of female offenders which 'finds them needy, not fully responsible for their actions, and requiring, above all else, special protection and support' (Asquith and Samuel 1994, p.77). Consequently girls and young women are more likely to be placed in custody for less serious offences. Compared to male young offenders, a greater proportion of females are in prison for petty offences (principally dishonesty and petty assault) and with fewer previous convictions. Assumptions about girls' needs for protection result in discriminatory juvenile justice practices, resulting in girls being dealt with more punitively than boys for behaviour that would not be regarded as criminal in adults (Worrall 1999).

Again, largely due to their minority position within the criminal justice system, female young (and adult) offenders are further disadvantaged insofar as fewer penal institutions mean that they are often placed long distances from home, thereby weakening their ties to the community. In England and Wales, there are just 16 prisons that hold women (three are open prisons). Cornton Vale is the only female establishment in Scotland. This makes it difficult for families (and probation officers from the home area) to visit. The provision of programmes, vocational training and recreational facilities is also affected.

A difficult group to work with?

In a context of competition for scare resources, because males outnumber females in both the adult and juvenile justice systems and because girls and young women represent less of a threat to society generally, community-based provisions and programmes for girls and young women in custodial settings are relatively few and far between. In the USA, where the question 'what about girls?' has been more forcefully put, 35 per cent of US delinquency programmes serve only males and 42.4 per cent serve primarily boys. Only 2.3 per cent serve only girls and 5.9 per cent serve primarily girls (Girls Incorporated 1996). Equivalent figures are not available in Britain as there has yet to be a comprehensive review of provision of services for girls.

Establishing sustainable gender-specific criminal justice projects for female lawbreakers is particularly problematic because low numbers, short sentences and fluctuations in demand mean that facilities are often under-utilised and therefore are not seen as cost effective. This often results in pressure to extend provision to male offenders, which in turn leads to a decreased take-up among female offenders whose histories of violence mean they are reluctant to risk mixed projects (Carlen 2001).

Small numbers also mean that workers may have had minimal contact with young female offenders and so lack awareness of the specific needs of this particular client group.[6] A range of research, both in the UK and abroad, has suggested that working with girls causes anxiety among juvenile justice and related workers (Alder 1996; Aymer 1992; Brown and Pearce 1992; Hudson 1989; Pearce 1995; Spence 1996). Writing about troubled and troublesome girls in Australia, Baines and Alder (1996a, 1996b) have noted that people who work in the juvenile justice system often conceptualise the behaviours and needs of young men and young women differently. Whereas girls are variously described as 'hysterical', 'manipulative', 'verbally aggressive' and 'untrustworthy', boys are depicted as 'honest', 'open' and 'less complex' (Alder 1998). In the UK, Carpenter and Young (1986) have noted that youth workers find young women to be both 'bored' and 'boring' and 'more trouble' than boys. Girls are deemed as having 'emotional needs' that are difficult to address effectively and which render them difficult and demanding. In addition, girls are considered recalcitrant and unlikely to willingly engage in programmes and services or take up available support (Alder 1996; Worrall 2001).

Why is it that workers perceive girls and young women to be such a difficult and challenging client group? According to the sexualisation theory of female offending, 'troublesome' girls and young women are treated differently to young men as a consequence of a double standard of acceptable behaviour in which the deviant behaviour of women is interpreted as a symptom of problematic sexuality requiring welfare regulation not punishment (Worrall 2000). They are constructed within a range of legal, welfare and political discourses as, on the one hand, 'deeply maladjusted misfits and, on the other as dangerous folk devils, symbolic of post-modern adolescent femininity' (Worrall 1999). While welfare concerns have always dominated professional responses to girls 'in trouble', concerns to provide protection to girls have always been mingled with anxieties about the wildness and dangerousness of girls who are 'out of control' (Alder 1996). Consequently, girls and young women are more likely to become caught up in the juvenile justice system as a consequence of gender inappropriate behaviours such as unsanctioned sexual activity, running away and wilfulness – activities that question feminine stereotypes of passivity, chastity and submissiveness (Chesney-Lind 1973; Hudson 1989).

Gendering needs

Where programmes for girls do exist, many have the traditionally narrow focus of sexuality and pregnancy prevention which, although beneficial, are too restricted in scope to meet the complex needs of young women in trouble. A gendered reading of youth problems shows that, although young men and young women in trouble share a set of universal needs, there are also key differences in terms of behavioural issues, domestic expectations and risk factors. The different gendered experiences of young women render them in need of different and innovative strategies.

Girls in trouble are not only perpetrators of criminal behaviour, but also frequently have extensive experience of physical, sexual and emotional victimisation. Analysis of Scottish Children's Reporters' Administration (SCRA) data relating to girls referred to the Children's Hearing System on offence grounds has shown that, compared to boys, offending girls are more likely to have originally come to the attention of the Reporter for being the victim of an offence, such as neglect or sexual abuse (Social Work Services and Prisons Inspectorate for Scotland 1998, p.12). In her study of adult female prisoners in Scotland, Loucks (1997) revealed that one of the most universally shared attributes of female inmates was a history of violent victimisation (82% of respondents had experienced some form of abuse during their lives). Emotional abuse was most common (71%), followed by physical abuse (60%), then sexual abuse (47%).[7] This last form of victimisation was most common during childhood and was often perpetrated by fathers or other male relatives or guardians. Evidence from the USA shows that a third of women in prison there have been physically or sexually abused before the age of 18, a third have grown up in homes where adults abused alcohol and drugs, one in five have spent time in foster care and, by adulthood, nearly half have been the victims of sexual or physical violence at the hands of a partner or spouse (Chesney-Lind 1997).

The high proportion of child sexual abuse experienced by young female offenders may contribute to the commission of status offences such as truancy and running away from home, which in turn provide a pathway to offending behaviours such as drug or alcohol abuse and prostitution (Belknap and Holsinger 1998; Chesney-Lind 2001b; Chesney-Lind *et al.* 2001). Almost 90 per cent of the women in Loucks's study had experience of illicit drug use and about half felt their drug use was problematic. Academics and practitioners alike agree that clear correlations exist between the victimisation of women and girls and high-risk behaviours such as serious drug abuse, suicide and self-harm (Acoca and Dedel 1998; Boswell 1996; Covington 1998; Howard League 1997). One reason for this close connection is the capacity of both psychoactive substances and self-injury to (temporarily) block out distressing experiences and dull emotional pain (Motz 2001).

Working with girls and young women

Clearly any effort by the system to respond appropriately to the offending behaviour of young women needs to take account of their gendered experiences in order to be effective. But what exactly should effective provision/programmes look like? As the discussion above has indicated, in Britain, there are very few programmes or projects designed specifically for female offenders, with girls and young women perhaps the most neglected offender population. Inevitably, then, evaluations for these programmes/ projects are similarly scarce (Kendall 1998), particularly in the UK. Much of the existing research relating to work with female offenders originates in North America, particularly the USA, and tends to have been gathered in custodial rather than community settings (Durrance and Ablitt 2002). Nevertheless, a range of effective community-based programmes serving young women offenders in the USA have been identified, and successful programmes have been shown to share similar characteristics. These are outlined below.

Holism

Successful programmes and projects appear to employ a comprehensive and holistic strategy aimed at addressing girls' and young women's multiple needs in a continuum of care. Successful inter-agency communication is important both in terms of ease of access and minimisation of inter-agency distrust or subversion of each other's endeavours when sharing the same group of clients (Carlen 2001).

Developing a sense of self-efficacy and empowerment

For work with girls and young women to be effective, they need to feel confident that they are capable of making changes in their lives. To be confident, they have to achieve a sense of self-esteem, to feel that they have personal worth and something to contribute (Alder 1996; Eaton 1993). Allowing young female offenders to make informed decisions about issues that affect them promotes a sense of self-efficacy. If they are to make meaningful and responsible choices, they need to be advised as to the availability of resources and the implications of their decisions (Dauvergne-Latimer 1995).

Gender specificity

One of the key criticisms of the concept of 'empowering women' is that it has been appropriated by the *What Works* agenda as a means of 'responsibilising' women – making them responsible for engaging with programmes of change and managing their own risk assessment (Hannah-Moffat 2000; Shaw and Hannah-Moffat 2000). Yet the actual power of young female offenders to effect change is limited by oppressive structures such as age, gender, class and race. It is therefore important that those working with young female offenders acknowledge not only their individual agency, but also the wider structures that impose on them (Chesney-Lind 2001b; Kendall 1998). Young women will only change their lives 'if and when they have access to the structural preconditions of social justice – housing, employment and health facilities' (Worrall 1999).

Programmes, projects and services need, therefore, to be gender specific, age specific, and culturally specific. Gender-specific programming refers to programme models and services that comprehensively address the special needs of a targeted gender group, such as adolescent girls. Such programmes are rooted in the everyday experiences of girls and incorporate an understanding of female adolescent development (Greene, Peters and Associates 1998). In other words, they are not simply 'women only' programmes that were designed for men, but rather take account of the evidence in relation to the criminogenic needs and protective factors which are particularly associated with girls. Paradoxically, gender-sensitive programmes developed with women in mind are of questionable suitability for girls and young women. Age is a crucial factor both in defining and in meeting the needs of this particular group.

Recognising / addressing abuse issues

Where they are the survivors of – or currently in – an abusive relationship, girls' and young women's sense of self-efficacy is likely to be damaged. Work with young female offenders, therefore, must assist them in developing an understanding of their victimisation and encourage them to accept the power not to participate in abusive situations in the future (Greene, Peters and Associates 1998). They also need opportunities to address the feelings of anger and frustration that often contribute to their offending behaviour. Many girls inevitably require specialised counselling. However, research suggests that approaches which rely primarily on the provision of counselling alone are not likely to succeed (Chesney-Lind 1997).

Talking and listening to girls and young women

In addition to looking at issues surrounding abusive relationships, successful work with girls and young women who offend needs to develop resources that utilise the experiences of women themselves. Young female offenders frequently have a great deal to say for themselves (Batchelor 2002). They need to be listened to and their insights incorporated into work with them (Alder 1996; Burman, Batchelor and Brown 2001; Chesney-Lind 1997).[8]

The importance of involving participants in the development of meaningful programme initiatives has been highlighted by Dixon (2000). She criticises the rigidity of the current *What Works* ideology, arguing that a preoccupation with 'programme integrity' stifles spontaneity and creativity. This is seen to impact both on programme effectiveness and programme development:

> The point is that for change to occur offenders need to experience the value of change efforts for themselves. This is unlikely to emerge when offenders go through the motions prescribed to them by others. The

exchanges in the group have to strike a personal chord with each offender. Each has to feel that at various points something uniquely relevant to her or him has happened, and that the exchange makes sense to the person in terms of personal life experiences. (Dixon 2000, p.18)

According to a report by the National Council for Research on Women:

When girls' collaboration is solicited through authentic and meaningful ways, through involvement in the design and implementation of programmes, girls can gain leadership skills, develop supportive intergenerational relationships and experience themselves as active participants in social change. (1998, p.87, cited in Worrall 2001)

Relationships

This directs us towards the crucial significance of the relationships between workers and young people in supporting change (McNeill and Batchelor 2002). As Durrance and Ablitt note, in their evaluation of the Women's Probation Centre in England and Wales: 'Women respond to an environment that recognises their individual worth and provides a supportive and positive atmosphere. The examples set by staff in their interactions with others, and within the group are crucial' (2002, p.248). Whereas boys are more likely to adhere to rules because they respect rules or want to avoid consequences, girls are more likely to co-operate where they have established a relationship with workers and feel they respect them and have their best interests in mind (Ryan and Lindgren 1999). For many girls and young women who offend, their only other experience of relationships is subordination, exploitation and abuse. Interactions between young women and workers can provide a context for young female offenders to participate in positive relationships.

Another way of playing to young female offenders' strengths is by recognising the complex and often positive ways in which their relationships provide an opportunity for them to structure their lives and resolve conflicts (Worrall 2001). Whereas work with boys and young men tends to be more successful where it takes place in a structured, rule-bound environment, successful programmes for girls 'focus on relationships with other people and offer ways to master their lives while keeping these relationships intact' (Belknap *et al.* 1997, cited in Dougherty 1999, p.119). This highlights the advantages of community-based over custodial disposals, and in particular points to the possibility of utilising peer support and involving families in work with girls and young women. Research into the prevention of violence and antisocial behaviour in the USA points to the advantages of utilising informal interventions for young people aimed at peers and other key components of their social environments (National Institute of Mental Health 1999). Peer support programmes that tap into girls' affinities for close and supportive relationships are being successfully developed to combat bullying and physical violence in schools, and there are moves to extend these to probation programmes.

Informalism and reintegrative strategies

In recent years, the more informal approach offered by restorative justice has been heralded by some advocates as an appropriate means of controlling and dealing with the offending behaviour of young people (Morris and Maxwell 2001). Girls have long been seen as amenable to more informal elements of social control such as that exercised through the family and social networks (Cain 1989). Building on their 'natural' affinity for forming relationships and their verbal eloquence (compared to boys), the more informal strategies of mediation, family conferencing and programmes informed by the underlying principles of shame and reintegration have been put forward as viable alternatives to traditional approaches to female criminality. Some feminist writers, however, have counselled caution at the wholehearted adoption of the principles of restorative justice for girls and young women (Alder 1998; Worrall 2001). Many girls behave badly precisely because their experience of informal social control (particularly within the home) has been abusive and brutalising. What's more, the concept of 'shame' – which encourages self-blame – has certain connotations for girls, given that it is denotative of failure (Alder 1998).

Sustainability

The main reasons for winding down projects for female offenders are usually financial. However lack of funding can mask other shortcomings, notably: change of objectives; poor or adverse publicity; loss of gender specificity; non-use by the courts; and inappropriate expectations by funders. Based on the impressions and experiences of managers of gender-specific programmes in custodial and non-custodial settings, Carlen (2001) found a general convergence of opinion regarding attributes of sustainable projects. These include a resistance to the erosion of gender specificity; an evolutionary and flexible organisation (whereby the relationships between project provision and the varied or changing situations of those attending the project are monitored); an holistic (co-ordinated) approach to service delivery; a democratic model of policy formation to enhance staff morale and project success; and a principled approach to probity in human relationships. Successful projects are likely to have the ability to convince courts of a congruity of interest in reducing recidivism by improving the quality of clients' lives in the present.

Conclusion

Despite their growing numbers within the criminal justice system, girls and young women are generally not a priority for service and programme provision. In comparison with young men, the 'problem' posed by young women is small and resources therefore tend to be targeted at the former. Despite media accounts to the contrary, the risks posed by the majority of girls and young women who offend are relatively slight. Their offending is rarely serious and their needs are not best met within custodial settings. Nevertheless, the growing numbers of girls drawn into the criminal justice system cannot be ignored. This upward trend renders the question 'what about girls?' even more fraught. As this chapter has argued, girls who offend present very different circumstances and needs than their male counterparts. Effective gender-responsive programmes and interventions need to address this fact and take into account the multitude of unique issues that bring young women into contact with the law. The key lies in ensuring that any initiative developed to tackle the problems caused by 'troublesome girls' is flexible enough to address the specific experiences and concerns of those same girls. The challenge then is to develop effective and credible non-prison based programmes that take into account the social realities from which young female offenders come and to which they will return. This requires more research, more training and the informed development of more gender- and age-specific initiatives and, above all, a commitment to keeping girls' needs on the criminal justice policy agenda.

Notes

1   We are using the term 'girls' to refer to female offenders under the age of 16 and 'young women' to refer to those aged 16 to 20 years.

2   This is less the case in the USA where the US Office of Juvenile Justice and Delinquency Prevention (OJJDP) launched a multi-level approach designed to review the treatment of female juvenile offenders, develop an inventory of best practices, produce a training curriculum and develop gender-specific programmes (US Department of Justice, OJJDP, 1998).

3   In Scotland, children aged under 16 who commit offences are normally referred to the Children's Hearing System. Children's Hearings are administrative tribunals where lay members of the public determine whether compulsory measures of supervision are required. The determination of guilt or innocence is considered inappropriate.

4   This compares to 3808 men who had a charge of non-sexual violence proven against them, of which 38 per cent (1445) were aged under 21 (Scottish Executive 2001a).

5   In the USA girls are still likely to be detained and sent to institutions as a result of 'bootstrapping'. This occurs where girls originally charged with a status offence are subsequently re-arrested for the delinquent offence of 'probation violation', following the commission of another status offence, and are thus rendered liable for detention (Chesney-Lind 1997, 2001a).

6   Recent innovations in youth justice in England and Wales may however go some way to change this, although young males will still dominate in terms of numbers and degree of contact. Since April 2000, Youth Offending Teams (YOTs) consisting of social workers, probation officers, police officers, education and health staff have been operating in every local authority area. YOTs' responsibilities include supervision of community sentences, involvement in through-care and undertaking post-release supervision.

7   Young female offenders in Loucks's study shared broadly similar characteristics to the adult female population, but the small number involved made reliable comparisons difficult.

8   That said, a word of caution may be necessary insofar as not all young women may be able to participate meaningfully, or to the same extent, and so universal applicability of participation by girls and young women may be inappropriate. While a central principle of the Children's Hearing System in Scotland is the participation of young people, recent research suggests that many find it hard to express themselves and their contributions are notably brief (Hallett and Murray 1998).

References

Acoca, L. and Dedel, K. (1998) *No Place to Hide: Understanding and Meeting the Needs of Girls in the California Juvenile Justice System.* San Francisco: National Council on Crime and Delinquency.

Alder, C. (1996) 'Introduction.' In C. Alder and M. Baines (eds) *And When She Was Bad? Working with Young Women in Juvenile Justice and Related Areas.* Hobart: National Clearinghouse for Youth Studies.

Alder, C. (1998) 'Passionate and wilful girls: Confronting practices.' *Women and Criminal Justice 9*, 4, 81–101.

Asquith, S. and Samuel, E. (1994) *Criminal Justice and Related Services for Young Adult Offenders.* Edinburgh: HMSO.

Audit Scotland (2001) *Youth Justice in Scotland: A Baseline Report.* Edinburgh: Audit Scotland.

Aymer, C. (1992) 'Women in residential work.' In M. Langan and L. Day (eds) *Women, Oppression and Social Work.* London: Routledge.

Baines, M. and Alder, C. (1996a) 'Are girls more difficult to work with? Youth workers' perspectives in juvenile justice and related areas.' *Crime and Delinquency 42*, 3, 467–485.

Baines, M. and Alder, C. (1996b) 'When she was bad she was horrid.' In C. Alder and M. Baines (eds) *And When She Was Bad? Working with Young Women in Juvenile Justice and Related Areas.* Hobart: National Clearing House for Youth Studies.

Batchelor, S. (2001) 'The myth of girl gangs.' *Criminal Justice Matters 43*, 26–27. Reprinted in Y. Jewkes and G. Letherby (eds) (2002) *Criminology: A Reader.* London: Sage.

Batchelor, S. (2002) '"What's a nice girl like you doing in a place like this?" The experience of researching violent young women in prison.' Unpublished paper presented to the Department of Sociology and Anthropology Postgraduate/Staff Seminar, University of Glasgow, 12 February.

Batchelor, S., Burman, M. and Brown, J. (2001) 'Discussing violence: Let's hear it for the girls.' *Probation Journal 48*, 2, 125–134.

Batchelor, S. and McNeill, F. (forthcoming) 'The Young Person–Worker Relationship.' In T. Bateman and J. Pitts (eds) *The Russell House Companion to Youth Justice.* London: Russell House Publishing.

Belknap, J. and Holsinger, K. (1998) 'An overview of delinquent girls: How theory and practise have failed and the need for innovative changes.' In R. Zaplin (ed) *Female Offenders: Critical Perspectives and Effective Interventions.* Aspen: Maryland.

Boswell, G. (1996) *Young and Dangerous: The Backgrounds and Careers of Section 53 Offenders.* Aldershot: Avebury.

Brown, H.C. and Pearce, J. (1992) 'Good practice in the face of anxiety: Social work with girls and young women.' *Journal of Social Work Practice 6*, 2, 159–165.

Burman, M. (1999) 'Women and the Scottish criminal justice system.' In P. Duff and N. Hutton (eds) *Criminal Justice in Scotland.* Aldershot: Ashgate.

Burman, M., Batchelor, S. and Brown, J. (2001) 'Researching girls and violence: Facing the dilemmas of fieldwork.' *British Journal of Criminology 41*, 443–459.

Cain, M. (1989) *Growing up Good: Policing the Behaviour of Girls in Europe.* London: Sage.

Carlen, P. (2001) 'Gender-specific projects for female lawbreakers: Questions of survival.' *Criminal Justice Matters 46*, 44–45.

Carpenter, V. and Young, K. (1986) *Coming in from the Margins: Youth Work with Girls and Young Women.* Leicester: National Association of Youth Clubs.

Chesney-Lind, M. (1973) 'Judicial enforcement of the female sex role.' *Issues in Criminology 3*, 51–71.

Chesney-Lind, M. (1997) *The Female Offender: Girls, Women and Crime.* Thousand Oaks, CA: Sage.

Chesney-Lind, M. (2001a) 'Are girls closing the gender gap in violence?' *Criminal Justice*, Spring, 18–23.

Chesney-Lind, M. (2001b) 'What about the girls? Delinquency programming as if gender mattered.' *Corrections Today*, February.

Chesney-Lind, M., Artz, S. and Nicholson, D. (2001) 'Girls' delinquency and violence: Making the case for gender-responsive programming.' Paper presented at the American Society of Criminology Conference, Atlanta, Georgia, November.

Covington, S. (1998) 'The relational theory of women's psychological development: Implications for the criminal justice system.' In R.T. Zaplin (ed) *Female Offenders: Critical Perspectives and Effective Interventions.* Gaithersburg, MD: Aspen.

Dauvergne-Latimer, M. (1995) *Exemplary Community Programs for Federally Sentenced Women: A Literature Review.* Ottawa: Correctional Service of Canada.

Department of Health (2001) *Children Accommodated in Secure Units, Year Ending 31 March 2001: England and Wales.* Statistical Bulletin no. 2001/17. London: Department of Health.

Dixon, L. (2000) 'Punishment and the question of ownership: Groupwork in the criminal justice system.' *Groupwork 12*, 1, 6–25.

Dougherty, J. (1999) 'The relational theory of women's psychological development: Implications for the criminal justice system.' In R. Zaplin (ed) *Female Offenders: Critical Perspectives and Effective Interventions.* Gaithersburg, MD: Aspen.

Durrance, P. and Ablitt, F. (2002) 'Creative solutions to women's offending: An evaluation of the women's probation centre.' *Probation Journal 48*, 4, 247– 259.

Eaton, M. (1993) *Women after Prison.* Buckingham: Open University Press.

Gelsthorpe, L. (2000) 'Female crime in Britain.' In N.H. Rafter (ed) *Encyclopaedia of Women and Crime.* Phoenix, AZ: Oryx Press.

Girls Incorporated (1996) *Prevention and Parity: Girls in Juvenile Justice.* Indianapolis: IN Girls.

Greene, Peters and Associates in collaboration with the Northwest Regional Educational Laboratory (1998) *Guiding Principles for Promising Female Programming: An Inventory of Best Practices.* Washington, DC: US Department of Justice, Office of Justice Programs, Office of Juvenile Justice and Delinquency Prevention.

Hallett, C. and Murray, C. (1998) *Deciding in Children's Interests.* Edinburgh: Scottish Office.

Hannah-Moffat, K. (2000) 'Prisons that empower: Neo-liberal governance in Canadian women's prisons.' *British Journal of Criminology 40*, 3, 510–531.

Hogg, K. (1999) *Youth Crime in Scotland: A Scottish Executive Policy Unit Review.* Edinburgh: The Scottish Executive.

Home Office (2000) *Prison Statistics, England and Wales 1999.* Cm 8045. London: The Stationery Office.

Home Office (2001) *Statistics on Women and the Criminal Justice System. A Home Office Publication under Section 95 of the Criminal Justice Act 1991: Report 2001.* London: The Stationery Office.

Howard League (1997) *Lost Inside: The Imprisonment of Teenage Girls.* London: The Howard League.

Howard League (2001) *Suicide and Self-Harm Prevention: Repetitive Self-Harm Among Women and Girls in Prison.* London: The Howard League.

Hudson, A. (1989) 'Troublesome girls: Towards alternative definitions and policies.' In M. Cain (ed) *Growing up Good: Policing the Behaviour of Girls in Europe.* London: Sage.

Kendall, K. (1998) 'Evaluation of programmes for female offenders.' In R. Zaplin (ed) *Female Offenders: Critical Perspectives and Effective Interventions.* Gaithersburg, MD: Aspen.

Leschied, A., Cummings, A., Van Brunschot, M., Cunningham, A. and Saunders, A. (2000) *Female Adolescent Aggression: A Review of the Literature and the Correlates of Aggression.* User Report no. 2000-04. Ottawa: Solicitor General Canada.

Lippincott, W. (2000) 'Juvenile institutions.' In N.H. Rafter (ed) *Encyclopaedia of Women and Crime*. Phoenix, AZ: Oryx Press.

Loucks, N. (1997) *HMP Cornton Vale: Research into Drugs and Alcohol, Violence and Bullying, Suicides and Self-Injury, and Backgrounds of Abuse*. Scottish Prison Service Occasional Papers Report no. 1/98. Edinburgh: Scottish Prison Service.

McIvor, G. (1998) 'Jobs for the boys? Gender differences in referral to community service.' *Howard Journal of Criminal Justice 37*, 3, 280–290.

Morris, A. and Maxwell, G. (2001) (eds) *Restoring Justice for Juveniles: Conferencing, Mediation and Circles*. Oxford: Hart.

Motz, A. (2001) *The Psychology of Female Violence: Crimes Against the Body*. Hove: Brunner-Routledge.

NACRO (2001) *Youth Crime Briefing October 2001: Girls in the Youth Justice System*. London: NACRO.

National Institute of Mental Health (1999) *Preventing Destructive Behaviour by Harnessing the Power of Peers*. NIH publication no. 99-4588.

Pearce, J. (1995) 'The woman in the worker: Youth work with young women.' *Youth and Policy 52*, 1–11.

Reitsma-Street, M. (1999) 'Justice for Canadian girls: A 1990s update.' *Canadian Journal of Criminology*, July, 335–363.

Ryan, C.A. and Lindgren, S.J. (1999) 'How to work effectively with girls: Promising practices in gender-specific interventions.' *Reaching Today's Youth 3*, 3, 55–58.

Samuel, E. and Tisdall, K. (1996) 'Female offenders in Scotland: Implications for theory.' In S. Asquith (ed) *Children and Young People in Conflict with the Law*. London: Jessica Kingsley Publishers.

Schnelle, S. (2000) 'Juvenile delinquency and age.' In N.H. Rafter (ed) *Encyclopaedia of Women and Crime*. Phoenix, AZ: Oryx Press.

Scottish Executive (2000) *The Scottish Executive's Response to the Advisory Group Report on Youth Crime*. Edinburgh: The Scottish Executive.

Scottish Executive (2001a) *Criminal Proceedings in Scottish Courts, 2000*. Edinburgh: The Scottish Executive.

Scottish Executive (2001b) *Children in Residential Accommodation 1999–2000*. Edinburgh: The Scottish Executive.

Scottish Executive (2002) *A Better Way: The Report of the Ministerial Group on Women's Offending*. Edinburgh: HMSO.

Shaw, M. and Hannah-Moffatt, K. (2000) 'Gender, diversity and risk assessment in Canadian corrections.' *Probation Journal 47*, 3, 163–172.

Social Work Services and Prisons Inspectorate for Scotland (1998) *Women Offenders: A Safer Way: A Review of Community Disposals and the Use of Custody for Women Offenders in Scotland*. Edinburgh: HMSO.

Spence, J. (1996) 'Feminism in work with girls and women.' *Youth and Policy 52*, 38–53.

US Department of Justice, Federal Bureau of Investigation (1999) *Crime in the United States 1998*. Washington, DC: US Government Printing Office.

US Department of Justice, Office of Juvenile Justice and Delinquency Prevention (1998) *What About Girls?* OJJDP fact sheet. Washington, DC: US Government Printing Office.

Worrall, A. (1999) 'Troubled or troublesome? Justice for girls and young women.' In B. Goldson (ed) *Youth Justice: Contemporary Policy and Practice*. Aldershot: Ashgate.

Worrall, A. (2000) 'Governing bad girls: Changing constructions of female juvenile delinquency.' In J. Bridgeman and D. Monk (eds) *Feminist Perspectives on Child Law*. London: Cavendish.

Worrall, A. (2001) 'Girls at risk? Reflections on changing attitudes to young women's offending.' *Probation Journal 48*, 2, 86–92.

Wundersitz, J. (2000) 'Juvenile Delinquency, Australia.' In N.H. Rafter (ed) *Encyclopaedia of Women and Crime*. Phoenix, AZ: Oryx Press.

Zager, M.A. (2000) 'Gender and crime.' In N.H. Rafter (ed) *Encyclopaedia of Women and Crime*. Phoenix, AZ: Oryx Press.

The Contributors

Susan Batchelor is a research student in the Department of Sociology and Anthropology at Glasgow University. She has a long-standing interest in young women, crime and the criminal justice system and has been employed on a number of research projects, most recently 'A View from the Girls: Exploring Violence and Violent Behaviour'. Her current study focuses on violent young women (aged 16 to 24 years) in prison in Scotland.

Michele Burman teaches courses in Criminology, Research Methods and Criminal Justice at the University of Glasgow, where she is a Professor of Criminology and Director of the Criminology Research Unit. She has long-standing research interests in gender and violence, female offenders and troubled and troublesome girls.

Ruth Chigwada-Bailey is a consultant criminologist who has been running conferences addressing issues around race, gender and the criminal justice system (Criminology in the New Millennium) since 1991. She taught criminology at Birkbeck College, London University from 1987 to 2001 and in 1994 was the recipient of Black Woman of the Year award. Ruth has published widely, especially on issues around race, gender and the criminal justice system. She is the author of *Race, Gender and Criminal Justice Process* (Waterside Press 2002) and *Black Women's Experiences of the Criminal Justice System* (Waterside Press 1997).

Loraine Gelsthorpe is a University Senior Lecturer in Criminology at the Institute of Criminology and a Fellow of Pembroke College, University of Cambridge. Her research and teaching interests include gender and race issues in the criminal justice system, youth justice, restorative justice and the links between criminal and social justice. Her publications include: *Sexism and the Female Offender* (1989); *Feminist Perspectives in Criminology* (edited with A. Morris 1990); *Understanding the Sentencing of Women* (edited with C. Hedderman 1997); *Community Penalties: Change and Challenge* (edited with A.E. Bottoms and S. Rex 2001); 'Feminism and Criminology' in the *Oxford Handbook of Criminology* (eds M. Maguire, R. Morgan and R. Reiner 2002).

Carol Hedderman was Deputy Director of the Criminal Policy Research Unit, London South Bank University from 1999 to 2002. Her research interests include the imposition and enforcement of community penalties, sentencing disparities, parole decision-making, female offending, the treatment of women in the criminal justice system and strategies for improving services for the victims of domestic violence. She was a member of the Parole Board from 2001 to 2002 and has recently been appointed Assistant Director of the Home Office Research and Statistics Directorate where she will take on responsibility for research on courts, corrections and offenders.

Hazel Kemshall is Professor of Community and Criminal Justice at DeMontfort University. She has undertaken research on risk assessment and risk management, including evaluation of multi-agency public protection panels and the risk assessment and risk management of violent and sexual offenders. She has practice experience with offenders, young offenders and victims from her 11-year career in the Probation Service as an officer and manager. Her numerous publications include: *Good Practice in Risk Assessment and Management*, vols 1 and 2 (edited with Jacki Pritchard, Jessica Kingsley Publishers 1996, 1997); *Good Practice in Working with Violence* (edited with Jacki Pritchard, Jessica Kingsley Publishers 1999); *Good Practice in Working with Victims of Violence*, (edited with Jacki Pritchard, Jessica Kingsley Publishers 2000); and a recent literature review on *Risk Assessment and Management of Known Sexual and Violent Offenders*, and *An Evaluation of Multi-Agency Public Protection Panels* (with Maguire and Noaks) for the Home Office.

Nancy Loucks is an Independent Criminologist who specialises in prison policy and comparative penology. She has conducted extensive research into women in prison and acted as specialist advisor to the Inspectorates of Prisons and Social Work Services in Scotland for their Inquiry into female offenders, to the Inter Agency Forum on Women's Offending, and to the Ministerial Group on Women's Offending. Other research has included work on young offenders, remand prisoners, prison discipline, assaults and bullying in custody, the maintenance of prisoners' family ties and prisoners' rights.

Gill McIvor is Director of the Social Work Research Centre at the University of Stirling. Her previous research has focused primarily upon community penalties, young people and crime and women's experience of community sentences (community service and probation). She is currently involved in the evaluation of pilot Drug Courts in Scotland and in comparative research on drug courts and on women's experiences after prison. Her publications include *Sentenced to Serve*

(Avebury 1992), *Working with Offenders* (Jessica Kingsley Publishers 1995) and *Understanding Offending Among Young People* (edited with Janet Jamieson and Cathy Murray, The Stationery Office 1999).

Margaret S. Malloch is a Research Fellow in the Social Work Research Centre, University of Stirling. Her previous research has focused on the experiences of women drug users in prison, and women drug users' experiences of the criminal justice system. She is currently a member of the research team conducting an Evaluation into the Operation and Effectiveness of the Glasgow Pilot Drug Court, and the Scottish Prison Service Transitional Care Arrangements.

Judith Rumgay is Senior Lecturer in the Department of Social Policy, London School of Economics. She was a probation officer prior to her appointment at LSE, where she was responsible for the Home Office sponsored probation stream on the postgraduate social work programme. Her teaching currently focuses on psychology and crime, rehabilitation of offenders and criminal justice policy. Her research interests include alcohol- and drug-related offending, the Probation Service, female offenders and voluntary sector involvement in offender rehabilitation. She is the author of *Crime, Punishment and the Drinking Offender* (Macmillan 1998) and *The Addicted Offender: Developments in British Policy and Practice* (Palgrave 2000).

Jacqueline Tombs is a Senior Fellow at the Universities of Stirling and Edinburgh and Director of the Scottish Consortium on Crime and Criminal Justice. She has a PhD from Edinburgh University, an MA from the University of Pennsylvania, a Diploma in Criminology from Cambridge University and an MA from Glasgow University. From 1976 until 1997 she was responsible for criminological and social policy research in The Scottish Office. She previously held research and teaching appointments at the Universities of Cambridge and Pennsylvania. From 1984 to 1985, she was a Visiting Fellow at La Trobe University and has held appointments as a Visiting Scholar and Professor at Universities in New Zealand, the USA and Europe. She is author of: *Rethinking Criminal Justice in Scotland* (2000); *Social Work and Criminal Justice: The Impact of Policy* (edited with Fiona Spencer, 1998); *The British Crime Survey: Scotland* (edited with Gerry Chambers, 1984); and *Prosecution in the Public Interest* (edited with Sue Moody, 1982). She is a member of the Editorial Board of the *British Journal of Criminology* and a Committee Member of the Howard League for Penal Reform in Scotland.

Christine Wilkinson is a Lecturer in Criminology at the Scarman Centre, University of Leicester where she directs the campus-based MSc programmes in Criminology, Criminology (Clinical) and Criminology (Applied). She has published (with Professor Allison Morris) a number of articles on the imprisonment of women, particularly the problems and difficulties faced on and after release. Her current research interests centre on the problems of dealing with drug use, especially in a criminal justice context, and the problems of implementing drug prevention initiatives.

Subject Index

abuse 25–7, 29, 31, 53, 69, 70, 74, 76, 102, 106, 108, 109, 112, 117, 142, 144, 145, 148, 151–4, 156, 161, 163, 164, 167, 184, 191, 196, 201, 202, 216–19, 230, 234, 238, 240–2, 261, 275, 276, 278, 279
  backgrounds of 145
  of mental health powers, and police 196–8
  physical and sexual 238
  recognising/addressing issues 278
access 111–13
Accreditation Panel 228
act of desperation, crime as 28
acting out, crime as 19
addiction 151
Advisory Council on the Misuse of Drugs 255, 262
Africans 183, 193, 204
Afro-Caribbean women 184, 192, 197
aggression 16, 17, 19, 20, 187, 198, 216, 274
alcohol 144
  dependency 234
Alien Deportation Group 192
Allitt, Beverly 219, 220
Anti-Drugs Co-ordinator 255, 261, 262
antisocial attitudes 231–3
antisocial/criminal models, strong ties/identification with 233
Arrest Referral Schemes 75
arrests of notifiable offences by offence group 47
Asians 192, 202
assault 43, 47, 49, 54, 56, 57, 63, 152, 195, 202, 215, 267–9, 273
AUDIT scale 144
Audit Scotland 267, 283
Auld Report 159, 180

Australia 43, 267, 274

Bail Support Schemes 253
Bangladesh(is) 186
Beck Hopelessness Scale 148
Better Way, A (Scottish Executive) 77–9
biological theories 16–18
Black Female Prisoners Scheme 174
black women
  and courts 198–200
  and criminal justice system 183–204
    background 183–4
    economic pressure 185–7
    mainstream criminology 184–5
    stereotyping motherhood 187–90
    stereotyping womanhood 187–90
  and police 195–6
  and abuse of mental health powers 196–8
  in prison 200–2
  as suspects 192–5
Black Women in Prison 201, 205
breach of the peace 267, 268
Britain/UK 7, 27, 41, 42, 71, 100, 127, 132, 135, 138, 183, 186, 188, 195, 197, 201, 204, 207, 219, 228, 246, 250, 253, 254, 259, 261, 266, 270, 272, 273, 276
British Crime Survey (1998) 14
bullying 152–3
burglary 14, 47–52, 54, 59, 88, 91, 162, 234

Cabinet Office 109, 125
'Campaign Against Racism and Fascism' 196
Canada 43, 49, 53, 57, 145, 212, 228, 241, 267, 271

Canadian Center for Justice Statistics 53, 63
Canadian Crime Statistics (1997) 43
CARATS schemes 168
Caribbeans 183, 188, 191, 194, 204
cautions and convictions for indictable offences, changes in (1992 and 2000) 87
Correctional Drug Abuse Treatment Effectiveness Project (CDATE) 229, 237, 241
Chicago ecologists 21
Chief Inspector of Prisons 179
Chief Inspector of Social Work Services for Scotland 69
children 149–50
Children's Hearing System 269, 275, 282
Chinese 204
community 'punishment', women and 126–39
  effectiveness of community service 130–2
  use of community service with women who offend 127–30
Community Punishment Pathfinders 137, 139
Community Rehabilitation Orders 99
Community Research Associates 106, 119
community service
  effectiveness of 130–2
  use of with women who offend 127–30
  women's experiences of 132–6
community supervision of women offenders 99–118
  gender-specific programming 106–10
  programmes in practice 110–16
    access 111–13
    mutual help 114–15
    programme sustainment 115–16
    service integration 113–14

Author Index